TRADE AND DEVELOPMENT

New Silk Roads

TRADE AND DEVELOPMENT

A series of books on international economic relations and economic issues in development

Edited from the National Centre for Development Studies, Australian National University, by Helen Hughes

Advisory editors

Juergen Donges, *Universität zu Köln, Wirtschaftspolitisches Seminar*
Peter Lloyd, *Department of Economics, University of Melbourne*
Gustav Ranis, *Department of Economics, Yale University*
David Wall, *Department of Economics, University of Sussex*

Titles in the series

Helen Hughes (ed.), *Achieving industrialization in East Asia*
Yun-Wing Sung, *The China–Hong Kong connection*
Kym Anderson (ed.), *New silk roads: East Asia and world textile markets*
Rod Tyers and Kym Anderson, *Disarray in world food markets: a quantitative assessment*

NEW
SILK ROADS

East Asia and World Textile Markets

Edited By

KYM ANDERSON

Economic Research and Analysis Unit,
General Agreement on Tariffs and Trade, Geneva.

The right of the
University of Cambridge
to print and sell
all manner of books
was granted by
Henry VIII in 1534.
The University has printed
and published continuously
since 1584.

CAMBRIDGE UNIVERSITY PRESS
CAMBRIDGE
NEW YORK   PORT CHESTER   MELBOURNE   SYDNEY

Published by the Press Syndicate of the University of Cambridge
The Pitt Building, Trumpington Street, Cambridge CB2 1RP, UK
40 West 20th Street, New York, NY 10011-4211, USA
10 Stamford Road, Oakleigh, Victoria 3166, Australia

Printed in Hong Kong by Colorcraft

National Library of Australia cataloguing-in-publication data:
New silk roads.
Bibliography.
Includes index.
ISBN 0 521 39278 0.
1. Textile industry. 2. Textile industry — East
Asia. I. Anderson, Kym. Series : Trade and
development.
338.47677

Library of Congress cataloguing-in-publication data:
New silk roads : East Asia and world textile markets / edited by
Kym Anderson.
. – (Trade and development)
Includes bibliographical references and index.
ISBN 0 521 39278 0.
1. Textile industry—East Asia. I. Anderson, Kym. II. Series:
Trade and development (Cambridge, England)
HD9866.E18N49 1991
382'.45677'00951—dc20
91-3276
CIP

A catalogue record for this book is available from the British Library
ISBN 0 521 39278 0

Contents

Figures

Tables

Contributors to this volume

KYM ANDERSON is Director, Centre for International Economic Studies, University of Adelaide, Adelaide, Australia (currently on leave at the GATT Secretariat, Geneva, Switzerland).

CARL HAMILTON is Research Fellow and former Acting Director, Institute for International Economic Studies, University of Stockholm, Stockholm, Sweden.

PETER LLOYD is Professor and Dean, Faculty of Commerce and Economics, University of Melbourne, Melbourne, Australia.

YOUNG-IL PARK is Associate Professor, Department of International Trade, Inha University, Inchon, Republic of Korea.

JOSEPH PELZMAN is Professor and Chairman, Department of Economics, George Washington University, Washington, DC, United States.

PRUE PHILLIPS is Director, International Economic Data Bank, Australian National University, Canberra, Australia.

SUPHAT SUPHACHALASAI is Lecturer, Department of Economics, Thammasat University, Bangkok, Thailand.

JOHN WHALLEY is Professor and Director, Centre for the Study of International Economic Relations, University of Western Ontario, London, Canada.

HIDEKI YAMAWAKI is Professor, Department of Economics, Catholic University of Louvain, Louvaine-la-Neuve, Belgium.

Preface

For centuries East Asia has been home to an important part of the world's textile industry. Its role for most of that period has been as a supplier of natural fibres which were exported to Europe via the so-called Silk Road. During recent decades, however, East Asia's production and exports of textile products have expanded dramatically, transforming the region into a major net importer of natural fibres. Even by the first half of the 1960s its net imports of natural fibres represented one-sixth of world fibre trade, compared with Western Europe's two-fifths. But, by the first half of the 1980s, East Asia's share had doubled while Western Europe's had almost halved.

This dramatic redirection of world fibre trade was driven initially by the success of Japan and then Northeast Asia's newly industrialized economies in developing export-oriented textile and clothing industries and penetrating the markets of more advanced industrial economies. Then in the 1980s China joined its neighbours as a rapidly expanding producer and exporter of textiles and clothing. At the same time, however, China also began to expand its domestic production of fibres. This raised questions in the minds of traditional fibre exporters such as Australian wool producers and US cotton growers as to the net impact China would have on world fibre markets. As a result, the Australian Wool Research and Development Fund in 1987 commissioned a study to address those questions. The Australia–Japan Research Centre (AJRC) of the Australian National University, Canberra, coordinated the three-year project and provided additional funding to ensure its satisfactory completion.

The present volume is one of the products of that endeavour. The AJRC, in collaboration with the University of Adelaide's Centre for International Economic Studies and its Chinese Economy Research Unit, invited several economists to contribute specific papers to a conference in August 1989. A selection of these papers have since been revised substantially to provide an integrated picture of past, present and prospective developments in East Asia as they relate to world fibre, textile and clothing markets, and of the ways in which advanced industrial economies are responding to these developments. The latter papers, which form Part II of this volume, were commissioned by the AJRC, as was the August 1989 conference.

The editor and authors are grateful to the Australian Wool Research and Development Fund and the Australia–Japan Research Centre for financial support for the research on which the volume is based; to Peter Drysdale and Christopher Findlay for their untiring support throughout the project; to the people who kindly acted as discussants at the August 1989 conference at which earlier versions of the chapters were discussed, namely, Rod Falvey, Brian Fisher, Helen Hughes, Ji Hong Kim, John Lowe, John O'Connor, Yoko Sazanami, Ben Smith, Francis Teal, Rod Tyers, Peter Warr and Yongzheng Yang; to the publishers of the journals *Economic Development and Cultural Change* and *Weltwirtschafliches Archiv* (Kiel Institute of World Economics) for permission to reprint, in Chapters 1 to 3, some material from two Anderson/Park papers which they published; to Cambridge University Press for including the volume in its Trade and Development Series; to Prue Phillips of ANU's International Economic Data Bank for providing data on which many tables are based; to Maree Tait at ANU's National Centre for Development Studies and Shirley Purchase for editorial assistance; and to Debbie Beckman at the University of Adelaide for coordinating the word processing of the manuscript. The editor would also like to express his gratitude not only to his employer, the University of Adelaide, but to the Institute for International Economic Studies at the University of Stockholm, where he was a Visiting Fellow during 1988 when early versions of Chapters 1–3 were drafted and when ideas for the volume were being shaped. After completing this volume the editor took leave from Adelaide to take up an assignment with the economic research division of the GATT Secretariat in Geneva. Needless to say, none of the views expressed in this volume are intended to reflect the views of the GATT Secretariat or GATT Contracting Parties.

Kym Anderson

Abbreviations and acronyms

ASEAN	Association of South East Asian Nations, comprising Brunei, Indonesia, Malaysia, the Philippines, Singapore and Thailand
ASIC	Australian Standard Industrial Classification
China	People's Republic of China (excluding Taiwan)
Eastern Europe	The seven main centrally planned European economies (Bulgaria, Czechoslovakia, the former Democratic Republic of Germany, Hungary, Poland, Romania and the USSR)
EC	European Community of twelve member countries (Belgium, Denmark, Federal Republic of Germany, France, Greece, Ireland, Italy, Luxembourg, the Netherlands, Portugal, Spain and the United Kingdom)
EFTA	European Free Trade Association of six member countries (Austria, Finland, Iceland, Norway, Sweden and Switzerland)
ERA	Effective rate of assistance
GATT	General Agreement on Tariffs and Trade
GDP	Gross domestic product
ISIC	International Standard Industrial Classification
Korea	Republic of Korea (or South Korea)
LTA	Long Term Agreement
MFA	Multi-fibre Arrangement
MFN	Most-favoured-nation
MITI	Ministry of International Trade and Industry of the Japanese Government
MTE	Import tariff equivalent
NIEs	Newly industrializing economies
NTBs	Non-tariff barriers to international trade
OECD	Organization for Economic Co-operation and Development

SIC	Standard Industrial Classification (Japan)
SITC	Standard International Trade Classification
Taiwan	Republic of China, Taiwan Province
VER	Voluntary export restraint

Symbols

n.a.	not applicable
..	not available
—	zero or insignificant

Introduction and summary

Kym Anderson

There seems to be a happy concurrence of causes in human affairs, which checks the growth of trade and riches, and hinders them from being confined entirely to one people; as might naturally at first be dreaded from the advantages of an established commerce. Where one nation has gotten the start of another in trade, it is very difficult for the latter to regain the ground it has lost; because of the superior industry and skill of the former, and the greater stocks, of which the merchants are possessed, and which enable them to trade on so much smaller profits. But these advantages are compensated in some measure, by the low price of labor in every nation which has not an extensive commerce, and does not much abound in gold and silver. Manufactures therefore gradually shift their places, leaving those countries and provinces which they have already enriched, and flying to others, whither they are allured by the cheapness of provisions and labor, till they have enriched those also, and are again banished by the same cause.

David Hume, *Essays Moral and Political* (1748), ed. E. Rotwein, London, Nelson, 1955, pp. 34–5

The changing patterns of production and international trade in fibres, textiles and clothing provide a classic study of the dynamics of our interdependent world economy. Nowhere has that pattern changed more dramatically than in East Asia during the past few decades. For centuries before that, Asia supplied the textile manufacturers of Europe with natural fibres, including silk from East Asia along the route known as the Silk Road. Today East Asia exports virtually no natural fibres and instead has become the most important region of the world both as an importer of raw cotton and wool and as an exporter of manufactured textile products and clothing.

One of the main purposes of this volume is to ask whether advanced industrial countries will continue to make room for further generations of newly industrializing countries seeking to export their way out of poverty. Or will the recent growth in textile exports from countries such as China simply cause high-wage countries to raise their import barriers? To answer that properly requires first addressing questions such as the following:

— How is the relative importance of fibre, textile and clothing production and trade in an economy likely to change as that economy and the rest of the world grow?

— To what extent has the economic growth of first Japan and then East Asia's advanced developing economies altered the location of production of textile products and the pattern of global trade in fibres, textiles and clothing?

— Has China been following a similar development path to its neighbours, particularly since its dramatic reforms began in the late 1970s?

— Given China's already prominent position in international markets for fibres, textiles and clothing, what would be the impact on those markets of further economic reforms in China, particularly with respect to its trade and exchange rate policies?

— Are smaller economies such as Thailand able to develop in this way also, or are China's expansion and the Multi-fibre Arrangement thwarting their prospects?

These questions are the focus of the chapters in Part I of this volume, before attention is turned in Part II to the structural adjustments and policy responses of more advanced industrial economies.

Chapter 1 draws on trade and development theory to suggest that a poor country opening up to international trade will tend to specialize in the export of primary products, though less so the more densely populated the country. If its domestic incomes grow more rapidly than the rest of the world's, its export specialization will gradually switch away from primary products to manufactures. The manufactured goods initially exported will be more labour-intensive the more resource-poor or densely populated the country. Since many processes in textile and clothing production tend to be intensive in the use of unskilled labour, they will be among the items initially exported by a newly industrializing, densely populated country. And as the demands for textile raw materials by that country's expanding textile industry grow, so the country's net exports of natural fibres will diminish, or net imports of natural fibres will increase, *ceteris paribus*. On the other hand, since synthetic fibre production is an extremely capital-intensive activity, its products will tend to be imported by the newly industrializing country from relatively capital-abundant industrial countries. If this newly industrializing country is growing more rapidly than other countries, it will initially increase its shares of world production and exports of textiles and clothing and of world imports of fibres at the expense of more mature industrial economies. In time, another generation of newly industrializing countries would duplicate this process, so gradually displacing the former in those world markets but providing them with a growing export market for capital-intensive manufactures, including synthetic fibres.

The economic growth of Japan since the deregulation and opening up of that economy, which began with the Meiji Restoration in 1868, has been more than twice as fast as growth in the more mature economies. Chapter 2 shows that, during the twelve decades since then, Japan's economy has developed precisely as theory would suggest. What was mainly an agrarian economy before the 1870s has been transformed into one in which the primary sector accounts for less than one-tenth of employment and one-thirtieth of GDP and exports. The shares of textiles and clothing in GDP, employment and exports, on the other hand, rose from low levels in the 1870s to substantial peaks in the middle of this century, before falling as comparative advantage switched to manufactures that are more intensive in the use of Japan's increasingly more abundant human and physical capital. Even *within* the textile/clothing sector, production and exports of the more capital-intensive activities have gradually increased in relative importance in that sector. Given these structural changes, it is not surprising that the share of natural fibres in Japan's exports fell to virtually zero by the middle of this century and that the fibre share of Japan's imports grew initially before falling, along with the relative rise and demise of textiles and clothing.

Nor is it surprising, given also that Japan's total trade grew ten times as fast as world trade between the 1870s and 1930s, that this period was characterized by a steady decline in Britain's once-dominant share of world exports of textiles and clothing and world imports of natural fibres. Britain was the world's first major exporter of industrial products, beginning with textiles. In the nineteenth century it supplied more than half the world's trade in textile products. (Most of the remainder came from France and Germany.) During the Industrial Revolution Britain was also the destination for the vast majority of the world's trade in natural fibres because its own domestic suppliers (principally woolgrowers) were incapable of matching the growth in fibre demand by British factories.

The importance of these products to Britain is reflected in their dominance in British trade. In the latter half of the eighteenth century textiles accounted for more than half of Britain's exports, and by the 1840s this share had risen to almost three-quarters. The share of natural fibres in British imports grew in parallel fashion: by the mid-nineteenth century fibres accounted for about one-third of total imports.

Competition then began to erode both the importance of Britain in world textile markets and the importance of textiles in British exports. Japanese industrial development had an especially dramatic effect on these traditional industries. Japan's share of world exports of textiles and clothing grew from less than 2 per cent in 1899 to 22 per cent by 1939. Over the same period Britain's share of world trade in textiles and clothing fell from 47 to 37 per cent. By the 1930s, the share of textiles and clothing in Britain's exports had fallen to one-quarter, and the share of natural fibres in imports had fallen to one-tenth, from three times these levels a century before.

The growth in Japanese competitiveness in textile production was reflected also in Japan's changing role in natural fibre markets. Its importance as an exporter of raw silk gradually declined and its importance as an importer of raw cotton and wool expanded dramatically during the first half of this century. By the 1950s, Japan accounted for one-quarter of US cotton exports and one-fifth of Australian wool exports – and the latter share was two-fifths by the early 1970s. By contrast Britain, which had provided a market for three-quarters of US cotton exports and virtually all Australian wool exports before the 1870s, has accounted for less than 5 per cent of these fibre exports since the early 1970s.

Jápan's share of those world markets continued to grow until the take-off of another generation of newly industrializing economies (NIEs), notably Hong Kong, (South) Korea and Taiwan from the late 1950s/early 1960s. The rise of these economies caused the textile industries in Japan to decline in relative importance domestically and internationally in the same way as had occurred in Europe and the UK in response to Japan's economic growth. Moreover, this subsequent decline in Japan occurred first for labour-intensive clothing and last for capital-intensive synthetic fibres, again as we would expect from standard trade theory.

This pattern of development is now being repeated in another generation of NIEs. Chapters 3 and 4 show that during the 1980s the textile and clothing industries of both China and Thailand have grown extremely rapidly as those countries have adopted more outward-looking policies. Both are expanding their shares of GDP, employment and exports accounted for by these manufactures, and are becoming more dependent on imports of fibres.

Moreover, the emergence of China especially as a major exporter of textile products is now putting competitive pressure on Asia's advanced developing economies as well as adding to pressure on manufacturers in high-income countries. The growth in exports of these products from Korea and Taiwan slowed down considerably in the 1980s, but China's expansion is more than compensating so that the importance of East Asia in world textile and clothing exports has continued to grow, just as it did in the previous three decades when Hong Kong, Korea and Taiwan overshadowed Japan in these markets. Over the same period the rapidly developing economies of East Asia – like Japan before them – have switched from being important exporters of natural fibres to being gradually more and more important as fibre importers. It is true that China's development slowed in the late 1980s as a consequence of macroeconomic difficulties and political unrest. However, long-run trends are likely to resume in the 1990s, particularly if the Chinese government were to introduce further marcroeconomic policy reforms.

In short, the decline of Britain and Europe as exporters of textiles and clothing and importers of natural fibres has been accompanied by the increasing importance of first Japan, then Hong Kong, Korea and Taiwan and now mainland China and some Southeast Asian countries in these markets. The emergence of East Asia's second and third generation NIEs in turn has contributed to the relative demise of Japan's producers, and China's emergence is now beginning to have the same effect on the more advanced Asian NIEs as well. These developments are thus tracing out a landscape of hills through time formed by the different countries' importance in world textile and clothing exports, and this landscape is mirrored in their changing importance in world imports of natural fibres as agricultural comparative advantage declines with the industrial development of each country. And within each densely populated economy we are seeing first a rise and then demise of the relative importance of the textile/ clothing sector.

A major policy interest in this long-run process of rise and decline of the textile industries is the pace of adjustment in the established supplier countries and the scope that adjustment creates for newcomer suppliers. These market access issues are critical for countries like China and Thailand that are at the beginning of a process of industrial development and economic reform, for they would pursue more vigorously their outward-looking strategy if convinced that export expansion would be accommodated rather than thwarted by trade barriers. (The same issues will arise if and when South Asian and some Sub-Saharan African and Latin American countries alter their trade policies in the same direction.) Now is an especially opportune time to provide Chinese policymakers with evidence that will give them confidence to proceed with their reform process: the Chinese leadership is understandably concerned that the potentially very large volume of their textile and clothing exports may trigger import barriers which would substantially depress international prices. But the issue of market access for exports of these labour-intensive products in which NIEs have their strongest comparative advantage is of great importance to advanced industrial economies also, for without open export markets the NIEs will grow slower and thereby be less of a market for the exports of advanced economies.

The history of structural transformation in earlier-developed economies summarized in the first part of this volume suggests that the world economy has adjusted amply in the past to major new suppliers of textile and clothing exports. This experience suggests that the current emergence of another generation of exporters, dominated by

China but including smaller countries like Thailand, may well stimulate
further reductions in production growth in advanced economies. In
that case the prospects for successfully pursuing a more open trade
policy in countries like China and Thailand would look rosy.

To reduce even further the uncertainty about the prospects for new
textile and clothing exporters, Part II of this volume looks in detail at
the adjustment experiences of the advanced industrial countries. It
begins with an analysis in Chapter 5 of the Multi-fibre Arrangement
(MFA) and the role it has played in limiting the penetration of imports
from developing countries into industrial-country markets. That evidence, from a global computable general equilibrium model, suggests
that while it is true that developing countries have penetrated those
markets very considerably, liberalization of the MFA would allow a
great deal more penetration. This latter point is also the conclusion
drawn for Thailand in particular from the modelling results presented
in Chapter 4.

A number of adjustment strategies are open to and have been
adopted by the mature economies and would be pursued even more
if the MFA were to be liberalized. One is specialization *within* the
textiles and clothing sector of their economy. A point not often stressed
in discussions of these industries is that there is a wide range of factor
intensities of production within this industry group. For example,
finished textiles and standard clothing production is very intensive in
the use of unskilled labour while synthetic yarn production is extremely
capital intensive. Clothing and finished textiles are thus the first items
to emerge in the exports of a resource-poor, newly-industrializing
country and the first to decline as an economy matures. Synthetic
fibres and yarn tend to be the last to begin to be exported, and
comparative advantage in that product group tends to linger. The
emergence of new generations of textile and clothing producers thus
puts greatest pressure on the segments of the industry that are least
capital intensive, but it enhances the prospects of other segments. The
differences in factor intensity of different production processes can
result in a high degree of complementarity between new and established
suppliers. As a result, the degree of intra-industry trade increases.

Subcontracting or licensing of firms in newly industrializing countries, perhaps with the help of direct foreign investment joint ventures,
is another way in which firms in more developed economies can
respond to potential new suppliers. Indeed the MFA's preferential
access arrangements for established suppliers as compared with newcomers encourages this strategy. Another strategy is to invest heavily
in research and development to produce new techniques of production
which are more labour saving. Advanced-economy producers have in
many cases argued successfully for high levels of protection from
import competition to give them time to become more labour
productive.

Chapter 6 shows that Japan has adopted all of these strategies in its efforts to restructure in the face of both new opportunities in high-tech manufacturing and increasing competition from neighbouring countries in standard-technology textile and clothing activities. Japan's comparative advantage in some textile product areas has lingered as a result of these successful structural changes, although the strength of the yen in the latter 1980s has added to the pressure on these industries to decline in relative importance.

The myriad changes currently underway in Europe also include the above adjustments in the most advanced of Europe's economies. But there are major international relocations of production taking place *within* Europe that have potentially very important implications for low-cost suppliers of textiles and clothing in East Asia and elsewhere. Three simultaneous developments are highlighted in Chapter 7. One is the removal by 1992 of remaining barriers to market integration within the European Community (EC). This includes the completion of the integration with EC-9 of the three most recent and poorest members (Greece, Spain and Portugal). The latter Southern European countries are seeking to have the EC retain high external barriers to imports of labour-intensive manufactures such as clothing, to enable them to expand their share of the markets of high-wage EC countries to their north.

The second development involves the request by Turkey to be granted full membership of the EC. While this is unlikely to occur in the near future, the EC may well grant freer access of manufactures from Turkey (and other associate member countries around the Mediterranean). Again this preferential treatment would make it more difficult for Asian and other developing country exporters of textiles and clothing to penetrate EC markets.

Thirdly, the rapid thawing of relations between East and West Europe will result in increased opportunities for trade specialization between these groups of countries. The potentially much lower wage costs in East Europe, should market forces and hence productivity incentives be given freer reign there, should ensure that textiles and clothing become major export items from East to West. This too would dampen Asia's hopes to expand its market share in West Europe, particularly as preferential access has already been recommended for those neighbours by the EC Commission.

The situation in the United States is analysed in Chapter 8, where details of the restrictive MFA limitations are outlined. What comes out clearly from that case study is that even though there have been severe limitations on US imports of textiles and clothing from developing countries and rapid growth in unrestricted imports from Europe, East Asia has been able to increase its share of the US domestic market quite rapidly, and certainly faster than its shares of other industrial-country markets. In the decade to 1986, developing East Asia's share of the US market for textiles and clothing rose from 3 to 11 per cent, compared with an increase from 4 to only 8 per cent of the market of all advanced industrial countries. Moreover, the increased penetration into the US market by the developing economies of East Asia was faster for the heavily restricted textiles and clothing group of products than for other, less restricted labour-intensive manufactures. The latter fact underscores the point that textiles and especially clothing are products in which newly industrializing, densely populated economies initially have a very strong comparative advantage.

While Australia and New Zealand are small players in the global markets for textiles and clothing, the adjustments there have been sufficiently different to those in the northern hemisphere to warrant some discussion. Chapter 9 draws attention to the fact that, while they have a strong comparative advantage in natural fibre production (fine wool and cotton in Australia's case, coarser wool in New Zealand's), they have a strong comparative disadvantage in manufactured goods, including textiles and clothing. These two phenomena are both related to the extremely low population density of these countries. Even so, the clothing markets of these economies have not been penetrated as heavily as one might expect from neighbouring East Asia, and indeed New Zealand has been a net exporter of clothing in recent years. The movement towards a free trade area between Australia and New Zealand and their extremely high levels of assistance to knitting mills and clothing producers are important parts of the explanation for these trade patterns. With continuing liberalization of the restrictions on imports of these products, however, the extent of import penetration by East Asian and other newly industrializing producers will continue to increase.

The final chapter draws out the lessons that emerge from East Asia's experience in becoming involved in world markets for textiles, clothing and fibres. It then reviews what this implies for China in the 1990s and for the countries with which China would look to trade, and what the dramatic political changes in Eastern Europe could mean for East Asian and other exporters of textiles and clothing. The study concludes with an assessment of the prospects for liberalization of trade in these products, a few suggestions of ways to enhance those prospects for reform, and a brief mention of some implications from this case study for policies affecting other manufacturing industries in advanced industrial economies.

I
FIBRES, TEXTILES AND ECONOMIC DEVELOPMENT

1

The changing role of fibres, textiles and clothing as economies grow

Kym Anderson

This chapter addresses the first of the questions posed above in the introduction, namely: how is the relative importance of fibre, textile and clothing production and trade in an economy likely to change as that economy and the rest of the world grow? It begins by drawing on trade and development theory to develop hypotheses about the changing patterns of trade specialization, and then examines global evidence to show the extent to which those hypotheses are supported. In fact the available evidence provides very strong support for the theory. This allows that theory to be drawn on with confidence in subsequent chapters which explore in more depth the recent and prospective experiences of the rapidly industrializing economies of East Asia.

Standard trade and development theory

Much of the production and employment of a low-income economy involves the provision of essentials, namely food and fibre. Agriculture's shares of GDP and employment thus start at high levels. However, as economic development and commercialization proceed, agriculture's relative importance typically falls. This phenomenon is commonly attributed to two facts: the slow rise in the direct demand for food and to a lesser extent fibre as compared with other goods and services as incomes rise, and the rapid development of new technologies for agriculture relative to other sectors which leads to expanding farm output per hectare and per worker (Schultz 1945: chs 3–5; Kuznets 1966: ch. 3; Johnson 1973: ch. 5). Together these two facts ensure that in a closed economy (including the world as a whole) both the quantity and the price of agricultural relative to other products will decline, as will the share of employment in agriculture. The evidence certainly supports the declining relative importance of agriculture in world production and employment, and even appears to support the view that the long-run trend in agricultural prices relative to industrial product prices during this century has been downward.[1]

But what about an open economy which has the opportunity to trade at the international terms of trade? Consider a small open agrarian economy which could trade all of its primary products at those declining international terms of trade. Its primary sectors would decline in relative importance unless its own productivity growth is biased toward agriculture and mining sufficiently for the relative output changes to more than offset the adverse change in the terms of trade that result from economic growth abroad. This bias in productivity growth would have to be even stronger in a *large* open economy because its own contribution to world exports of primary products would depress the terms of trade even further.

Moreover, in reality many goods and services are such that transaction costs make them prohibitively expensive to trade internationally. In so far as these nontradables as a group tend to have a high income elasticity of demand and/or to be produced in industries which have relatively low rates of labour and total factor productivity growth, the share of nontradables in output and employment will rise over time. There is strong evidence to suggest the income elasticity of demand for services is above unity,[2] so that may well be true for nontradables as a group too, given that the bulk of nontradables are services. Evidence on the productivity growth of nontradables in total is difficult to find, but it would not be surprising if it was below that for tradables simply because the cold-shower effect of international competition on the former is absent. For these two reasons the shares of tradables in GDP and employment are more likely to decline than to increase in a growing economy.

If there is a tendency for the primary sector's relative importance in the tradable part of an open growing economy to decline, and if the tradables part of the total economy is likely to decline, then the combined effects of these tendencies multiply the likelihood of the primary sector's relative demise over time. For that *not* to happen, productivity growth in that sector has to be sufficiently greater than productivity growth in the other sectors so as to offset the effects of the decline in the relative price of primary products.[3]

1 The latter conclusion, which can be generalized to include all primary products, is still somewhat controversial, however. See, for example, Spraos (1980), Sapsford (1985) and Grilli and Yang (1988).

2 See, for example, Lluch, Powell and Williams (1977), Kravis, Heston and Summers (1983), and Theil and Clements (1987).

3 For a more detailed treatment of the above argument, see Anderson (1987; 1990a: ch. 2).

One might also expect the share of primary products in a country's exports to decline over time, though again this could be avoided by rapid productivity growth in the primary sector of the economy. The decline in the relative price of primary products in international markets due to the rest of the world's economic growth would, *ceteris paribus*, discourage domestic primary production and encourage domestic consumption of primary products while doing the opposite in the domestic market for manufactured goods. Only by exceptionally rapid primary productivity growth in one's own country could this be avoided. Even then for a large country its growth would have to be fast enough to offset the adverse effects its own expansion would have on further depressing the international terms of trade for primary products.

Must self-sufficiency in primary products such as natural fibres also decline as an economy grows? According to the standard Heckscher–Ohlin–Samuelson model of international trade, each country would export commodities which require relatively intensive use of the country's relatively abundant factors of production, and import commodities which would demand much of the country's relatively scarce factors. Empirical tests in the early postwar years failed to support this model of comparative advantage in its simplest form, giving rise to numerous attempts in modifying the theory to make it more applicable to the real world. Many of the earlier modifications were synthesized by Harry Johnson in his 1968 Wiksell Lectures. He suggested that the two-sector, two-factor, Heckscher–Ohlin–Samuelson model is more applicable, at least for manufactured goods, if capital is defined broadly to include not only physical capital equipment but also human skills, social capital, technological and organizational knowledge, and natural resources, while labour is defined in the narrow sense of human labour time availability. The relative capital intensity of different activities is then reflected in flow terms by relative value added per unit of labour time input.[4]

Anne Krueger has further modified the model to allow it to explain trade in primary products as well.[5] This modification separates out natural resources from Johnson's broad definition of capital, and integrates the model with the specific-factors model that has become popular again. It then becomes a model of an economy with two tradable sectors, producing primary products and manufactures, and three factors of production: natural resources which are specific to the primary sector, capital which is specific to the manufacturing

[4] The use of value added per worker as a measure of the overall capital intensity of production was first used to discuss US imports of manufactured goods from developing countries by Lary (1968).

[5] See Krueger (1977). Key elements of Krueger's model are presented more formally in Deardorff (1984). See also Eaton (1987) and Grossman and Helpman (1989a).

sector, and labour which is used in both sectors, is intersectorally mobile and exhibits diminishing marginal product in each sector. In this model, at a given set of international prices, the real wage rate is determined by the overall per worker endowment of natural resources and capital, as in the Johnson synthesis, while the pattern of comparative advantage between manufactures and primary products is influenced largely by the relative endowments of capital and natural resources in this country as compared with the rest of the world.

An underdeveloped country with little capital will produce mostly primary products and export them (in raw or lightly processed form) in exchange for manufactures. As the stock of industrial capital per worker expands in this as compared with other countries, relative wages increase and labour is attracted to the manufacturing sector. The country gradually switches from being predominantly a primary producer to being predominantly an exporter of (non-resource-based) manufactured goods, with the capital intensity of manufacturing activities increasing over time. Labour begins to be attracted to manufacturing at an earlier stage of economic development, and the non-resource-based manufactured goods initially exported use unskilled labour relatively more intensively, the lower the country's natural resources per worker and hence initial relative wage rate. This is because the relatively low wage will give the resource-poor country an international comparative advantage initially in labour-intensive, standard-technology manufactures.

Allowing for the fact that capital is required in addition to natural resources and labour in primary production strengthens the above conclusion. At a particular level of capital per worker, a country would tend to employ a greater share of its available capital in primary production rather than in manufacturing, the greater its agricultural land and mineral resource endowment per worker. This is because an abundance of natural resources per worker keeps down the price of those resources relative to labour and hence boosts the return from investing capital in the primary sector. This is a further reason for expecting that natural-resource-poor, densely populated countries will begin manufacturing at an earlier stage of capital availability per worker than will resource-rich countries. These changes in comparative advantage can proceed even more rapidly when barriers to foreign capital inflow are lowered.

The demand for food increases with population and per capita income while the demand for industrial raw materials increases with industrial production. Thus, relatively rapid increases in a country's national income and manufacturing output raise domestic relative to overseas demand for primary products and hasten the country's switch from being a net exporter to being a net importer of primary products, including natural fibres in the case of resource-poor economies whose industrialization begins with labour-intensive products such as textiles and clothing.

To summarize, this theory suggests that a poor country opening up to international trade will tend to specialize in the production and export of primary products, though less so the more densely populated the country. If its domestic incomes grow more rapidly than the rest of the world's, its export specialization will gradually move away from primary products (in raw or lightly processed form) to manufactures. The manufactured goods initially exported will be more labour intensive the more resource-poor or densely populated the country. Since many processes in textile and clothing production tend to be intensive in the use of unskilled labour, they would be among the items initially exported by a newly industrializing, densely populated country. And as the demands for textile raw materials by that country's expanding textile industry grow, so the country's net exports of natural fibre would diminish, or net imports of natural fibre would increase, *ceteris paribus*. On the other hand, since synthetic fibre production is an extremely capital-intensive activity,[6] it will tend to be imported by the newly industrializing country from relatively more capital-abundant countries. If this newly industrializing country is growing more rapidly than other countries, it will initially increase its shares of world production and exports of textiles and clothing and of world imports of fibres at the expense of more mature industrial economies. In time, another generation of newly industrializing countries would duplicate this process,[7] so gradually displacing the former in those world markets but providing a growing export market for capital-intensive synthetic fibres. Meanwhile, slower-growing, land-abundant economies – even rich ones – may retain an export specialization in natural fibres or other primary products and import textiles, clothing and other labour-intensive manufactures from densely populated lower-wage economies.

[6] Perhaps the best single indicator of (physical and human) capital intensity of production is value added per worker (Johnson 1968; Lary 1968). According to 1980 data for industry value added, from the Japanese input-output table published by the Bank of Japan in its *Economic Statistics Yearbook* (Tokyo, 1984), and for number of employees, published by the Ministry of International Trade and Industry in its *Textile Statistics Yearbook* (Tokyo, 1981), the value added per worker in 1980 in Japan's clothing industries averaged 4 million yen, while in the natural-fibre spinning and weaving industries it averaged 4.8 million yen, and in the synthetic fibre and spinning industries it was 24.1 million yen. Similar data for Korea from the Bank of Korea's 1985 *Input-Output Table* (Seoul, 1986) also show value added per worker to be highest in synthetic fibre production (12.8 million won), intermediate for yarns and fabrics (4.6 million won) and lowest for finished textiles (3.9 million won) and clothing (2.4 million won).

[7] For more on these changes in comparative advantage that accompany economic growth and their effects on global patterns of production and trade, see Akimatsu (1961), Balassa (1979), Leamer (1984), and Balassa and Bauwens (1988).

Empirical support for the theory

This theory has strong empirical support from both cross-sectional and time-series evidence.[8] For example, the theory suggests the share of primary products in total exports (PRI) would be negatively related to both per capita income (Y, a crude index of the endowment of capital per worker) and population density (PD, a crude index of the endowment of natural resources per capita),[9] and this is what is obtained in estimating ordinary-least-squares regression equations from cross-sectional data. For example, using the data available for the year 1983 from the World Bank (1985a, 1986) for 69 countries with populations exceeding one million, one obtains the following regression result (t-values in parentheses):

$$PRI = 180.4 - 9.75\ln Y - 11.52\ln PD, \overline{R}^2 = .54$$
$$\quad\quad\quad\quad (5.68)\quad\quad (7.15)$$

The theory suggests also that the share of labour-intensive goods such as textiles and clothing in total exports of manufactures would be very high at first as per capita income and industrialization increase from a low base and then would fall, and would tend to be higher the greater the population density of the country. Recent data from the World Bank (1988) provide 1986 shares of textiles and clothing in manufactured exports (TEX) as well as Y and PD data for 63 countries, from which the following regression equation is obtained:

$$TEX = 25.6 + 7.77\ln Y - 0.523(\ln Y)^2 + 0.00136 PD, \overline{R}^2 = 0.52$$
$$\quad\quad\quad (5.6)\quad\quad (5.7)\quad\quad\quad\quad (6.3)$$

These regression equations are clearly consistent with the theory of changing comparative advantage presented above, with the latter equation suggesting the share of textiles and clothing in manufacturing exports declines at an increasing rate as income per capita rises.

The four key conclusions that can be drawn from these statistical relationships are confirmed also in the first two columns of Table 1.1. They are (a) that the shares of primary products in total exports and of textiles and clothing in manufactured exports will be higher in developing economies than in advanced industrial economies, (b) that these shares will tend to decline over time in all economies, (c) that the declines will be faster in economies that are growing relatively

---

[8] Since many empirical studies are available with such evidence, only a small sample is presented here. For more detailed evidence, see, for example, Kuznets (1971), Chenery and Syrquin (1975) and Chenery, Robinson and Syrquin (1986).

[9] On the usefulness and limitations of population density as a proxy for primary resources per worker, see Keesing and Sherk (1971) and Bowen (1983).

Table 1.1:   Export specialization and net exports as a share of world trade in primary products, fibres, textiles and clothing,[a] industrial and developing economies, 1965 to 1987

	Primary products' share (%) of total exports	Textiles and clothing's share (%) of manufactured exports	Index of export specialization[b] in					Net exports as a % of world trade in:			
			All primary products	Natural fibres	Textiles	Clothing	Synthetic fibres	Natural fibres	Textiles	Clothing	Synthetic fibres
All advanced industrial economies											
1965–69	29	9	0.70	0.64	1.03	0.98	1.29	–29	11	–10	38
1970–79	27	7	0.64	0.70	1.05	0.79	1.34	–17	6	–32	39
1980–87	25	6	0.66	0.80	0.95	0.60	1.25	–4	2	–44	37
All developing economies											
1965–69	84	38	2.02	2.23	0.93	1.05	0.11	38	–9	9	–22
1970–79	80	32	1.98	1.73	0.90	1.50	0.09	24	–3	28	–30
1980–87	68	27	1.76	1.42	1.20	1.98	0.37	10	—	40	–30
Japan											
1965–69	7	16	0.17	0.14	2.60	1.81	2.96	–15	13	10	16
1970–79	5	7	0.13	0.07	1.59	0.44	2.79	–18	8	–1	19
1980–87	4	4	0.12	0.05	1.12	0.15	1.66	–15	6	–3	14
Northeast Asian NIEs[c]											
1965–69	20	47	0.48	0.40	2.89	14.40	0.01	—	–1	15	–5
1970–79	11	39	0.29	0.44	3.11	12.10	0.39	–1	1	25	–7
1980–87	8	29	0.21	0.19	2.84	7.51	1.20	–4	2	25	–1

[a] All primary products are SITC 0 to 4 plus 68 less 266; natural fibres are SITC 26 less 266; textiles are SITC 65; clothing is SITC 84; and synthetic fibres are SITC 266.
[b] The index of export specialization is the share of a commodity group in an economy's exports as a ratio of that commodity group's share of world exports, following Balassa (1965).
[c] Hong Kong, Korea and Taiwan.
Source: International Economic Data Bank, Trade Data Tapes, Australian National University, Canberra, 1990.

rapidly, and (d) that within each of these two groups, relatively densely populated economies will tend to have lower shares of exports due to primary products and higher shares due to textiles and clothing. The experiences of Japan and Northeast Asia's newly industrializing economies (NIEs) illustrate the latter two points since they are very densely populated and have been the world's fastest-growing economies.

There are two other indicators of changes in comparative advantage which are useful for present purposes. One is an index of export specialization, or what Balassa (1965) called an index of 'revealed' comparative advantage, defined as the share of a product group in an economy's exports as a ratio of that commodity group's share of world exports. Table 1.1 shows this index over time for all primary products, natural fibres, textiles, clothing and synthetic fibres. Clearly, developing economies as a group have a much stronger comparative advantage in primary products in general and in natural fibres in particular than do industrial economies as a group, by a factor of two or three. For both groups this index has been declining for all primary products and especially for natural fibres in the case of developing economies. Comparative advantage in textiles and clothing as measured by this index has been declining for industrial economies and increasing for developing economies, with the trend much stronger for clothing. And industrial economies have a much stronger comparative advantage in capital-intensive synthetic fibres than do developing economies, although the Northeast Asian NIEs have rapidly strengthened their competitiveness in that product group.

Japan, being very densely populated, has a much stronger comparative disadvantage (advantage) in primary products (manufactures) than the average industrial country. Hence its export specialization index in the 1960s was much lower for primary products including natural fibres and much higher for textiles and clothing than other industrial countries. And since Japan's economy has grown faster than other industrial economies its comparative advantage in these products has declined faster too, according to Table 1.1.

The NIEs of Northeast Asia (Hong Kong, Korea and Taiwan) also are endowed with few natural resources per worker and so their rapid economic growth has resulted in a much lower level of and sharper decline in their index of export specialization in primary products compared with other developing economies, while their indexes of export specialization in textiles and clothing are very high. Note, however, that the latter indexes have been declining since the 1960s for labour-intensive clothing, had begun to decline in the 1970s for textiles, and have been rising rapidly for capital-intensive synthetic fibres. These changes reflect the fact that the comparative advantage of these NIEs is gradually moving away from unskilled labour-intensive manufacturing towards more capital-intensive processing.

Notice also from Table 1.1 that in industrial countries textiles have a higher and a less rapidly decreasing index of export specialization than clothing, and conversely in developing economies, reflecting the fact (see footnote 6 above) that clothing production is more intensive in the use of unskilled labour than textile production on average.

This export specialization index is less than ideal as an indicator of comparative advantage because it ignores what is happening to a country's import pattern. An indicator which better captures both trade patterns is shown on the right-hand side of Table 1.1, namely, net exports as a percentage of world trade. The story is much the same, however. Industrial (developing) economies as a group are net importers (exporters) of natural fibres and net exporters (importers) of clothing, while textiles are in between: they switched in the mid-1980s from being a net export group to a net import group for industrial countries, and conversely for developing economies.

It should be kept in mind that textiles and clothing comprise a heterogeneous set of commodities which not only use a wide range of production techniques in terms of their labour or capital intensity but also face widely varying elasticities of demand. Thus France until the 1980s had remained a net exporter of clothes in terms of value by exporting high-priced fashion clothing, and Italy is still a net clothes exporter. Moreover, as real ocean transport costs and international communication costs continue to diminish, countries are becoming more specialized in producing intermediate goods. This is reflected in the changes that are taking place in the extent of intra-industry trade, that is, in the extent to which imports fail to dominate exports or vice versa.

Advanced industrial economies are gradually reducing the degree of their intra-industry trade in clothes, but some are increasing their intra-industry trade in intermediate textile products as their textile firms specialize more heavily in modern capital-intensive processes and leave the more labour-intensive processes (including the final assembly of clothing) to lower-wage countries (Table 1.2). This point, which is taken up again in Chapter 9 by Peter Lloyd, can also be seen from the data in Table 1.3 on shares of different country groups in gross imports and gross exports of the world as a whole. All groups are participants in both imports and exports of natural fibres, textiles, clothing and synthetic fibres, but textiles stand out as having the highest degree of intra-industry trade among these four commodity groups. For industrial countries as a whole, imports as a share of consumption and exports as a share of production have been increasing at about the same rate for textiles while the former has increased much faster than the latter for clothing (Table 1.4).

As is evident from Table 1.3, developing countries now supply more than half the world's exports of clothing and a third of global textile exports, double their shares of the late 1960s. This is reflected in the dramatic increase in the penetration of imports into industrial country markets for these products. The self-sufficiency of industrial countries

Table 1.2: Index of intra-industry trade[a] in textiles and clothing, various industrial market economies, 1965 to 1987 (per cent in value terms)

	Australia	Canada	France	West Germany	Hong Kong	Italy	Japan	Sweden	United Kingdom	United States
Textiles										
1965–69	91	72	–32	7	31	–52	–86	60	–20	25
1975–79	87	73	5	1	44	–32	–49	44	5	–8
1985–87	77	64	12	–10	58	–27	–39	31	30	38
Clothing										
1965–69	66	54	–27	32	–86	–85	–90	52	10	59
1975–79	90	65	–6	48	–86	–79	44	60	21	74
1985–87	91	67	25	46	–47	–72	63	67	31	91

[a] Imports minus exports as a percentage of imports plus exports. The closer this number is to zero, the greater the degree of intra-industry trade. The closer a number is to +100 (–100) the more imports dominate exports (imports are dominated by exports). Grubel and Lloyd (1975) define their index of intra-industry trade in an equivalent form, namely 100 minus the modulus of the above number, divided by 100, so that their index is closer to unity the more intra-industry trade is present.

Source: International Economic Data Bank, Trade Data Tapes, Australian National University, Canberra, 1990.

Table 1.3: *Importance of industrial, developing, centrally planned and East Asian economies in world trade in fibres, textiles and clothing, 1965 to 1987[a]*
(per cent)

	Share of world exports of:				Share of world imports of:			
	Textiles	Clothing	Synthetic fibres	Natural fibres	Textiles	Clothing	Synthetic fibres	Natural fibres
Industrial market economies								
1965–69	75	71	95	47	64	81	57	71
1970–74	74	59	95	47	67	86	56	63
1975–79	71	50	91	50	66	87	52	59
1980–84	65	42	85	53	60	83	44	55
1985–87	62	38	83	55	63	87	52	57
Developing economies								
1965–69	19	21	2	45	28	13	24	15
1970–74	20	32	1	44	24	8	29	19
1974–79	24	41	3	39	26	9	34	24
1980–84	29	49	8	36	32	12	41	29
1985–87	33	54	11	37	31	10	37	30
Centrally planned Europe[b]								
1965–69	6	8	3	8	8	6	19	14
1970–74	6	9	4	9	9	6	15	18
1975–79	5	9	6	11	8	4	14	17
1980–84	6	9	7	11	8	5	15	16
1985–87	5	8	6	8	6	3	11	13
East Asian economies[c]								
1965–69	22	28	17	5	11	3	11	24
1970–74	22	31	22	6	13	5	16	31
1975–79	23	34	20	6	13	6	17	34
1980–84	28	41	20	7	17	8	22	37
1985–87	30	43	20	12	22	10	23	37

[a] SITC categories are as follows: textiles 65, clothing 84, synthetic fibres 266, natural fibres 26 less 266.
[b] Based on the trade of these non-reporting countries with reporting countries, and hence excluding trade within centrally planned Europe.
[c] Japan; the Northeast Asian NIEs of Hong Kong, Korea and Taiwan; China; and the members of ASEAN.
Source: International Economic Data Bank, Trade Data Tapes, Australian National University, Canberra, 1990.

Table 1.4: *Trade specialization in textiles and clothing, industrial market economies,[a] 1970 to 1986*
(per cent)

	Gross imports/ consumption	Net imports/ consumption	Gross exports/ production	Net imports/ imports plus exports
Textiles				
1970–73	14.5	–0.3	14.7	–1.1
1974–77	17.5	–0.2	17.7	–0.5
1978–81	20.6	0.8	20.0	1.9
1982–85	20.8	2.0	19.2	5.1
1986	22.5	3.3	19.8	8.0
Clothing				
1970–73	13.5	4.0	9.9	17.6
1974–77	20.9	8.7	13.3	26.5
1978–81	27.6	12.8	17.0	30.1
1982–85	30.6	16.8	16.6	37.8
1986	35.9	19.9	20.0	38.3

[a] Australia, Belgium, Canada, Finland, France, West Germany, Italy, Japan, the Netherlands, Norway, Sweden, the United Kingdom and the United States only.
Source: See Appendix to this volume.

in textiles declined from just over 100 per cent in the early 1970s to less than 97 per cent in the mid-1980s, while for clothing the decline in self-sufficiency was from 96 to 80 per cent over the same period (column (2) of Table 1.4). As Table 1.5 shows, the share of developing country imports of textiles, clothing and footwear in domestic sales in industrial countries trebled between the early 1970s and the mid-1980s, and the increase occurred in virtually all industrial countries. These import items are now as dominant as all other light manufactures put together, and are far more dominant than other, more capital-intensive manufactures. It is the inexorable increase in import penetration by developing country producers of textiles and clothing that makes these items important for newly industrializing countries and at the same time of concern to politicians in high-wage countries who are worried about job losses in their constituencies.

Conclusion

Brief though this evidence is, it strongly suggests that the theory presented earlier in the chapter is helpful in explaining the changing pattern of world production and trade in fibres, textiles and clothing, notwithstanding the prevalence of trade-distorting barriers provided by the MFA and related policies. The experiences of Japan and East Asia's NIEs, reflected in Table 1.1, are especially dramatic and are deserving of closer attention. Hence they are examined in a longer historical perspective in the next two chapters.

Table 1.5: *Import penetration into various industrial-country markets for textiles, clothing and other manufactures,*[a]
1970 to 1986
(imports as a per cent of domestic consumption)

	All industrial market economies	EC	EFTA	Japan	United States	Canada	Australia
IMPORTS FROM ALL COUNTRIES							
Textiles, clothing, footwear and other leather products (ISIC 32)							
1970–73	13.8	22.6	41.8	6.6	6.1	19.5	18.1
1974–77	18.3	30.6	48.7	7.8	7.2	22.8	22.7
1978–81	22.6	37.6	58.0	9.3	10.5	22.3	24.1
1982–85	24.1	43.0	64.0	9.9	14.4	22.7	25.8
1986	26.8	44.8	67.1	8.5	18.7	27.0	26.1
Other light manufactures (ISIC 39)							
1970–73	20.4	42.8	42.2	8.9	11.5	22.0	27.7
1974–77	25.2	54.3	48.0	8.5	13.6	25.3	36.0
1978–81	34.1	75.8	55.0	9.5	18.2	40.1	39.7
1982–85	30.7	77.0	58.1	8.8	22.1	31.9	41.4
1986	30.7	61.8	56.0	9.0	26.8	34.0	43.8
All manufactures (ISIC 3)							
1970–73	12.4	21.3	31.2	4.5	6.1	28.2	15.2
1974–77	15.1	26.2	34.3	5.1	7.4	30.3	18.5
1978–81	17.0	30.1	35.7	5.3	9.0	32.0	20.2
1982–85	17.7	34.4	38.0	5.5	11.1	30.6	22.0
1986	17.6	33.3	36.8	4.3	12.2	34.4	24.5
IMPORTS FROM DEVELOPING ECONOMIES							
Textiles, clothing, footwear and other leather products (ISIC 32)							
1970–73	3.6	3.7	4.2	4.3	3.0	4.0	6.1
1974–77	5.8	6.6	7.3	5.1	4.9	6.6	9.9
1978–81	8.1	9.0	9.2	6.0	7.9	7.7	11.9
1982–85	10.4	11.1	11.3	6.6	11.1	9.9	13.6
1986	11.4	11.4	11.5	5.9	14.1	12.4	13.9
Other light manufactures (ISIC 39)							
1970–73	4.5	4.8	2.2	4.5	4.4	2.⁷	5.6
1974–77	6.0	7.5	3.7	4.4	6.0	3.6	8.8
1978–81	8.5	11.1	6.4	5.3	8.7	5.0	12.3
1982–85	10.7	16.4	8.7	5.0	11.7	5.1	16.1
1986	11.5	14.1	9.6	5.1	14.2	6.8	19.3
All manufactures (ISIC 3)							
1970–73	1.5	1.8	1.4	1.4	1.3	1.2	1.5
1974–77	2.1	2.3	1.7	1.9	2.1	1.5	3.0
1978–81	2.6	2.8	2.0	2.0	2.7	1.8	3.7
1982–85	3.1	3.5	2.1	2.0	3.5	2.3	4.2
1986	2.9	3.0	1.9	1.5	3.6	3.0	4.3

Source: See Appendix to this volume.

2

The experience of Japan in historical and international perspective

Young-Il Park and Kym Anderson*

In recent decades producers of textiles and clothing in advanced industrial economies have been the first large group of manufacturers to come under pressure to decline as a result of import competition from newly industrializing economies (NIEs). The main reason for this phenomenon, as pointed out in the previous chapter, is that many processes in textile and clothing production tend to be intensive in the use of unskilled labour so, as unskilled labour becomes relatively scarce in the advanced economies, comparative advantage gradually moves to countries less well endowed with physical and human capital per worker. However, only a subset of countries with low capital–labour ratios are likely to become exporters of labour-intensive manufactures. The theory summarized in Chapter 1 suggests that subset is limited to NIEs that are poorly endowed with natural resources per worker and hence characterized by low real wages for labour attracted from primary production to industry, and whose stock of industrial capital per worker is expanding relatively rapidly from a low base. The increasing dominance of East Asia's resource-poor, rapidly growing economies in the growth of imports of textiles and clothing into the advanced industrial economies, as depicted in Table 1.5 above, is certainly consistent with that theory.

One of the purposes of this chapter is to show that this theory is also supported strongly by evidence provided over a much longer term by Japan's experience. That evidence shows that the resource-poor, rapidly industrializing Japanese economy gradually strengthened its comparative advantage in textiles and clothing from late last century but subsequently lost it steadily during the postwar period as exports of these items dwindled and imports from newly industrializing

* The authors are grateful for helpful comments from Peter Drysdale, Christopher Findlay and Ben Smith. The chapter was written in part while Kym Anderson was a Visiting Fellow in the Institute for International Economic Studies at the University of Stockholm. Earlier versions of parts of it appeared as Park (1988) and Park and Anderson (1991).

neighbours rose. In addition, the Japanese experience supports two corollaries to that theory. One is that the importance of natural fibres in imports of such an economy gradually rises and then falls as that economy develops, as does its share of world fibre trade. The other is that the most (least) labour-intensive segments of the textile and clothing sector will be the first (last) to become important in the economy's exports and in world trade. In particular, Japan's comparative advantage in synthetic fibres, production of which is extremely capital intensive, is only now beginning to come under competitive pressure from later-developing economies, long after the demise of Japan's more labour-intensive sub-sectors began.

The chapter begins by specifying more precisely what the standard trade and development theory outlined in the previous chapter would predict for textiles, clothing and fibre markets during the past 120 years of Japan's economic development. It then looks at the changing status of these industries within Japan, at Japan's impact on older economies such as the United Kingdom, and at the impact on Japan since the 1960s of the rapid development of a subsequent generation of NIEs. As well, the changes in Japan's fibre trade and its effects on the trade pattern of fibre-exporting countries are examined.

Given that the experience of Japan and its interrelationships with earlier and later industrializing countries and with fibre suppliers provides strong support for the trade and development theory summarized in Chapter 1, it is possible to discuss with some confidence both the likely pattern of future developments in world fibre, textile and clothing markets and the appropriate policy responses of different countries to these developments. In particular, the final section of the chapter highlights the impact China is making – and is likely to continue to make – on textile and clothing markets in Japan and the rest of the world, which leads into the analysis of China in Chapter 3.

What theory would predict

Japan's rapid economic growth began with the Meiji Restoration in 1868. The deregulation and opening up of the largely agrarian economy at that time was followed by a century of growth in Japanese incomes and capital formation at rates that were more than twice as fast as in the more mature economies (Kuznets 1966; Maddison 1982). The share of Japan's GDP that was exported also rose dramatically so that Japan's trade grew almost ten times as fast as world trade between the 1870s and the 1930s. Also, Japan was then and still is one of the most densely populated large economies in the world with a very poor endowment of agricultural land and mineral resources per worker.

From the theory outlined in Chapter 1 it would therefore be reasonable to expect the following:

— the primary sector's shares of GDP, employment and exports in Japan to have fallen from a high level around 1870;
— the shares of textiles and clothing in Japan's GDP, employment and exports to have risen from 1870 but subsequently to have fallen as comparative advantage moved towards more capital-intensive manufactures;
— the share of natural fibres in Japan's exports to have fallen continually and its share of Japan's imports to have grown initially before falling, along with the relative rise and demise of textiles;
— the production and export of the more capital-intensive activities within Japan's textiles/clothing sector to have gradually increased in importance in that sector;
— the shares of world exports of textiles and clothing from and world imports of natural fibres by older industrial economies such as the United Kingdom to have fallen as Japan expanded;
— Japan's shares of world exports of textiles and clothing and of world imports of natural fibres to have grown until the take-off of another generation of NIEs (e.g. Hong Kong, South Korea and Taiwan from the1960s, mainland China from 1978); and
— the subsequent decline in Japan's importance in international markets for textiles and clothing to have occurred first for labour-intensive clothing and last for capital-intensive synthetic fibres.

That is, in addition to the relative importance of textiles and clothing in Japan's *domestic* economy rising and then falling, the shares of Japan in world exports of textiles and clothing and world imports of natural fibres also would be expected to trace out a hill-shaped path over time, the latter being part of a landscape in which the hill for older economies would be to the left of Japan on this time path and that for more recent industrializers would be to the right.

Evidence from the Japanese experience
The domestic economy

Table 2.1 provides evidence which clearly supports these expectations concerning the changing importance of various commodities to the Japanese economy. At the time of the Meiji Restoration, the primary sector accounted for about half of Japan's GDP and more than three-quarters of employment and exports (columns (1) to (3)). Since that time those shares have declined steadily so that at present the primary sector is contributing less than 10 per cent of employment and less than 3 per cent to GDP and to exports.

Table 2.1: *Importance of textiles, clothing and fibres in production, employment and trade, Japan, 1874 to 1987 (percentage shares)*

	Primary products' share of:			Textiles and clothing's share of total:				Textiles and clothing's share of manufacturing:			Natural fibre's share of total imports	Index of export[c] specialization in textiles and clothing	Index of import[c] specialization in natural fibres
	GDP[a]	Employment	Exports[b]	GDP[a]	Employment	Exports	Imports	GDP[a]	Employment	Exports			
	(1)	(2)	(3)	(4)	(5)	(6)	(7)	(8)	(9)	(10)	(11)	(12)	(13)
1874–79	45	73	83 (38)	..	..	4	54	10	..	25	1	..	..
1880–89	44	71	77 (37)	2	.	9	44	18	..	36	6	..	..
1890–99	43	67	55 (29)	4	..	23	19	26	..	51	21	1.2	1.1
1900–09	35	65	45 (26)	5	7	28	11	26	62	51	26	..	..
1910–19	34	59	34 (23)	7	8	34	8	28	61	52	32	1.5	1.4
1920–29	30	50	38 (32)	8	9	34	5	30	55	56	27	1.9	1.5
1930–39	18	45	20 (13)	9	6	35	3	28	37	44	25	3.4	2.4
1950–59	18	39	12 (1)	3	4	36	–	11	22	38	23	5.4	3.5
1960–69	10	24	7 (–)	2	3	19	1	7	14	19	10	2.9	1.5
1970–79	5	13	3 (–)	1	2	6	3	5	11	6	3	1.2	0.9
1980–84	3	9	2 (–)	1	2	4	3	4	8	4	2	0.8	0.8
1985–87	3	9	1 (–)	1	2	3	3	3	8	3	2	0.5	0.8

[a] Gross domestic product shares in the prewar period are at constant 1934–36 prices, thereafter at current prices.

[b] Numbers in parentheses are for raw silk (the only natural fibre exported).

[c] Indexes of import and export specialization are the share of these items in Japan's trade as a ratio of the share of those items in world trade. Textiles and clothing are SITC items 65 and 84; natural fibres are SITC items 26 less 266. Over the pre-1950 period these indexes are for the single years 1899, 1913, 1929 and 1937, global data for which are from Maizels (1963).

Sources: United Nations, *Yearbook of National Accounts Statistics*, New York, various issues; International Labour Organization, *Yearbook of Labour Statistics*, Geneva, various issues; Bank of Japan, *Economic Statistics Annual*, Tokyo, various issues; K. Ohkawa and M. Shinohara (eds), *Patterns of Japanese Economic Development: A Quantitative Appraisal*, New Haven, Yale University Press, 1989; and I. Yamazawa and Y. Yamamoto, *Estimates of Long Term Economic Statistics of Japan Since 1868*, Tokyo: Toyo Keizai Shimposha, various years.

Second, the contributions of textiles and clothing to Japan's economy grew steadily from the 1870s to the 1930s (columns (4) to (6) of Table 2.1). Around 1930, those manufacturing industries provided one-tenth of GDP and employment in Japan and one-third of the country's total export earnings. Their importance within the rapidly expanding manufacturing sector peaked a decade or so earlier, when they accounted for 30 per cent of manufacturing value-added and about 60 per cent of both industrial employment and exports of manufactures (columns (8) to (10)). Initially, half of all imports expenditure was on manufactured inputs for the textile sector (predominantly yarns and fabrics) but, as domestic production of yarns and fabrics expanded, imports of natural fibres were required instead (compare columns (7) and (11)).

As the Japanese economy matured, these labour-intensive manufacturing industries rapidly lost their competitiveness internationally as NIEs with less capital per worker emerged in the postwar years. Today the textiles/clothing sector accounts for less than 2 per cent of GDP and employment in Japan and contributes less than 5 per cent of manufactured exports, which is less than is spent on fibre, textile and clothing imports.

A corollary to the loss in Japan's comparative advantage in primary products and the growth in demand by textiles manufacturers for natural fibres is the dramatic fall in the contribution of natural fibres to export earnings and initial rise in the share of fibres in import expenditure. In the 1870s raw silk accounted for about 40 per cent of exports, but this contribution had fallen to virtually zero by the 1940s (column (3) of Table 2.1). Meanwhile, raw cotton began to be imported in the 1870s and raw wool at the turn of the century. By about 1920, these fibres were accounting for almost one-third of Japan's total import bill (column (11)), a share that is comparable to the importance of energy products in Japan's imports in recent years. In the 1950s, when fibre prices were very high, this share was still about one-quarter, but it has since fallen to only 2 per cent with the declines in the textile industry and in fibre prices.

The growth and then decline in Japan's comparative advantage in textiles and clothing is summarized in column (12) of Table 2.1, which shows the importance of these products in Japan's exports as a ratio of their importance in world trade. This ratio rose from around unity late last century to a peak of 5.4 in the 1950s, before falling to below unity again in the 1980s. The peak in this index is later than in the earlier-mentioned indicators because the share of these items in world trade started falling earlier than did the share in Japan's exports, reflecting Japan's late emergence as an advanced industrial economy. The parallel index of import specialization in natural fibres shows a similar hill-shaped trend from below unity last century to a peak of

Table 2.2:   *The trade dependence of Japan's textile and clothing manufacturing industries, 1874 to 1988*
(per cent, value based)

	Share of production exported	Share of domestic sales supplied by imports
1874–81	2	42
1882–91	5	29
1892–1901	13	16
1902–11	26	15
1912–21	27	5
1922–31	27	7
1932–39	29	3
1951–55	24	1
1956–60	23	1
1961–65	18	1
1966–70	17	2
1971–75	14	5
1976–80	13	7
1981–85	13	8
1986–88	9	10

Sources: Calculated from production and trade data in Statistical Bureau, Management and Coordination Agency, *Japan Statistical Yearbook*, Tokyo, various issues, and I. Yamazawa and Y. Yamamoto, *Estimates of Long Term Economic Statistics of Japan Since 1868*, Tokyo, Toyo Keizai Shimposha, various years.

3.5 in the 1950s and a subsequent decline to below unity from the 1970s (column 13)).[1]

This hill-shaped development pattern can be summarized in two additional ways. One is the changing trade dependence of Japan's textile/clothing sector. Table 2.2 shows the clear increase and then decrease in the share of Japan's production of textiles that are exported, starting from zero before 1870, peaking at around 30 per cent in the 1930s and falling to the still substantial level in the latter 1980s of 9 per cent (primarily synthetic fibres, which are extremely capital intensive). That table also shows that imports accounted for more than a third of domestic textile and clothing consumption in the early years of Japan's industrial development (primarily cotton yarns and fabrics needed as inputs for producing finished textiles and clothing), that this import dependence fell to almost zero in the 1950s and early 1960s with the growth in domestic production, but that it had since

[1] This is not to say the *volume* of Japan's exports of textiles and clothing declined in the postwar period. In fact the volume kept growing, but at a slower rate than Japan's other exports whereas the reverse was true before World War II. During the six decades to the 1930s Japan's volume of total exports grew at an average annual rate of 7 per cent while its textile and clothing exports grew at more than 9 per cent, whereas in the three decades from the early 1950s the total export volume grew at more than 13 per cent while textile and clothing export volumes grew at 5 per cent per year on average, according to data in Yamazawa and Yamamoto (1979).

Table 2.3: *Net exports as a ratio of exports plus imports in fibres, textiles and clothing, Japan, 1874 to 1987*[a]

| | Natural fibres | Textiles, clothing and synthetic fibres | | | |
| | | Total | Clothing | Natural-fibre textiles | Synthetic fibres and textiles |
	(1)	(2)	(3)	(4)	(5)
1874–79	0.88	–0.93	–1.00	–0.88	—
1880–89	0.84	–0.65	–0.70	–0.65	—
1890–99	0.10	0.00	–0.48	–0.01	—
1900–09	–0.04	0.38	0.14	0.38	—
1910–19	–0.18	0.63	0.96	0.83	–1.00
1920–29	–0.04	0.67	1.00	0.68	–0.77
1930–39	–0.32	0.84	1.00	0.86	0.83
1951–60	–0.85	0.96	0.93	0.96	0.98
1961–70	–0.89	0.73	0.89	0.81	0.96
1971–80	–0.95	0.37	–0.21	0.30	0.96
1981–84	–0.94	0.29	–0.50	0.23	0.93
1985–87	–0.95	0.17	–0.63	..	0.89

[a] The Standard International Trade Classifications for these four commodity groups are as follows: natural fibres, SITC 26 less 266; clothing, SITC 84; natural-fibre textiles, SITC 651, 652 and 653 except 6516-8 and 6535-8; and synthetic fibres and textiles, SITC 266, 6516-8 and 6535-8.
Sources: United Nations, *Yearbook of International Trade Statistics*, New York, various issues and Yamazawa and Yamamoto (1979).

grown to more than one-tenth by the late 1980s as low-cost imports of labour-intensive items have become available from nearby NIEs.

The other way used here to demonstrate the rise and demise of the competitiveness of Japan's textiles and clothing sector and the gradual decline in Japan's self-sufficiency in natural fibres is to express net exports as a ratio of the sum of exports and imports of these products. This indicator has the advantage of showing the net trade situation rather than just gross exports or imports, and of removing scale effects by being confined to the range –1 to +1. Columns (1) and (2) of Table 2.3 show that in the 1870s Japan's trade in textiles and clothing was almost entirely imports (yarn and fabric) and its trade in natural fibres was almost entirely exports (silk). Since then, these two ratios have moved steadily in opposite directions. In recent decades, Japan's trade in natural fibres has been almost all imports, while its exports of textiles and clothing have grown almost to match its imports: the net export ratio had fallen from 0.96 in the 1950s to 0.23 in the early 1980s.

Columns (3) to (5) of Table 2.3 show the net export ratio for three sub-groups of products within the textiles and clothing group. Clothing is the least intensive in the use of capital per worker among these three sub-groups, and synthetic fibres and textiles is the most capital

intensive (see footnote 6 of Chapter 1). Thus it is not surprising that
the net export ratio rises to near unity first for clothing and last for
synthetic fibres and textiles and that the ratio becomes negative first
for clothing (in the 1970s), is currently in the mid-range for natural-
fibre textiles and is still close to unity for capital-intensive synthetic
fibre and yarn production.

The international markets

In addition to developments in Japan itself, the country's changing
role in international markets is also as expected from theory. First,
Japan's share of world exports of textiles and clothing rose and then
fell. At the turn of the century Japan's share was only 2 per cent, but
by the mid-1930s it exceeded 20 per cent before falling gradually from
the 1950s to only 3 per cent in 1988 as newly industrializing countries
became more competitive (Table 2.4). The emergence of Japan clearly
put downward pressure on exports from older industrial economies.
The United Kingdom, for example, was responsible for the majority
of the world's exports of textiles and clothing during most of the
nineteenth century. During the first three decades of this century the
UK's share had fallen to around 40 per cent, by the mid-1950s it was
down to 20 per cent and by the mid-1980s only 3 per cent. Similar if
less spectacular declines occurred in the shares due to France.

This change was accompanied by changes in the importance of
fibres, textiles and clothing in these older economies' trade, and in
their fibre self-sufficiency, in a manner analogous to Japan except that
it occurred earlier. The experience for the UK, for example, is clear
from Table 2.5. The shares of other West European countries also fell
until the 1940s. The latter then rose for a time, because of the reduction
in trade barriers within Europe which stimulated the expansion of
exports especially from lower-wage members of the European Community such as Italy, but it has since resumed its decline. The share
of textiles and clothing in total exports peaked a century earlier for
the UK than for Japan, at more than 70 per cent in the 1820s,[2] after
which it declined monotonically and is now less than 5 per cent
(column (1) of Table 2.5). Likewise, the share of natural fibres in total
UK imports rose steadily until the mid-nineteenth century, but again
is now close to zero (column (2)). During the eighteenth century the
UK was virtually self-sufficient in wool (column (3)). Import dependence grew with industrialization until the 1950s, but with the demise

[2] This high peak share of textiles and clothing in total exports of 70 per cent for the
United Kingdom compares with subsequent peaks of less than 50 per cent for Japan and
its newly industrialized neighbours. Lower peaks are to be expected given the increasing
array of labour-intensive manufacturing possibilities that face NIEs as new products
come on to the market and their production processes become standardized.

Table 2.4: *Major industrial countries' shares in world exports of textiles and clothing, 1899 to 1988*
(per cent)

	Japan	United Kingdom	France	Other Western Europe	United States	Others[a]	Total
	(1)	(2)	(3)	(4)	(5)	(6)	(7)
1899	2	47	15	29	2	5	100
1913	4	43	15	29	3	6	100
1929	9	43	14	23	5	6	100
1937	22	37	6	23	3	9	100
1955	15	21	11	30	12	10	100
1965	13	8	8	38	6	27	100
1975	8	5	6	42	5	33	100
1988	3	3	4	39	3	48	100

[a] Since Canadian and Australasian exports were minimal, and East European exports are not included for the postwar period because of lack of data, this column from 1955 almost entirely refers to developing countries.
Sources: United Nations, *Yearbook of International Trade Statistics*, New York, various issues; and Maizels (1963).

Table 2.5: *Importance of textiles, clothing and fibres in trade, and wool self-sufficiency, United Kingdom, 1750 to 1988*
(per cent, value terms)

	Share of textiles and clothing in total exports (1)	Share of natural fibres in total imports (2)	Wool self-sufficiency[a] (3)
1750–99	52	12	98
1800–19	64	11	91
1820–39	71	21	80
1840–59	64	28	68
1860–79	61	27	50
1880–99	46	20	35
1900–19	38	18	21
1920–29	34	14	20
1930–38	24	10	16
1950–59	11	9	17
1960–69	7	5	22
1970–79	6	2	34
1980–88	4	1	52

[a] Domestic wool production as a percentage of apparent domestic wool consumption, the latter being defined as domestic production plus imports minus exports and re-exports, all measured in terms of volume of clean wool.
Sources: Derived from data from the United Nations, *Yearbook of International Trade Statistics*, New York, various issues; Food and Agriculture Organisation, *Production Yearbook*, Rome, various issues; and Mitchell (1962).

of textile production there in recent decades and the boost to UK sheep production following increased government assistance to farmers, the ratio of production to consumption of wool in the UK has actually risen in recent decades, although the volumes involved have been relatively small.

Meanwhile, in recent years countries with less capital per worker than the UK, such as Italy and some rapidly industrializing developing countries, have increased dramatically their shares of world exports of these products, in the case of developing countries from less than 10 per cent prior to the 1960s to more than 45 per cent today (column (6) of Table 2.4). Indeed the rapidly developing economies of Northeast Asia (South Korea, Taiwan, Hong Kong and mainland China) alone now account for about one-third of world exports of textiles and clothing. As it happens, the growth in their share has more than offset the decline in Japan's share in recent years, so East Asia has become steadily more important as a source of these manufactures. And since each of these developing economies is relatively densely populated, East Asia's importance as an importer of natural fibres has also been rising steadily.[3]

These changes in competitiveness and hence in the international location of textile production away from Western Europe towards first Japan, then the newly industrialized economies of Hong Kong, Korea and Taiwan, and now also to mainland China, are reflected in the changing direction of fibre trade. British imports of cotton and wool continued to grow through the nineteenth century and until World War I for cotton and the 1930s for wool. Throughout this period Britain was the destination for the vast majority of the world's fibre exports, part of which was for re-export to continental Europe. But, as Japan's competitiveness increased and Britain's entrepot role declined, the quantity of fibres imported by Britain declined also (Table 2.6). By the early 1980s Britain accounted for only 1 per cent of world cotton imports and 9 per cent of world imports of wool. Meanwhile, Japan's imports of fibres rose dramatically from late last century until the early 1970s, at which time its annual imports of cotton especially were almost as large as Britain's record imports half a century earlier. Then Japan's fibre imports began declining also as the textile industries in East Asia's NIEs expanded. As with textile and clothing exports, however, aggregate imports of fibres in East Asia as a region continued to grow (Table 2.6). The region's share of world imports of natural fibres had reached 40 per cent by the early 1980s, up from 20 per cent in the mid-1960s (Anderson and Park 1989: Fig. 2). These changes are reflected clearly in the changing direction of fibre exports of the world's largest exporters of cotton and wool, the United States and Australia respectively (Table 2.7).

[3] For details see, for example, Park (1988) and Anderson and Park (1989).

Table 2.6: *Imports (and consumption) of cotton and wool by the United Kingdom, Japan, Northeast Asian NIEs and China, 1770 to 1988[a]*
(annual average, kt)

	United Kingdom		Japan		Northeast Asian NIEs[b]		Mainland China	
	Cotton	Wool	Cotton	Wool	Cotton	Wool	Cotton	Wool
1770–79	3 (3)	1 (42)	—	—	—	—	—	—
1780–99	10 (10)	1 (46)	—	—	—	—	—	—
1800–19	38 (35)	4 (50)	—	—	—	—	—	—
1820–39	124 (110)	15 (66)	—	—	—	—	—	—
1840–59	348 (300)	39 (89)	—	—	—	—	—	—
1860–79	582 (458)	128 (141)	1	—	—	—	—	—
1880–99	793 (702)	271 (178)	47	1	—	—	—	—
1900–19	928 (818)	323 (253)	294	9	—	—	—	—
1920–39	712 (615)	384 (273)	665	65	—	—	—	—
1950–59	347 (340)	314 (273)	489	68	98	2	63 (1149)	3 (22)
1960–69	215 (213)	262 (253)	714	246	287	5	114 (1314)	14 (69)
1970–79	125 (124)	104 (141)	744	231	550	25	418 (2451)	23 (149)
1980–88	52 (52)	70 (119)	723	101	930	41	583 (4390)	95 (258)

[a] Numbers in parentheses are imports plus domestic production minus exports and re-exports. The latter three items are virtually zero for East Asia other than China, so consumption roughly equals imports.

[b] Hong Kong, South Korea and Taiwan.

kt = kilotonne, 1,000 metric tons.

Sources: Food and Agriculture Organisation, *Production Yearbook* and *Trade Yearbook*, Rome, various issues; Council for Agricultural Planning and Development, *Taiwan Agricultural Statistics*, Taipei, various issues; Allen (1981); and Mitchell (1962).

Finally, what has been the changing pattern of comparative advantage *within* Japan's textiles and clothing sector? An indication is provided in Table 2.8, which shows the commodity composition of exports and imports for that sector. Before this century the sector's exports were almost entirely silk yarns and its imports were cotton and wool yarns and fabrics. Then during the first half of this century

Table 2.7: *Direction of exports of cotton from the United States and of wool from Australia, 1800 to 1987* [a]

	United Kingdom	Japan	Northeast Asian NIEs [b]	China	Other	*Total*	Volume (kt per year)
United States cotton							
1800–19	72	—	—	—	28	100	23
1820–39	72	—	—	—	28	100	130
1840–59	68	—	—	—	32	100	403
1860–79	72	—	—	—	28	100	412
1880–99	52	4	—	—	44	100	1149
1900–19	41	9	—	—	50	100	1710
1920–39	22	24	—	—	54	100	1644
1950–59	11	22	5	—	62	100	1061
1960–69	5	23	13	—	59	100	1020
1970–79	3	22	37	4	34	100	1005
1980–85	2	32	40	5	21	100	1381
Australian wool							
1860–79	97	—	—	—	3	100	80
1880–99	74	—	—	—	26	100	221
1900–19	69	8	—	—	23	100	203
1920–39	44	18	—	—	38	100	319
1950–59	27	18	—	—	55	100	515
1960–69	12	35	1	1	51	100	655
1970–79	4	39	8	2	47	100	598
1980–85	2	33	12	8	45	100	513
1986–87	3	20	12	12	53	100	677

[a] The limited availability of data requires that shares in the prewar period are based on volume, whereas for the postwar period value data could be used to better account for quality differences. The 1986–87 wool data refer to the financial year ending June 1987.
[b] Hong Kong, South Korea and Taiwan.
Sources: United Nations, *Commodity Trade Statistics*, New York, various issues; United States Department of Commerce, *Historical Statistics of the United States* (bicentennial edition), Washington, DC, 1976; Mitsubishi Economic Research Bureau, *Japanese Trade and Industry*, London, Macmillan, 1936; Australian Bureau of Agricultural Economics, *Statistical Handbook of the Sheep and Wool Industry* (4th edition), Canberra, 1973; Barnard (1958); and Mitchell (1962).

Table 2.8: Composition of Japan's trade in textiles and clothing, 1880 to 1985[a] (per cent)

| | Yarns and fabrics | | | | | Synthetic fibre (266) | Finished textiles (654–7) | Clothing (841) | TOTAL[b] | |
	Silk	Cotton (6513+652)	Wool (6512+6532)	Synthetic (6516–9+ 6536–8)	Sub-total					
Exports										
1880–82	99	1	—	—	100	—	—	—	100	(1)
1890–92	90	1	—	—	91	—	9	—	100	(7)
1900–02	88	6	—	—	94	—	5	1	100	(49)
1911–13	76	17	—	—	93	—	3	4	100	(130)
1924–26	62	35	—	—	97	—	1	2	100	(659)
1934–36	39	44	3	7	93	—	2	5	100	(1082)
1953–55	4	42	6	25	77	—	11	12	100	(685)
1963–65	4	23	8	29	64	6	11	19	100	(1446)
1973–75	7	7	2	52	68	12	9	11	100	(3681)
1983–85	8	9	3	51	71	9	9	11	100	(6675)
Imports										
1880–82	—	80	20	—	100	—	—	—	100	(18)
1890–92	—	78	22	—	100	—	—	—	100	(20)
1900–02	—	60	39	—	99	—	—	1	100	(38)
1911–13	—	35	62	2	99	—	—	1	100	(39)
1924–26	8	8	77	7	100	—	—	—	100	(150)
1934–36	36	24	22	18	100	—	—	—	100	(30)
1953–55	n.a.	n.a.	n.a.	n.a.	45	1	30	24	100	(14)
1963–65	23	6	34	6	69	1	17	13	100	(106)
1973–75	21	16	6	7	50	—	10	40	100	(1895)
1983–85	12	17	5	6	40	—	10	50	100	(3533)

[a] Standard International Trade Classifications are shown under each column heading. Silk yarns and fabrics are SITC 615 and 653 not elsewhere specified.
[b] Numbers in parentheses refer to value in millions of yen prior to 1950 and in millions of US dollars thereafter.
Sources: United Nations, *Yearbook of International Trade Statistics*, New York, various issues and Yamazawa and Yamamoto (1979).

cotton yarns and fabrics increasingly dominated exports and diminished as import items. Woollen textiles started to be exported in the 1930s but declined in importance after the 1960s with the growth of synthetics. In the 1970s and 1980s the capital-intensive synthetic yarn and fabric sub-sector accounted for about 60 per cent of Japan's total exports of textiles and clothing, while labour-intensive finished textiles and clothing have come to account for 60 per cent of all textile and clothing imports (and only 20 per cent of exports). With these changes it is not surprising that Japan's share of world exports of clothing has diminished, from more than 10 per cent in the 1960s to well below 5 per cent in the 1980s, whereas its share of world exports of more capital-intensive synthetic fibres and fabrics kept rising until the mid-1970s, to close to 25 per cent, and in the mid-1980s was still above 20 per cent although it is now beginning to be taken over by the country's newly industrializing neighbours.

Conclusions and policy implications

The rise and demise of Japan's textile and clothing sector is clear from a number of perspectives: the relative importance of these industries in Japan's total and manufacturing value-added, employment and exports, the importance of Japan in world markets for textiles and clothing, and Japan's importance in international fibre markets. Japan's rise was at the expense of more advanced economies such as the United Kingdom, while its demise is closely associated with the rapid industrialization of neighbouring parts of East Asia. What is also clear is that this hill-shaped development pattern has peaked at different times for different sub-sectors. The industries which use unskilled labour most intensively, namely producers of finished textiles and standard clothing, were the first to come under pressure to decline, while Japan's capital-intensive synthetic fibre and fabric producers are still competitive in international markets (although pressure from Korea and Taiwan has been increasing rapidly during the past decade).

All of these trends are consistent with standard trade and development theory. They do *not* support the claim sometimes made by developing countries that Japan is not adjusting to allow later-industrializing countries to enter its and other countries' markets for products such as textiles and clothing. It is true that the share of developing country imports of textiles and clothing in Japanese consumption has been below the average for industrial countries, and that this import penetration ratio for Japan is growing more slowly for Japan than for other advanced economies (Table 2.9). However, it has been suggested that this may have more to do with Japan's lingering comparative advantage in some segments of the textile and

Table 2.9: *Import penetration ratios for textiles, clothing and all manufactures from developing countries into Japan and other industrial countries, 1970 to 1986*
(imports as a percentage of domestic sales)

	Textiles (ISIC 321)		Clothing (ISIC 322)		All manufactures (ISIC 3)	
	1970–73	1982–86	1970–73	1982–86	1970–73	1982–86
Japan	4.6	5.6	4.1	9.7	1.4	1.9
France	1.5	4.8	1.5	10.6	1.3	2.5
West Germany	3.8	10.3	5.6	27.4	1.6	3.7
Italy	3.1	6.5	0.9	13.7	1.5	3.4
United Kingdom	3.8	7.5	7.5	19.6	2.0	3.2
United States	2.3	5.0	4.1	20.1	1.3	3.5
All industrial countries	3.3	6.3	4.4	18.0	1.5	3.1

Source: See Appendix to this volume.

clothing sector, due to rapid technological change, than to exceptionally high import barriers.[4] If new technologies are the explanation for Japan's low import penetration ratios today, then it is likely that those ratios will soon increase as Japan's newly industrialized neighbours adopt those same technologies in due course.[5]

Regardless of whether Japan's barriers to textile and clothing imports are higher than those of other high-wage countries, the fact is that all advanced industrial countries heavily protect their domestic producers of textiles and clothing.[6] Given the unequivocal evidence from Japan that producers of labour-intensive products in advanced economies will come under pressure to decline as successive generations of NIEs emerge in the course of global economic growth, it is clear that policies aimed at slowing this adjustment process will simply frustrate economic growth at home and abroad. In particular, they are likely to slow the export growth in the 1990s of lower-cost producers in countries such as China, as discussed in the next chapter. This in turn would weaken the overall demand for natural fibres from countries like Australia and the United States and for synthetic fibres from countries such as Japan and Korea. It is in the interests of these various fibre producers to join the developing countries in lobbying for a more liberal Multifibre Arrangement when the MFA comes up for renegotiation in 1991 and/or for bringing textiles and clothing into the normal disciplines of the GATT during the current Uruguay Round of multilateral trade negotiations – a point that is raised again in the final chapter of this volume.

[4] See, for example, Yamazawa (1983) and Chapter 6 in this volume.

[5] This process of international technology transfer is discussed in Vernon (1966) and Grossman and Helpman (1989, 1990).

[6] See, for example, Keesing and Wolf (1980), Cline (1987) and Hamilton (1990).

3

Effects of China's dramatic reforms on its neighbours and on world markets

Kym Anderson and Young-Il Park*

The dramatic reforms to China's economic policies which began in the late 1970s, particularly the opening up of China to international trade and investment, stimulated very rapid growth in this populous economy. During the first decade of the reforms China's real GDP per capita and volume of exports grew at more than 6 and 10 per cent per year, respectively, three times the rates for other developing countries and for the world as a whole and close to the remarkable performance of East Asia's more advanced developing economies. It is true that China still accounts for only about 2 per cent of world GDP and 1 per cent of world exports in aggregate, but for some basic commodities its importance in world markets is much closer to, and in some cases exceeds, the country's 22 per cent share of world population. Food, some minerals and metals, and fibres, textiles and clothing are in that exceptional category.

This chapter addresses the question: how important is China becoming in world textile and clothing markets? In particular, to what extent is China contributing to the international relocation of textile and clothing activity to the East Asian region? Will its growth in textile and clothing production lead to increased imports of fibres or will domestic fibre production expand to meet the fibre needs of Chinese manufacturers?

The evidence is clear that China has already become a substantial player in world textile and clothing markets. As Table 3.1 shows, China's share of world production of cotton textiles has gone up from 20 to 26 per cent since the economic reforms began, while its shares of wool textiles, synthetic textiles and blankets have trebled. That table also shows that China's share of global production of raw wool has crept up and its share of raw cotton increased phenomenally to 30 per cent in 1984, double its share in the late 1970s. The latter change not only put downward pressure on the international price of

* Parts of this chapter are drawn from Anderson and Park (1989) and Anderson (1990a,b).

Table 3.1:   *China's shares of world production of natural fibres and*
textiles, 1976 to 1986
(per cent, volume based)

	1976–78	1982–84	1985–86
Cotton textiles	19.7	25.9	..
Wool textiles	1.6	4.3	..
Synthetic textiles	0.5	1.5	..
Blankets	4.1[a]	11.5[b]	..
Raw cotton	14.8[c]	23.4[d]	22.0
Raw wool	5.2[c]	6.6[d]	6.1

[a] 1976   [c] 1975–79
[b] 1983   [d] 1980–84

Sources: State Statistical Bureau, *Statistical Yearbook of China*, Beijing, various issues;
United Nations, *Yearbook of Industrial Statistics*, New York, various issues; and the
Appendix to this volume (for production of cotton and wool).

cotton lint (which in 1985 was at its lowest level in real terms since
1950) but also left traditional natural fibre exporters doubtful as to
whether China would become a large market for their products.

Drawing on the standard trade and development theory summarized
in Chapter 1, the present chapter argues that those recent rates of
increase in natural fibre production in China are likely to slow down
and that China in the longer term will steadily become a larger net
importer of natural fibres as its comparative advantage in manufactured goods strengthens. The chapter also argues that China is becoming a large importer of synthetic fibres, which will allow the textile
industries in the more advanced industrial economies of East Asia and
perhaps Europe greater scope for specialization in this (and other)
more capital-intensive area of textiles production as China displaces
them from world markets for unskilled labour-intensive products such
as finished textiles and standard clothing.

Much depends, however, on the extent to which the Multi-fibre
Arrangement (MFA) limits China's capacity to exploit its strengthening
comparative advantage in labour-intensive manufactures, a point taken
up in the final section of the chapter on the implications of China's
growth for neighbouring and other countries' trade in fibres, textiles
and clothing.

Comparative advantage in fibres,
textiles and clothing

The standard trade and development theory in Chapter 1 suggests
that a poor country opening up to international trade will tend to
specialize in the export of primary products, though less so the more

densely populated the country. If its domestic incomes grow more rapidly than the rest of the world's, its export specialization will gradually switch away from primary products (in raw or lightly processed form) to manufactures. The manufactured goods initially exported will be more labour intensive, the more resource-poor or densely populated the country. Since many (though by no means all) textile and clothing production activities tend to be intensive in the use of unskilled labour, they would be among the items initially exported by a newly industrializing, densely populated country. And as the demands for textile raw materials by that country's expanding textile industry grow, so the country's net exports of natural fibre would diminish, or net imports of natural fibre would increase, *ceteris paribus*.[1]

How well does China's experience fit these patterns? The two regression equations in Chapter 1 predict China's share of primary products in its total exports in 1985 to average 65 per cent, and its share of textiles and clothing in its exports of manufactured goods to average 54 per cent. The first of these predicted shares is well above the actual 1983–85 share of 50 per cent, but the second is identical with the actual share for 1983–85 (see Table 3.2 below).

One of the reasons for the actual share for primary products being below that predicted has to do with China's previous development strategy, which was perhaps more extreme than that of other developing countries in discouraging food exports in an attempt to keep down domestic prices of these basic consumer items and in discouraging the export of industrial raw materials and energy products to keep down the cost of industrial production.

With the recent dramatic reforms to China's development strategy, involving substantial liberalization to these distortions in producer incentives, one might therefore expect to see China's shares of primary products in total exports rise at first, before declining in the manner suggested by the first regression equation in Chapter 1. And in fact this has happened: according to the data reported below in Table 3.2 that share of primary products in China's exports rose slightly from 50.1 per cent in 1979 to 51.4 per cent in 1985 before declining rapidly, to 32.1 per cent in 1987.

Japan and the newly industrialized economies of Hong Kong, South Korea and Taiwan are, like China, among the world's most densely populated countries. They also have had the enviable reputation for a long time of enjoying extremely rapid rates of economic growth, as has China since 1978. Thus the above theory suggests that all five of these economies should lose their comparative advantage in primary

[1] Needless to say, these supply- and demand-side influences on the pattern of export specialization can be affected by, among other things, changes in government policies affecting relative domestic prices and by inter-sectoral differences in rates of technological change.

products at a relatively early stage of their economic development and have an initial strengthening of comparative advantage in unskilled-labour-intensive manufactured products, such as finished textiles and clothing, which will eventually diminish.

This is indeed what the historical record shows. Japan's share of primary products in total exports was above 70 per cent in the first decade of the Meiji Restoration last century, but it has steadily fallen since then and is now close to zero. The NIEs of Korea and Taiwan also exported mostly primary products prior to their industrial take-off, in their case in the early 1960s, but in just two decades their primary export shares have fallen to less than 10 per cent. And the same pattern has occurred in China. Column 1 of Table 3.2 suggests the share of China's exports due to primary products was three-quarters in the mid-1950s, two-thirds in the mid-1960s and less than half in the 1980s.

It is also clear from Table 3.2 that, consistent with the above theory, the shares of textiles and clothing in East Asia's total exports first increased and then declined as these economies grew and, soon after their industrial take-offs, the shares of textiles and clothing in their *manufacturing* exports began to fall.[2] For China also this has been the case although, as mentioned earlier, since 1982 the latter share has been rising – and may rise further still – simply as a result of the Chinese economy adjusting to the economic reforms of recent years.

Of more importance from the point of view of this chapter is the change in comparative advantage in (rather than just export shares of) textiles and clothing. One indication of this would be revealed, if there were no distortions, by the share of these goods in a particular country's total exports relative to the importance of those goods in world trade (Balassa 1965). This index of export specialization is reported in the final column of Table 3.2. What is clear from those data is that even though the share of textiles and clothing in manu-factured exports has been falling, those goods' share of total exports from industrial Asian economies, relative to the global export share, kept rising for some time after each economy's industrial take-off – despite increases in protection in advanced industrial economies aimed at reducing their imports of these goods. This index peaked at 5.5 in the mid-1950s for Japan and at between 5 and 9 in the 1970s for the newly industrialized East Asian economies, in each case having risen from less than half that value. That is, textiles and clothing were five to nine times as important in East Asia's exports as in world exports at those peak times.

---

[2] In some cases the share of these goods in manufactured exports only increased initially, but then declined as per capita incomes rose. The initial increase in this latter share reflects the fact that in the pre-industrialization phase exports may include some lightly processed primary products which are classified as manufactures, in which case it takes a little time for labour-intensive goods to dominate manufactured exports.

Table 3.2: *Importance of primary products and textiles and clothing in exports from East Asia, 1874 to 1987*[a]

	Primary products' share (%) of total exports	Textiles and clothing's share (%) of:		Index of export specialization in textiles and clothing[b]
		total exports	manufactured exports	
Japan				
1874–83	82	4	25	..
1882–91	75	9	35	..
1892–1901	54	23	52	1.5
1902–11	45	28	51	..
1912–21	34	34	51	2.6
1922–31	34	35	53	2.9
1930–39	20	35	44	4.1
1954–56	13	35	40	5.5
1965–69	7	15	16	2.4
1970–74	5	8	9	1.4
1975–79	3	5	5	0.9
1980–84	3	4	4	0.8
1985–87	2	3	3	0.5
Hong Kong				
1954–56	25	36	48	5.4
1965–69	5	48	51	7.8
1970–74	4	48	50	8.1
1975–79	3	47	48	9.0
1980–84	3	40	41	8.1
1985–87	3	41	41	6.6
Korea				
1954–56	94	..	..	..
1965–69	30	34	49	5.5
1970–74	16	36	43	6.0
1975–79	13	33	38	6.3
1980–84	9	27	30	5.4
1985–87	8	24	26	3.9
Taiwan				
1954–56	90	..	..	..
1965–69	41	21	35	3.4
1970–74	18	29	35	4.8
1975–79	14	24	28	4.6
1980–84	10	20	23	4.1
1985–87	8	18	20	2.9

Table 3.2: *(cont'd)*

| | Primary products' share (%) of total exports | Textiles and clothing's share (%) of: | | Index of export specialization in textiles and clothing[b] |
		total exports	manufactured exports	
China				
1910–29[c]	85	6	40	..
1955–57[d]	70	14	47	2.1
1965–69	57	20	46	3.2
1970–74	53	20	46	3.4
1975–79	52	22	46	4.2
1980–82	51	24	49	4.9
1983–85	50	27	54	5.1
1986	39	33	54	5.2
1987	32	34	49	5.0

[a] Primary products cover SITC sections 0 to 4 plus division 68 (non-ferrous metals) less 266 (synthetic fibres); textiles and clothing cover SITC divisions 65 and 84.
[b] The index of export specialization is defined as the share of a product group in total exports of an economy as a ratio of the share of that product group in world exports, following Balassa (1965). The four pre-1950 values for Japan are calculated using world trade data for 1899, 1913, 1929 and 1937, from Maizels (1963).
[c] From Hsiao (1974).   [d] From Eckstein (1971).
Sources: International Economic Data Bank, Trade Data Tapes, Australian National University, Canberra, 1990; United Nations, *Yearbook of International Trade Statistics*, New York, various issues; Council for Economic Planning and Development, *Taiwan Statistical Data Book*, Taipei, 1985; Ohkawa *et al.* (1979); Maizels (1963).

Further insights can be gained by disaggregating this index of export specialization and comparing it with the index for other commodity groups, as in Table 3.3. At least four points can be made from the data in that table. First, China's export specialization in agricultural products in total halved between the early 1970s and mid-1980s, a much faster rate of decline than for East Asia's other rapidly developing economies. But, because of a change in producer price incentives for cotton relative to grain in China (see below), cotton production and exports rose in the mid-1980s so the declining comparative advantage in primary products begins to show up in the natural fibre index of export specialization for China only after 1986, whereas it steadily declines for the period shown for all other East Asian economies. Recall, however, that this index reflects only the export part of the trade pattern: China has been a net importer of natural fibres throughout the postwar period with the exception of 1984–86.

Second, China's index of export specialization was greater for textiles than for clothing before the mid-1980s, in strong contrast to

Table 3.3: *Index of export specialization for various product groups, China, other East Asian economies and all developing economies, 1965 to 1987*[a]

	All agriculture	Natural fibres	Textiles	Clothing	Other labour-intensive manufactures	Synthetic fibres
China						
1965–69	2.1	2.2	3.8	1.8	1.2	—
1970–74	2.4	4.1	3.9	2.5	1.2	—
1975–79	2.1	4.6	4.9	3.2	1.4	—
1980–84	1.6	4.3	4.9	5.3	1.4	—
1985	1.6	6.2	4.4	5.1	1.5	0.1
1986	1.6	6.0	4.6	5.9	1.7	0.1
1987	1.3	5.4	4.4	5.5	2.2	0.1
Northeast Asian NIEs						
1965–69	0.7	0.4	2.9	14.4	3.1	—
1970–74	0.5	0.6	3.0	12.9	2.7	—
1975–79	0.5	0.3	3.3	11.2	3.1	0.1
1980–84	0.4	0.2	3.0	8.6	4.0	1.2
1985–87	0.4	0.2	2.5	5.6	3.3	1.3
ASEAN						
1965–69	2.6	0.7	0.3	0.3	0.2	—
1970–74	2.5	0.5	0.4	0.6	0.3	—
1975–79	2.3	0.3	0.5	0.8	0.5	0.1
1980–84	1.9	0.2	0.5	1.0	0.6	0.2
1985–87	1.9	0.2	0.7	1.4	0.8	0.2
All developing economies						
1965–69	1.8	2.2	0.9	1.1	0.4	0.1
1970–74	1.4	2.0	0.9	1.4	0.4	0.1
1975–79	1.2	1.5	0.9	1.5	0.5	0.1
1980–84	1.1	1.3	1.0	1.7	0.8	0.3
1985–87	1.3	1.6	1.5	2.4	1.2	0.5
Japan						
1965–69	0.2	0.2	2.6	1.8	2.8	2.9
1970–74	0.2	0.2	1.8	0.6	2.4	3.0
1975–79	0.1	0.1	1.4	0.2	2.0	2.5
1980–84	0.1	0.1	1.3	0.2	1.6	1.9
1985–87	0.1	—	0.8	0.1	1.1	1.3

[a] The index of export specialization is defined as the share of a product group in an economy as a ratio of the share of that product group in world exports, following Balassa (1965). The product groups have the following SITC classifications: all agriculture 0,1,4 and 2 less 266,27,28; natural fibres 26 less 266; textiles 65; clothing 84, other labour-intensive manufactures 632, 633, 664, 665, 666, 722, 735, 821, 831, 894, 895, 899; and synthetic fibres 266.
Source: International Economic Data Bank, Trade Data Tapes, Australian National University, Canberra 1990.

the pattern for other developing economies and more like the pattern for advanced industrial countries. As China develops its skills in satisfying the needs of clothes buyers in richer countries this pattern is changing, however. It may be that during the 1990s China's index of export specialization in clothing will double or more to the levels experienced in the late 1960s and early 1970s by the Northeast Asian NIEs.

Third, China already has diversified its manufacturing export base beyond textiles and clothing and has an index of export specialization in other labour-intensive manufactures well above that for ASEAN and other developing countries. The recent growth in that index for China has no doubt contributed to the decline in that index for its Northeast Asian neighbours, as they adjust their production to specialize in more capital-intensive products.

Fourth, China exports virtually no synthetic fibres, but note that the Northeast Asian NIEs have rapidly increased their competitiveness in this capital-intensive product group, at the expense of Japan.

If China's trade pattern were to follow that of the other East Asian economies, it is likely that China's export specialization in natural fibres and other primary products will steadily decline as specialization in clothing and other labour-intensive products strengthens, and that the Northeast Asian NIEs will lose comparative advantage in the latter goods – just as their development affected Japan's export specialization during the past two or three decades.

China and the international relocation of production and trade
Textiles and clothing

How are these changes in comparative advantage affecting the international location of production and international trade in textiles and clothing? Textile and clothing output has grown much more rapidly in East Asia than it has in the rest of the world. It grew especially rapidly in Japan in the 1950s and 1960s, in Korea and Taiwan in the 1960s and 1970s, and in China since its opening up in 1978 (Table 3.4). Notice, however, that these industries declined in Japan (and other industrial countries) from the early 1970s as comparative advantage there moved away from labour-intensive manufactures, because of competition from NIEs, and moved towards more capital-intensive products. This development is also reflected in the data in Table 3.4 on export growth rates, with Japan's textiles and clothing export growth slowing down below the world and industrial-country averages since the 1960s and making way for burgeoning exports from East Asia's developing economies.

Table 3.4: *Growth in production and exports of textiles and clothing in East Asia and the world, 1954 to 1984*
(per cent per year)

	Real value-added[a]			Nominal (US$) value of exports[b]		
	1954–56 to 64–66	1964–66 to 71–73	1971–73 to 81–83	1954–56 to 64–66	1964–66 to 71–73	1971–73 to 82–84
World	3.7	4.1	1.5	7.5	13.9	11.1
Japan	9.8	7.0	–0.2	7.4	9.1	7.5
NIEs[c]	9.1	26.2	14.3	9.5	32.8	16.9
China	..	..	15.0[d]	8.0	10.8	21.5
ASEAN	..	..	..	8.1	21.5	20.1
Other developing economies[e]	4.7[d]	4.3[d]	3.4	7.6	6.4	13.5
Other industrial market economies[3]	3.7	2.4	–0.3	7.2	8.4	8.8

[a] The footwear and leather industry is included in world value-added. The final value-added column refers to 1973–80 for Taiwan and 1977–83 for China.
[b] Imports by the rest of the world are used to obtain proxy export data for China from 1964 and for Taiwan from 1982.
[c] The newly industrialized Northeast Asian economies of Hong Kong, South Korea and Taiwan, except that Hong Kong is excluded from the first two columns because of lack of data.
[d] Textiles only, because of unavailability of clothing data.
[e] Includes the above East Asian countries in the case of value added data.
Sources: Export data are from the International Economic Data Bank, Trade Data Tapes, Australian National University, Canberra, 1988. Production data are from the United Nations, *Monthly Bulletin of Statistics* and *Yearbook of Industrial Statistics*, New York, various issues; Economic Planning Board, *Handbook of Korean Economy*, Seoul, 1985; and the Council for Economic Planning and Development, *Taiwan Statistical Data Book*, Taipei, 1985.

As a consequence of these high rates of growth of production and exports, the share of East Asia in world exports of textiles and clothing has grown dramatically. Notwithstanding the decline in Japan's share, East and Southeast Asia now account for 40 per cent of that trade, double the share of three decades ago and now similar to the combined share of Western Europe and North America (Figure 3.1). This has occurred despite the fact that within the textile industry grouping there are some industries which through technological change have become extremely capital intensive and thereby expanded in some of the advanced industrial countries (Yamazawa 1983).

The large jump in China's share since 1978 may well slow the growth in the share of the three newly industrialized East Asian economies during the next decade or so, as happened for Japan from the mid-1960s – although the new capital-intensive technologies being

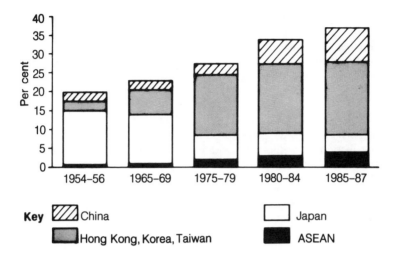

Figure 3.1: *East Asia's shares of world exports of textiles and clothing, 1954 to 1987*
(Textiles and clothing cover SITC divisions 65 and 84)

Sources: International Economic Data Bank, Trade Data Tapes, Australian National University, Canberra, 1990; and United Nations, *Yearbook of International Trade Statistics*, New York, 1956 and 1957.

developed by textile firms in advanced industrial countries will no doubt be adopted by Korean and Taiwanese firms which will help maintain their market share. But even if a slowdown of the growth of the Asian NIEs' share does occur, it is probable, given the likelihood of China's strengthening comparative advantage in labour-intensive manufactures and continuing rapid growth in total exports, that East Asia's total share of world exports of textiles and clothing will continue to expand into the 1990s.

Southeast Asia's share may also keep growing, but it is now much less significant than China's share of world trade in these products. Indeed, China may well prove too strong a competitor for the higher-wage ASEAN countries in the most labour-intensive segments of these markets, so ASEAN's performance will depend very much on wage pressures in Indonesia and Thailand and on reducing political uncertainties in the Philippines (see Garnaut and Anderson 1980; Tyers, Phillips and Findlay 1987, and Chapter 4 below).

In summary, just as rapid economic growth in first Japan and then the more recently industrialized economies of East Asia led to a gradual relocation of world textile and clothing activity away from Europe (see Chapter 2 above), so China's growth is beginning – and is likely to continue – to add to that tendency for relocation in East Asia. Thus suppliers of textiles and clothing in higher-income countries can expect continuing increases in competition from East Asia as China's industrialization proceeds.

Natural fibres

A corollary to the increasing importance of East Asia in world production of textiles and clothing and the region's declining comparative advantage in primary products is the growth in the region's share of world imports of natural fibres. Japan's share of global imports of natural fibres has declined somewhat since the early 1970s, but this has been more than compensated for by the steady growth in natural fibre imports by the NIEs of East Asia (and ASEAN) since the early 1960s and by China since the late 1970s (Figure 3.2).

The reason for faster growth in the newly industrialized economies' share of world exports of textiles and clothing than in their share of world imports of natural fibres has to do with the changing fibre

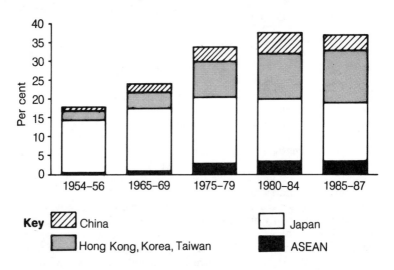

Figure 3.2:   *East Asia's shares of world imports of natural fibres, 1954 to 1987*
(Natural fibres covers SITC division 26 excluding 266)

Sources: International Economic Data Bank, Trade Data Tapes, Australian National University, Canberra, 1990; and United Nations, *Yearbook of International Trade Statistics*, New York, 1956 and 1957.

composition of their textile industries. Prior to the mid-1960s, Korean and Taiwanese textile firms were using cotton almost exclusively. However, the imposition in the early 1960s of the Long-term Arrangement (LTA) limiting international trade in cotton textiles encouraged these firms to switch to synthetic fibres. They therefore changed from using much less synthetic fibre than the rest of the world's producers around 1960 to using much more than the world average by the 1970s (Table 3.5). As in Korea and Taiwan in the early 1960s, the textile industry in China has been very strongly cotton-based until recently, but Table 3.5 shows there are now signs of decline in the importance of cotton as China's use of synthetic fibres increases too.

The suggestion that China is likely to contribute to the increase in East Asia's share of world imports of natural fibres may seem at odds

Table 3.5: *Fibre composition of textile production in East Asia, 1959 to 1983*
(per cent)

	Synthetic	Cotton	Wool	Other natural	Total
World					
1959–61	22	68	10	—	100
1969–71	38	55	7	—	100
1981–83	51	45	4	—	100
Japan					
1959–61	19	58	14	9	100
1969–71	41	37	13	9	100
1981–83	54	35	9	2	100
Korea					
1959–61	2	92	5	1	100
1969–71	42	54	3	1	100
1981–83	70	26	4	—	100
Taiwan					
1959–61	6	90	3	1	100
1969–71	27	70	3	—	100
1981–83	78	21	1	—	100
China					
1970	7	89	2	2	100
1980	9	85	2	4	100
1983	14	80	3	3	100

Sources: Textile Economic Bureau, *Textile Organon*, London, various issues; Bureau of Statistics, Office of the Prime Minister, *Japanese Statistical Yearbook*, Tokyo, various issues; Economic Planning Board, *Korean Statistical Yearbook*, Seoul, various issues; Council for Economic Planning and Development, *Taiwan Statistical Yearbook*, Taipei, various issues; and (for Chinese data), Japanese Spinning Association, *Monthly Report*, Tokyo, various issues.

with the tendency in the first half of the 1980s for China to *reduce* its imports of cotton: China's self-sufficiency in raw cotton increased from 70 per cent in 1980 to virtually 100 per cent in 1985, during which time the ratio of stocks to annual Chinese production also rose dramatically, from 15 to 100 per cent. However, this recent trend for cotton is a reversal of the longer-run trend, still evident for wool, which involves China becoming less self-sufficient in natural fibres (Table 3.6).

There are reasons to suggest that the trend reversal for cotton self-sufficiency will be short-lived.[3] The main reason for the surge in China's cotton output in the first half of the 1980s has to do with changes in producer incentives. As shown in Table 3.7, average prices received by cotton producers increased 50 per cent between 1978 and 1984, as did prices for grain and many other farm products (but not wool, the real price for which hardly changed until 1985). The *marginal* producer price for cotton – for over-quota deliveries or sales to the free market – increased even faster than for grains. Moreover, producers of cotton received preferential access to grain and fertilizer during 1978–82, and by switching from grain to cotton production farmers were able to avoid fulfilling their grain quota at the relatively low quota price (Sicular 1988). These changes to producer incentives understandably stimulated a massive increase in cotton output. (Almost half of that increase was due to increased acreage planted to cotton, because of the increase in its profitability relative to grain's. The other half was the result of increased yields per hectare due to the expanded use of fertilizer, pesticides, etc., the purchase of which was now economically profitable.) However, it is unlikely that such an expansion in output will continue indefinitely. Indeed cotton output was much lower in 1985 and 1986 than in the record year of 1984, partly in response to a further change in government-imposed incentives which resulted from concerns about declining grain self-sufficiency.

Even if China's production of natural fibres *does* contine to grow, domestic demand for those fibres may grow even faster. Continuing rapid growth in manufacturers' demands for fibres is to be expected because of not only export growth but also the expected rapid growth in domestic demand for finished textiles and clothing (from a low base) following the increases in disposable incomes in China and the relaxation of clothing conformity. Hence the expectation that China's

---

[3] A similar turnaround also occurred in 1984 in the long-term decline in China's food self-sufficiency, and for similar reasons to the turnaround for cotton. Anderson and Tyers (1987) and Anderson (1990a) argue that for food, too, the reversal is likely to be short-lived, although in both cases it is difficult to predict the outcome because so little is known about the potential for further agricultural productivity growth in China and its distribution across commodities.

Table 3.6: *China's production, trade and self-sufficiency in raw cotton and raw wool, 1961 to 1986*
('000 metric tons per year)

	Production (1)	Exports (2)	Imports (3)	Change in stocks (4)	Availability[a] (5)=(1)−(2)+(3)−(4)	Self-sufficiency (%) (6)=(1)/(5)x100
Raw cotton						
1961–64	1150	5	105	..	1249	92
1965–69	2326	7	131	44	2405	97
1970–74	2373	21	281	135	2498	95
1975–79	2378	45	369	−168	2870	83
1980–84	4305	89	535	873	3878	111[a]
1985–86	4491	387	6	−1006	5116	88[a]
Raw wool[b]						
1961–64	96	14	22	..	104	92
1965–69	106	15	10	..	101	106
1970–74	125	6	9	..	128	98
1975–79	139	7	13	..	145	96
1980–84	189	3	59	..	245	77
1985–86	180	1	162	..	341	53

[a] The changes in cotton stocks in the 1980s were substantial; on average for the 1980–86 period China was just a little over 100 per cent self-sufficient in cotton.
[b] Raw wool production statistics are assumed to refer to greasy wool and are converted to a clean equivalent basis by multiplying by 0.45. Trade statistics are assumed to refer to clean wool.
Source: See Appendix to this volume.

Table 3.7: *Average and marginal prices received by farmers for agricultural products, China, 1978 to 1987*
(1978 = 100)

	Cotton		Wool	Grain			Average, all agricultural products	Industrial products sold in rural areas
	Average	Marginal	Average and marginal	Average	Marginal, wheat	Marginal, rice		
1978	100	100	100	100	100	100	100	100
1979	118	150	100	126	140	138	n.a.	100
1980	139	165	101	137	133	138	131	101
1981	137	167	102	145	133	138	139	102
1982	142	167	105	149	133	138	142	104
1983	150	167	108	149	133	138	148	105
1984	150	..	110	150	..	138	154	108
1985	141	..	148	158	..	..	..	..
1986	..	..	..	177	..	..	..	..
1987	156	..	..	193	..	..	..	..

Source: State Statistical Bureau, *Statistical Yearbook of China*, Beijing, 1985, and Sicular (1988).

self-sufficiency in natural fibres is likely to trend downwards again from the mid-1980s.[4]

To obtain some idea of likely magnitude of the growth in China's domestic demand for natural fibres, it is insightful to look at the growth in fibre use in Korea. In the 1960s, Korea used about the same quantities of natural fibres per capita as China did in the 1970s: around 3 kilograms of cotton and 0.15 kilograms of wool. By the early 1970s Korea's use of cotton and wool had risen to 4 kilograms and 0.3 kilograms, respectively, which again was almost the same as China's consumption in the mid-1980s. However, Korea's use of cotton has more than doubled again and wool use has trebled since the early 1970s, and cotton usage at least has gone to even higher levels in the other Asian NIEs (Table 3.8). So if China were to continue to duplicate the experience of its neighbours in this respect, exporters of cotton and wool could look forward to a healthy growth in China's demand for their products in the decade or so ahead, as it is inconceivable that China could supply more than a small fraction of such an increased demand from domestic production given the competing demands for agricultural resources for food production.[5]

Synthetic fibres

Just as the expansion in China's production of finished textiles and clothing is stimulating its domestic demand for natural fibres, so too is it stimulating a greater demand for synthetic fibres. The question arises as to whether that growing demand for man-made fibres will be met by Chinese or foreign firms.

Since the production of synthetic fibres tends to be much more capital intensive than yarn and fabric production and, even more so, finished textiles and clothing,[6] one would expect China to find it less costly to import those fibres at this early stage of its economic development than to produce them domestically. This is in fact what the NIEs found in the 1960s and early 1970s: they imported them from Japan, so that while Japan lost out in international markets for labour-intensive finished textiles and clothing (and at a later stage for synthetic yarns and fabrics) it gained market share in capital-intensive

---

[4] While data more recent than 1986 were not available for China's total fibre imports at the time of writing, other data show China's wool imports from Australia (its major source) continued to increase rapidly in the latter 1980s. In the twelve months to June 1984 they amounted to 26,000 tonnes, but in the four subsequent years they were 51,000 tonnes, 77,000 tonnes, 105,000 tonnes and 94,000 tonnes, before dropping to 59,000 tonnes for the politically unstable year of 1988–89.

[5] For further details on this point, see Anderson (1991).

[6] See Chapter 1, note 6.

Table 3.8: *Apparent per capita use of raw cotton and wool, China and other Northeast Asian economies, 1961 to 1986*[a] (kg per year)

| | China ($500) | Northeast Asian NIEs | | | | Japan ($11,330) |
		Korea ($2180)	Taiwan ($3100)	Hong Kong ($6200)	All three NIEs ($2770)	
Cotton						
1961–64	1.8	2.7	6.3	37.1	6.5	8.9
1965–69	3.2	3.0	7.0	41.0	7.2	8.5
1970–74	2.9	4.2	9.7	38.2	8.5	8.3
1975–79	3.1	8.3	12.7	46.4	12.6	7.5
1980–84	3.9	10.4	14.6	30.4	13.2	7.6
1985–86	4.9	9.7	16.6	24.0	12.8	6.6
Wool						
1961–64	0.15	0.11	0.10	0.10	0.11	2.90
1965–69	0.13	0.27	0.54	0.49	0.37	3.30
1970–74	0.15	0.48	1.06	0.76	0.67	3.34
1975–79	0.15	0.90	1.09	0.63	0.93	2.37
1980–84	0.24	1.25	1.21	0.34	1.17	1.79
1985–86	0.33	1.42	1.27	0.43	1.30	1.85

[a] Per capita incomes for 1985 are shown in US dollars at the top of each column, from the World Bank's *Atlas 1987* except for China for which the 'guesstimate' by Perkins (1988) is shown. China's per capita income in 1985 was equivalent to Korea's in 1964 and Taiwan's in 1958. If China achieves its goal of quadrupling its living standard between 1978 and 2000, its income will be a little under $1100 (in 1985 prices) in 2000. That was the living standard in Korea in 1974, Taiwan in 1970 and Hong Kong in 1955, approximately.
Source: See Appendix to this volume.

synthetic fibres. Similarly, the East Asian NIEs became exporters of synthetic yarns and fabrics somewhat later than was the case with clothing and only now are they becoming significant exporters of synthetic fibres, while growth in their share of the international market for more labour-intensive items such as clothing is levelling off as China's share grows (Figure 3.3). Thus by successful structural adjustments both Japan and the East Asian NIEs are making way for China in world markets for labour-intensive goods and at the same time are benefiting, as Europe also may do, from China's growing import demands even within the textile and clothing group of commodities for capital-intensive intermediate goods. Even though China's annual production of synthetic fibres trebled between 1977 and 1983, so too did the volume of its synthetic fibre imports (Park 1988). The extent to which China's imports of synthetic (and also natural) fibres continue to increase will depend, however, on the extent to which China limits the availability of foreign exchange for this purpose.

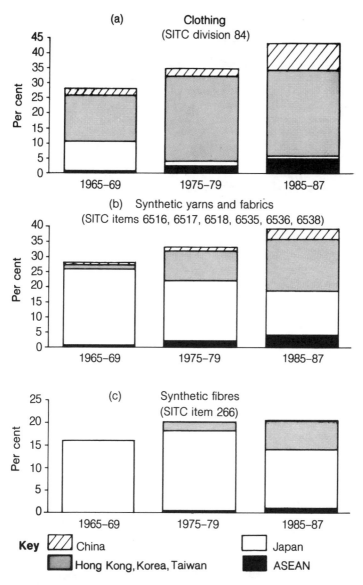

Figure 3.3: *East Asia's shares of world exports of clothing, synthetic yarns and fabrics, and synthetic fibres, 1965 to 1987*

[a] SITC division 84.
[b] SITC items 6516, 6517, 6518, 6535, 6536, 6538.
[c] SITC item 266.
Source: International Economic Data Bank, Trade Data Tapes, Australian National University, Canberra, 1990.

Conclusions and policy implications

Clearly, China is adding significantly to the international relocation of fibre, textile and clothing activity to the East Asian region. Its expanded production and exports of finished textiles and standard clothing are leading to increased imports of fibres, both natural (from the United States and Australasia) and synthetic (from Japan and newly industrialized East Asia). Notwithstanding rapid increases in natural fibre production in China during the first half of the 1980s, China's self-sufficiency in both cotton and wool is likely to continue its decline of the 1960s and 1970s as its comparative advantage in such primary products weakens. The latter will occur not only because of growth in export-oriented manufacturing production but also because of a likely bias in China's agricultural prices in favour of ensuring foodgrain self-sufficiency rather than cotton output growth. Moreover, there are likely to be rapid increases in domestic consumer demand for finished textiles and clothing as Chinese incomes rise and clothing conformity relaxes, which will put further downward pressure on fibre self-sufficiency.[7]

True, this prognosis assumes that economic growth in China will continue to be above the global average in the 1990s as it has been in the past decade or so, and that the economy will continue to remain open to foreign trade in goods, capital and technology. The Chinese government's reactions to the events of Tiananmen Square in mid-1989 may have cast doubt on the validity of that assumption in the short term, but there are very good reasons for expecting the long-run trend rate of Chinese economic growth to continue to be relatively high.[8]

The first is that China has already achieved the most difficult of tasks required to emulate its East Asian neighbours, namely, getting the growth process started. Now that it has behind it a decade in which average real incomes doubled, the Chinese leadership is keen to see that performance repeated with another doubling of China's per capita income by the turn of the century or soon afterwards. The economic and political instability of 1988–89 has if anything hardened the government's resolve to achieve that object.

Second, all of China's neighbouring industrialized market economies managed to double their per capita incomes not only in their first but also in their second (and subsequent) decades of reform-driven growth. That is, relevant precedents exist for sustained rapid economic growth beyond just one decade.

[7] See Anderson (1990a) for a more detailed analysis of the reasons for these likely future trends.

[8] The comments to follow have benefited from careful assessments by various analysts, including Garnaut (1988) and Perkins (1986).

Third, China has many of the same features that have been conducive to the rapid-growth performance of its neighbours. One of these is simply being close to similar societies that are demonstrating that rapid growth is indeed possible. Another is sharing cultural features that are growth-enhancing such as valuing formal education highly and having a capacity for social cohesion that brings with it a tolerance for the inconvenient disruptions to life that necessarily accompany rapid growth. China also shares with its neighbours similar structural features that are conducive to growth, particularly an equitable distribution of land and productive capital and a heavy reliance on labour and invested savings rather than on the relatively small stock of natural resources per capita as the main source of growth. The latter features ensure that the benefits of growth are distributed widely, thus providing a broad base of support for growth-oriented economic policies.

A fourth point to remember about East Asia's more advanced developing economies is that, as in China, their economic development has outpaced their domestic political development. Political freedom is much more limited than economic freedom in all those societies. However, the nature of restrictions on political freedoms in East Asia's market economies has been such that sufficient political stability has prevailed to allow rapid growth to continue in the long run, notwithstanding periodic short-term macroeconomic and political crises. Again, therefore, relevant precedents exist for the Chinese leadership to hold on to power and yet continue to achieve political stability and rapid economic growth.

Thus while it is too soon after the Tiananmen Square incident to say with a great deal of certainty that rapid economic growth will continue in China unabated, there is a reasonable possibility that it will, just as it has occurred following political disruptions in South Korea – and particularly if there is some acceleration of the political reform process in China in the 1990s and if the stalled economic reforms in urban areas regain momentum.

Assuming, then, that the Chinese economy does enjoy above-average growth rates, the development of China's export capacity will continue to add to the pressure on firms in more advanced industrial economies to move out of labour-intensive manufacturing such as finished textiles and standard clothing. To some extent the competitive pressure from China on high-income countries will be offset by reduced pressure from the East Asian NIEs, but only at the labour-intensive end of the spectrum. As firms in the Asian NIEs upgrade to capital-intensive textile processes in response to competitive pressure from China, they in turn will pressure Japan, the United States and Western Europe at the more capital-intensive end of the spectrum of textile and clothing activities. Thus total exports of textiles and clothing from the East Asian region are likely to continue to increase in the foreseeable future.

That is, there is a high probability that China's industrial development will ensure that East Asia's share of world exports of these manufactures – and the region's share of world imports of fibres – keeps growing.

How the rest of the world responds to this competitive pressure from East Asia will have a critical bearing on China's future, as will its choice of development strategy for the 1990s. For China to increase its share of world markets for labour-intensive textiles and clothing in line with its changing comparative advantage, it is essential that advanced industrial countries allow the penetration of increasing volumes of imports of these products from China. Without that market access, China's export growth prospects will be thwarted, which in turn will dampen its overall economic performance and hence also its domestic demand for finished textiles and clothing.

The new MFA negotiated in 1986 between industrial and developing countries, and related agreements, allow for very little export growth from China relative to China's potential – even though China used its economic and political might to obtain larger quotas than normal MFA restrictions allowed (Cline 1987: 142–3).[9] If China's market access is not revised upwards, particularly to the United States where as much as one-third of China's textile and clothing exports are currently destined, one or both of the following outcomes seems likely. First, China could redirect its export production to rely more on other labour-intensive manufactured goods in which it already is a competitive exporter (see Table 3.3 above). This would result in (i) a transfer of import competition from one to another group of manufacturing firms in industrial countries, (ii) a reduced demand for American cotton and Australian and New Zealand wool, and (iii) a reduced demand for synthetic fibres from other East Asian economies. So while restrictions on China's textile and clothing exports serve one special-interest group in rich countries, they directly harm others, in both manufacturing and agriculture.

The second possibility is that China may become pessimistic about export-led growth prospects based on manufactures and return to a more insular development strategy, which would result in even slower overall economic growth than the first option. A reduction in growth and in the share of production that is traded necessarily would reduce the rest of the world's economic growth. It would affect exporters of primary products not only because it would reduce demand for specific raw materials needed by China's export manufacturing industries but also because China's own mobile resources (particularly labour) would be attracted less rapidly out of primary production. And it would

[9] China also benefited before the 1986 renegotiation of the MFA from a loophole in the import-restrictive arrangements which allowed Chinese firms to export clothing based on ramie (Cable 1987: 623–4).

reduce the role of Western Europe, the United States and Japan as suppliers of capital-intensive manufactured goods, services and technologies to China.

This second possibility would be especially unfortunate for the world economy, not to mention for China itself. One can only hope that sufficient reductions in protectionism will result to avert such an outcome when the current MFA agreement expires in July 1991 and the discussions concerning Europe 1992 and the Uruguay Round of multilateral trade negotiations are concluded.

4

Thailand's growth in textile and clothing exports

Suphat Suphachalasai*

The textile and clothing industry in Thailand has become particularly important to the Thai economy in recent years. Exports of its output have grown so rapidly that in the mid-1980s they became the country's highest foreign exchange earning commodity group. They contributed about one-quarter of manufacturing value-added and had the highest employment share of any sub-sector in the manufacturing sector. In 1988 exports of textiles and clothing amounted to US$2.4 billion (one-seventh of all exports) compared with $0.6 billion in 1983, with clothing exports alone valued at $1.9 billion in 1988. This rapid increase in the importance of textile and clothing production and exports suggests that Thailand is following the pattern of earlier industrial development of first Japan and then Hong Kong, the Republic of Korea and Taiwan.

This chapter has two main objectives: to explain why this sub-sector of manufacturing has grown so fast in Thailand, and then to analyse the effects of the Multi-fibre Arrangement (MFA) on the Thai clothing sector. The first two sections of the chapter provide some background on the development of Thai manufacturing in general and the growth of textile and clothing production and exports in particular. The government's role in the industry is then examined, and is followed by an analysis of the effect of the MFA. In the final section is a summary of conclusions and a discussion of Thailand's export prospects for the 1990s.

Growth and structural change in the Thai economy

Thailand has enjoyed having one of the fastest-growing economies in the world since 1960, surpassed only by the East Asian NIEs. Its real

* The author is grateful for helpful comments on an early draft from Will Martin of the Australian National University and Kym Anderson of the University of Adelaide. The penultimate version of this chapter was circulated as Suphachalasai (1989b).

gross domestic product (GDP) grew at an average rate of 8.2 per cent in the 1960s, 7.2 per cent in the 1970s and more than 6 per cent in the 1980s (Table 4.1).

During that period, industrial development far outpaced growth in the primary sector. Agriculture's share of GDP fell from more than 40 per cent before the 1960s to 17 per cent in 1987, while that of manufacturing doubled, from 12 to 24 per cent (Figure 4.1). Labour productivity also increased fastest in the non-farm sector, but even so agriculture's share of employment declined substantially, from 80 to 67 per cent between 1960 and 1986.

Table 4.1:   *Real growth of GDP, Hong Kong, Korea, Singapore and Thailand, 1960 to 1988*
(per cent per year)

	Hong Kong	Korea	Singapore	Taiwan	Thailand
1960–70	10.0	8.6	8.8	9.6	8.4
1970–80	9.3	9.5	8.5	9.7	7.2
1980–85	5.9	7.9	6.5	6.1	5.1
1986	9.0	12.5	1.9	10.6	4.3
1987	13.6	12.2	8.6	11.1	7.0
1988	7.5	11.0	11.0	7.1	10.6

Sources: World Bank, *World Development Report*, various issues, Washington, DC and International Economic Data Bank, World GNP Tapes (based on World Bank data), Australian National University, Canberra.

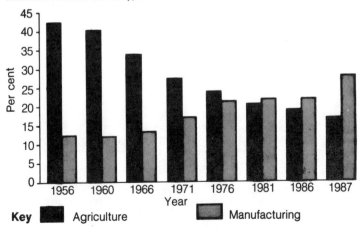

Figure 4.1:   *Shares of agriculture and manufacturing in Thailand's GDP, 1956 to 1988*

Source: National Statistical Office, *National Income Accounts*, Bangkok, various issues.

The industries being developed in Thailand are not just for import replacement but also for earning export income. Indeed the share of agricultural products in Thai exports fell from 86 per cent in 1961 to 45 per cent in 1987, while manufacturing (excluding processed food) increased its share from 2 to 52 per cent during that period. According to a study by Tambunlertchai (1987), the ratio of exports to output in manufacturing doubled between 1972 and 1980, from one-tenth to one-fifth.

These structural changes are reflected in the inter-sectoral pattern of exports shown in Table 4.2. Before the 1970s more than 90 per cent of Thailand's exports were primary products, and as recently as the early 1980s those products still accounted for three-quarters of all exports. But by 1987 manufactured goods contributed more than half of the country's export earnings, with textiles and clothing alone

Table 4.2: *Importance of primary products and textiles and clothing in exports from Thailand and all ASEAN countries, 1965 to 1988*[a]
(per cent)

	Primary products' share of total exports	Textiles and clothing's share of		Index of export specialization[b] in	
		total exports	manufactured exports	agricultural products	textiles and clothing[c]
Thailand					
1965–69	97	1	37	3.4	0.2(0.1)
1970–74	88	5	44	3.7	0.9(0.8)
1975–79	81	9	47	4.1	1.7(1.6)
1980–82	74	10	38	4.4	2.0(2.3)
1983–85	66	13	38	4.3	2.4(3.0)
1986–88	50	17	35	3.5	2.6(3.5)
All ASEAN[d]					
1965–69	90	2	18	2.6	0.3(0.3)
1970–74	84	3	17	2.5	0.5(0.6)
1975–79	80	3	17	2.3	0.6(0.8)
1980–82	74	3	15	1.9	0.7(1.0)
1983–85	70	4	14	1.8	0.8(1.1)
1986–88	59	6	16	1.9	1.0(1.4)

[a] Primary products cover SITC sections 0 to 4 plus division 68 (non-ferrous metals) less 266 (synthetic fibres); textiles and clothing cover SITC divisions 65 and 84; agriculture covers SITC sections 0,1,4, and 2 less 266, 27 and 28.
[b] The index of export specialization is defined as the share of a product group in total exports of a country as a ratio of the share of that product group in world exports, following Balassa (1965).
[c] The indexes in parentheses refer to clothing alone.
[d] Indonesia, Malaysia, Philippines, Singapore and Thailand (plus Brunei, not included here).
Source: International Economic Data Bank, Trade Data Tapes, Australian National University, Canberra, 1990.

contributing 18 per cent. These changes have been considerably more rapid in Thailand than in the other ASEAN countries (Table 4.2) and are comparable with the speed of change in China if not the more advanced NIEs of Northeast Asia (cf. Table 3.2 in Chapter 3 above). They are certainly faster than in the rest of the world, as reflected in Thailand's rapidly growing share of world textile and clothing exports and world imports of fibres (Table 4.3). It may be noticed from Table 4.3 and the final column of Table 4.2 that clothing exports from Thailand have grown especially rapidly, and that by 1987 the index of export specialization (Balassa's (1965) 'revealed' comparative advantage index) for clothing exceeded that for agricultural products.

The changing importance of key export items can be seen in Table 4.4. Food products such as tapioca pellets, sugar and canned pineapple were the major contributors to manufactured exports throughout the 1970s, but labour-intensive products such as textiles and clothing, integrated circuits, and precious stones and jewellery have become the principal manufactured exports during the 1980s. The share of these three labour-intensive products in manufacturing exports was only 30 per cent in 1970, but by 1985 it had doubled to about 60 per cent. Textile and clothing exports grew fastest of all these items during the 1980s, at more than 30 per cent per year in current US dollar terms.

Table 4.3: *Importance of Thailand and all ASEAN countries in world trade in fibres, textiles and clothing, 1965 to 1988[a]*
(per cent)

	Share of world exports of:		Share of world imports of:	
	textiles	clothing	natural fibres	synthetic fibres
Thailand				
1965–69	0.06	0.03	0.23	0.54
1970–74	0.26	0.21	0.63	0.90
1975–79	0.57	0.50	1.01	0.58
1980–82	0.66	0.84	0.94	0.80
1983–85	0.74	1.17	1.34	1.00
1986–88	0.81	1.35	1.46	0.81
All ASEAN				
1965–69	0.67	0.66	0.99	2.63
1970–74	0.97	1.32	1.86	4.25
1975–79	1.53	2.43	3.17	4.94
1980–82	1.83	3.48	3.35	6.05
1983–85	2.23	4.27	3.72	5.02
1986–88	2.31	4.47	3.77	4.04

[a] SITC categories are as follows: textiles 65, clothing 84, natural fibres 26 less 266, synthetic fibres 266.
Source: International Economic Data Bank, Trade Data Tapes, Australian National University, Canberra, 1990.

Table 4.4: *Thailand's seven most important export products, 1960 to 1988*
(share of total export value in parentheses)

Rank	1960	1976	1980	1988
1.	Rice (30%)	Rice (14%)	Rice (15%)	Textiles and clothing (14%)
2.	Rubber (29%)	Tapioca products (12%)	Tapioca products (11%)	Precious stones (8%)
3.	Maize (6%)	Sugar (11%)	Rubber (9%)	Rubber (7%)
4.	Tin (6%)	Maize (9%)	Tin (9%)	Rice (6%)
5.	Teak (4%)	Rubber (9%)	Textiles and clothing (8%)	Tapioca products (6%)
6.	Tapioca products (3%)	Tin (9%)	Maize (5%)	Integrated circuits (5%)
7.	Jute and kenaf (3%)	Textiles and clothing (5%)	Integrated circuits (5%)	Canned seafood (4%)
	(Sub-total 81%)	(Sub-total 69%)	(Sub-total 62%)	(Sub-total 50%)

Sources: Bank of Thailand, *Monthly Bulletin*, various issues, Bangkok, and Ministry of Commerce, Department of Economics and Business, Bangkok.

Developments in Thailand's textile and clothing industry

The Thai textile and clothing industry has undergone many changes since the 1950s when the first modern cotton spinning, weaving and knitting mills were established. Larger-sized plants began to operate with the assistance of protection that accompanied the introduction of the Industrial Promotion Act in 1960. In its early stages the industry concentrated on cotton-based products, but diversification to man-made fibres began in the mid-1960s with Thai–Japanese joint venture firms.

The Japanese joint venture companies, led by Toray and Teijin, have played an important role in the industry, contributing capital, technology and management. Katano (1981) notes that Japanese textile investment in Thailand was part of a strategy that also included investments in Indonesia, Malaysia and the Philippines. An important objective of the Japanese investors was to secure a share in the increasingly protected market of these ASEAN countries. Also relevant, however, was the fact that Japan's textile and clothing industry was subject to Voluntary Export Restraints (VERs) on cotton textiles to the United States under the Long Term Agreement (LTA) on textiles, and investing abroad was part of the Japanese companies' strategy of circumventing the LTA restrictions. In addition, by the mid-1960s

Japanese government policy was positively encouraging adjustments in the domestic textile industry (see Yamawaki in Chapter 6 below).

The large, integrated man-made fibre spinning, weaving and finishing firms in the Thai industry that were joint ventures with Japanese firms involved an average Japanese shareholding of only 36 per cent in 1978, but the Japanese controlled their management because Thai shareholders were fragmented (Tambunlertchai and Yamazawa 1981). Partly because of this, but also because Japanese supplies were competitively priced, most of the textile machines and technology used in Thailand came from Japan.

Then, from the mid-1970s, joint ventures began in Thailand with capital from Taiwan and Hong Kong as well. Firms from these economies were also seeking ways around the industrial countries' import controls that had now become part of the MFA. Moreover, in the 1980s they were trying to escape rising labour costs and the appreciation of their currencies at home.

Most Thai textile firms are located in or around Bangkok. There is a large number of firms in clothing and weaving, and these are at the labour-intensive end of the industry's spectrum; fewer firms are involved in the more capital-intensive activities of spinning and man-made fibre production. However, both ends of the spectrum are engaged in exporting.

There are at least 1500 clothing firms, ranging from those with fewer than ten sewing machines to those with more than one thousand. (This is almost certainly a substantial underestimate because small firms with fewer than 30 sewing machines are not required to be registered.) The clothing industry is characterized by low capital per worker and simple technology: in some areas there are few entry costs and thus the minimum efficient scale of production is quite small.

Weaving has fewer firms than the clothing component of the industry because it requires more capital and relatively sophisticated technology. In 1985 some 250 small firms with old semi-automatic and automatic looms produced for the domestic market and for the 'border' market that comprises Burma, Laos, Cambodia, Malaysia and Vietnam. Another 60 large firms with modern machines, ranging from modern automatic to waterjet looms, produce both for export and for the domestic market. These two groups of firms had almost equal shares in the number of looms in the mid-1980s, with approximately 80,000 each. There is a broad spectrum of weaving technology in Thailand, but it is concentrated at the labour-intensive end of the spectrum of technologies available globally.

At the more capital-intensive end of the industry there were 60 spinning firms in Thailand in 1985, using an average of 30,000 spindles each or a total of a little under 2 million spindles (Table 4.5). All but nine firms have more than 15,000 spindles, which was the

Table 4.5:   *Numbers of textile machines in Thailand, 1975 to 1985*
(thousands)

Year	Spindles	Looms	Knitting machines
1975	1094	53	17
1976	1112	56	22
1977	1129	57	23
1978	1168	59	24
1979	1300	63	26
1980	1320	67	30
1981	1547	70	31
1982	1642	72	33
1983	1791	77	35
1984	1872	79	39
1985	1963	80	41

Source: Thai Textile Manufacturing Association, Bangkok.

minimum economic size cited by Ajanant and Speafico (1984) for a spinning firm. Only seven firms produce filament and staple man-made fibres, mostly for import substitution in a highly protected domestic market.

Both small and large spinning and weaving concerns are internationally competitive. True, the physical labour productivity of large concerns in Thailand is lower than it is in Western Europe: in 1984 the output of the product known as Spinning Count No. 24 in Thailand was around 12 kg per worker per hour compared with 15 kg in West Germany, for example. However, labour costs in Thailand are substantially lower (in 1984 they were one-eighth of the costs of labour in Western Europe), ensuring that Thai production is very competitive internationally (Ajanant and Speafico 1984). It is therefore not surprising that Thai textile production more than doubled between 1975 and 1986 and that major new investments to expand capacity were under way in the late 1980s (Supachalasai 1989).

Thailand's competitiveness is evident in the increasing export orientation of its textile and clothing producers. In 1987 almost half (46 per cent) of clothing production was exported, compared with only 4 per cent in 1972. For fabrics the share exported rose from 8 to 22 per cent between 1972 and 1986, and for yarn it increased from less than 1 per cent to 22 per cent. For textiles and clothing as a whole about 35 per cent of production was exported in 1986, not counting border exports to neighbouring countries such as Burma, Cambodia, Laos and Malaysia.[1] This compares with only 20 per cent in 1972,

[1] Official data for this border trade are not available because domestic consumption and border trade use the same distribution channels through the central market in Bangkok. However, it is estimated that around one-eighth of total production is exported in this form across the border (IFCT 1986 and Theravaninthorn 1982), in which case by 1986 close to half of all textiles and clothing production in Thailand was being exported.

when Thailand was still a net importer of this aggregate group of commodities.

Domestic policies affecting Thai textiles and clothing production

Over the years the government has provided various forms of assistance to the industry. These have included promotion privileges and credit subsidies as well as protectionist import barriers, but there have been offsetting sales taxes and tariffs on intermediate inputs.

Textiles were among the first industries 'promoted' under the Industrial Promotion Act of 1960. However, promotion of textiles has been 'on and off'. The Board of Investment ceased granting privileges to the textile industry in 1971, started them again in 1974 and then ceased once more in 1978. In 1985 privileges were granted to export-oriented clothing firms but all clothing promotion was suspended in 1987 (Ministry of Commerce 1987). Meanwhile, spinning and weaving firms were granted promotion privileges in 1986. And in both 1970 and 1980 the government sought to reduce textile production because of an over-supply during the slump in international markets (Theravaninthorn 1982).

The promotion privileges granted to textiles and clothing have not been great. Except for man-made fibres, textiles and clothing were only given promotion at the lowest level of assistance. In the case of firms exporting more than 80 per cent of production, instruments of assistance included full exemption from import duties and business taxes, and up to a five-year holiday on income tax. As with other export activities, the draw-back system (providing a rebate of import tariffs paid on inputs) is also available for textile and clothing exporting firms, offsetting the costs of protection on imported intermediate products.

Credit subsidies have been available for production and export from the Bank of Thailand. Credit assistance has also been available for exports, in the form of discounted promissory notes. Discount rates vary with the market. The discount rate was raised close to the market rate of 14.5 per cent in March 1985, when the United States threatened to impose countervailing duties if Thai exports continued to be subsidized. If exporters received subsidized credit, a countervailing duty of 2.3 per cent was to be charged.

The government imposes sales taxes on intermediate goods such as fibres, yarns and fabrics. The tax is cumulative. As the intermediate products pass through subsequent processes the cost of production therefore rises progressively. However, according to a study by Hiranyakit (1986), these taxes do not encourage clothing producers to integrate vertically. Clothing manufacturers prefer not to be tied to woven product suppliers so that they can change inputs quickly in response to fashion changes: this flexibility advantage evidently outweighs the costs of the sales taxes that would be avoided via vertical integration. Hence integration has been confined to spinning and weaving, where economies of scale are possible.

Imported textile and clothing products have attracted tariffs. Import duties on fabrics and clothing have been among the highest, at about 60 per cent in 1985 and 80–100 per cent prior to 1978. Man-made fibres have had the second highest tariff rates, of 20–30 per cent in 1985 and subject also to surcharges before that. However, average import tariffs on textiles and clothing have been moderate in Thailand compared to other developing countries (Table 4.6), and Thailand has had virtually no effective quantitative restrictions on imports of these products.

Suphachalasai (1989a) estimates the overall effective rates of assistance (ERA) for the Thai textile and clothing industry in 1985 to be quite low, averaging 7 per cent for weaving and 6 per cent for clothing (Table 4.7).[2] Clothing that is exported attracts positive assistance, however (5 per cent ERA), suggesting that the structure of assistance is biased slightly towards exports. The main form of assistance to exports is the export credit assistance given by the Bank of Thailand.

It is true that the government has been trying to control domestic textile capacity and production since the 1978 slump by prohibiting investment in new capacity. However, the regulations were not implemented effectively. The number of spindles, looms and knitting machines continued to increase by approximately 10 per cent per year (Table 4.5): textile machines were simply imported and installed without being registered with the Ministry of Industry. As it happened, the rents created by the regulations were boosting the incentive for small firms to be established. The controls were therefore abandoned in May 1987, with the result that the expansion of existing firms and the establishment of new firms for spinning and weaving are now permitted. Promotion privileges, which ceased for the textile industry in 1986, have recently been resumed for both spinning and weaving and for firms that produce for domestic consumption as well as for those that export, if such firms locate in the investment promotion regions outside Bangkok.

Perhaps most importantly for the international competitiveness of textiles, Thailand – in contrast to many other countries – has steadily pursued prudent monetary and fiscal policies (Hughes 1985). The exchange rate for the Thai currency has been kept close to its

---

2 The effective rate of assistance is defined as the percentage by which an industry's value added has been raised as a result of government policies affecting output prices, input prices, tax concessions and the like.

Table 4.6: *Average tariffs on textiles and clothing in selected developing countries in the early 1980s*
(per cent)

Country	Average tariff
Argentina (1982)	37
Brazil (1983)	79
Colombia (1982)	66
Egypt (1982)	97
India (1983)	86
Republic of Korea (1982)	34
Malaysia (1981)	22
Pakistan (1981)	128
Sri Lanka (1983)	60
Taiwan (1983)	60
Thailand (1981)	53
Tunisia (1981)	31

Source: GATT, *Textiles and Clothing in the World Economy*, Geneva, 1984.

Table 4.7: *Effective rates of assistance for the textile and clothing industry, Thailand, 1985*
(per cent)

	All sales	Domestic sales	Export sales
Textiles (weaving)	6.5	6.3	8.2
Clothing	–6.1	–9.8	5.0

Source: Suphachalasai (1989a).

equilibrium rate for the last 20 years (Siamwalla and Setboonsarng 1987), and inflation has been remarkably low, averaging only 3 per cent per year between 1980 and 1986.

Thus the net effect of Thai government intervention on the textile and clothing industry has been close to negligible. That is, protection policy has not played a significant positive role in the industry's rapid growth, but government policies have not been penalizing exporting firms either. The growth of these industries is simply the result of changes in comparative advantage for this rapidly developing economy, subject to the limitations imposed by the MFA, to which we now turn.

Effects of the MFA on Thailand

The main external government influence on the Thai textile and clothing industry is via the MFA. The MFA involves agreements between developing country exporters of textiles and clothing and advanced industrial countries which limit bilateral trade between these two groups of countries. The net effect is to raise prices in the MFA importing countries but lower the volume of their imports. In so far as MFA-exporting countries divert their export production to other markets, prices in those markets will be depressed. Whether a country like Thailand gains or loses from the scheme therefore depends on the proportion of its export sales in the high-priced MFA-importing countries relative to those in other, lower-priced markets.

The effects can be seen from Figure 4.2, which depicts the world market for these products (call them simply homogeneous clothing). ES is the excess supply function of the developing country exporters of clothing. ED_M and ED_R are excess demand functions of the advanced industrial country importers of MFA clothing and of the rest of the world, respectively. ED is the sum of these two regions' excess demands. In a world of free trade in clothing, E would represent the point of market equilibrium: the world price would be P and the volume traded would be Q, of which Q_M would be sold to the advanced industrial country group and Q_R to the rest of the world. Suppose, however, that advanced industrial countries limit their imports under the MFA to L. This forces up the domestic price of clothing in those countries to P_L. It also effectively puts a kink in the world excess demand curve so that below point A it has the steeper slope of ED'. This causes the price of clothing in international markets to fall to P'. In the absence of tariffs in the MFA-importing countries, exporters as a group are better off by $P_L BCP$ in their high-priced but quota-restricted sales to those countries, but they are worse off by CDFE in their sales to the rest of the world. Clearly, the larger the proportion of any one exporting country's sales to the quota-restricted market, the more likely that country would benefit from the MFA-quota restrictions, other things being equal.

The critical share parameter has not been constant through time. As Table 4.8 shows, it has increased rapidly since 1975 for such countries as Indonesia, the Philippines, China, India and Pakistan, has been roughly constant at around 75–80 per cent for the NIEs, but it has decreased substantially for Thailand. According to official Thai statistics, 82 per cent of both the value and volume of clothing exports from Thailand went to MFA-restricted markets in 1977, while twelve years later only 36 per cent by volume and 51 per cent by value were destined for those high-priced markets (Table 4.7).

The EC and the United States are the main importing countries with a combined share of 50 per cent of Thai exports by value and 37 per cent of export volume. In contrast, in non-MFA markets the value share in 1988 was only 49 per cent while the volume share was 64 per cent. There are two main reasons for the difference between value and volume shares in the two markets: differences in desired product

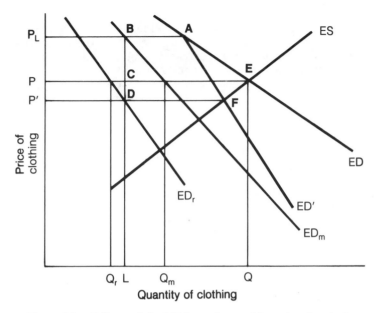

Figure 4.2: *Effects of the MFA on the world market for clothing*

Table 4.8: *Shares of clothing[a] exports from selected developing countries to MFA-restricted markets,[b] 1975 to 1986* (per cent, value based)

Countries	1975	1980	1985	1986
ASEAN				
Indonesia	33	51	97	94
Philippines	58	70	86	78
Thailand	80	63	71	63
Northeast Asian NIEs				
Hong Kong	80	81	86	86
Korea	77	72	74	73
Taiwan	80	66	74	73
Other Asia				
China	25	39	45	48
India	67	65	88	89
Pakistan	51	64	76	72
Latin America				
Brazil	49	62	77	96
Mexico	92	99	99	99

[a] Clothing includes all items in the Standard International Trade Classification 84.
[b] Austria, Canada, EC-12, Finland, Norway, Sweden and the United States.
Source: International Economic Data Bank, Trade Data Tapes, Australian National University, Canberra.

quality (as the MFA market is made up of higher-income countries), and the quota rents that are implicit in prices of exports to MFA markets. Moreover, since the quotas are volume-denominated, it pays exporters to raise the quality of their exports to MFA markets in order to maximize their quota rents. This upgrading is clearly evident in the slower decline in value as compared with volume shares shown in Table 4.9.

Quantitative estimates using a model of world clothing markets

An empirical simulation model of world markets for these products is needed to determine whether Thailand has been a net beneficiary or loser from the MFA. Such a model is provided, at least for clothing, by Suphachalasai (1989a). Basically it involves a set of partial equilibrium supply and demand equations for countries and country groups spanning the world. It does not have the virtue of Trela and Whalley's (1988b) model of being general equilibrium. However, unlike their model, its important feature is that clothing demand is differentiated by country of origin (the Armington assumption). The present model divides the world into the three groups of countries depicted in Figure 4.2, namely, MFA-restricted countries, unrestricted importing countries, and exporting countries. The latter group is divided so that the

Table 4.9: *The volume and value of Thai clothing exports to MFA-restricted markets, 1977 to 1988*

	Volume		Value	
	million pieces	share (%)[a]	US$ million	share (%)[a]
1977	37	82	68	82
1978	54	72	100	76
1979	57	65	132	60
1980	60	58	175	63
1981	74	56	226	63
1982	73	52	234	62
1983	89	54	276	72
1984	120	52	404	78
1985	122	51	419	71
1986	126	41	510	63
1987	183	40	800	55
1988	192	36	915	51

[a] Share of total volume or value of clothing exports from Thailand.
Source: Ministry of Commerce, Department of Economics and Business, Bangkok.

effects on Thailand and other groups can be distinguished. Figure 4.3 provides a flow chart of the interactions in these markets, which are assumed to clear simultaneously.

Only two sets of empirical results are presented here: the aggregate effect of the export volume, export price and net economic welfare of exporting countries; and some more detailed effects on Thailand in particular. Much more detailed results are available in Suphachalasai (1989a), along with a full specification of the model.

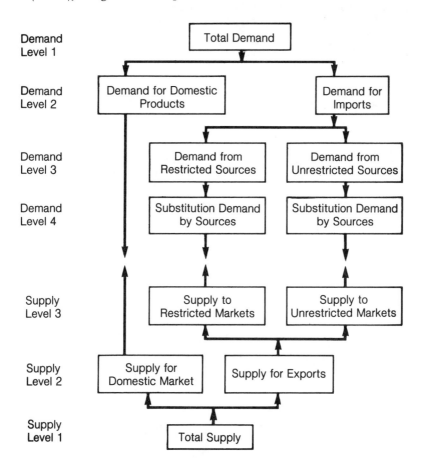

Figure 4.3:   *A flow diagram of the model of the world market for clothing*

Table 4.10 summarizes the estimated effects of the MFA on clothing export markets and exporters' welfare as of 1985. Those results suggest the volume of developing country exports of clothing was about one-third lower than it would have been in 1985 in the absence of the MFA. For Thailand the reduction is estimated to be 37 per cent, similar to the decline for the NIEs of East Asia.

The average export price is estimated to have been raised by the MFA, despite the fall in the non-MFA market. But the increase is not sufficient to offset the decline in export volumes, so the aggregate value of exports also has been lowered by the MFA.

The annual welfare cost of the MFA, according to these results, was around US$20 million in 1985 for Thailand and $1.8 billion for all exporting developing countries. This of course is a gross underestimate of the total cost because it does not include the administrative costs of controlling imports, of negotiating with each of the MFA importing countries, and the like.

These partial-equilibrium estimates of the welfare effects of the MFA are higher for MFA-importing countries (not shown here) and lower for exporting countries than the general-equilibrium results of Trela and Whalley (1988b). The main reason for the difference is the assumption regarding the elasticity of substitution in demand between restricted and unrestricted markets, for which no estimates are available. In this study it is assumed that the elasticity of substitution in demand between restricted and unrestricted markets is one, while Trela and Whalley assume it is five. This causes a lower estimation of the welfare effects on MFA-importing countries in the study from

Table 4.10: *Effects of the MFA on world clothing markets and on exporting countries' economic welfare, 1985*

	Thailand	Northeast Asian NIEs	Other exporting countries
Volume of exports (% change)			
MFA-restricted markets	−42	−41	−35
Other markets	30	15	10
Total	−37	−39	−30
Export prices (% change)			
MFA-restricted markets	27	32	25
Other markets	−15	−20	−13
Total	18	27	15
Net economic welfare change (1985 US$ billion)	−0.02	−1.51	−0.28

Source: Suphachalasai (1989a).

which the above results are quoted because of a lower degree of substitution between the two sources. On the other hand the exporting countries lose more in Trela and Whalley's estimation of the net welfare effects because the reduction of export quantity is higher.

Despite the differences in the size of the welfare effects in this study as compared with Trela and Whalley's (1988b), the important common conclusion is that exporting countries are losing from the MFA when compared with the free-trade situation. In the case of Thailand the welfare loss due to the MFA has increased with time. Because the model is comparatively static, linear, and homogeneous of degree zero, the percentage changes in each consecutive year are the same. Therefore if the necessary data (such as export and import values and production) are available, the same percentage change can be used to calculate the welfare effects for different years (assuming other things to be similar to the base year, most notably the tariff equivalent of MFA quotas). In the case of Thailand, the required data were available from national sources up to 1987. Thailand has had difficulties in expanding its exports to MFA-restricted markets because the export quotas allocated to Thailand are small and growing only slowly. It has thus had to diversify its exports to non-MFA markets. As a result, Thailand's welfare loss is estimated to have increased from $20 million in 1985 to $120 million in 1987. The more extensive the diversification of its exports, the more Thailand will lose from the MFA unless its export quotas in MFA markets are increased.

Lessons from Thailand and its future export prospects

Clearly the Thai economy is structurally adjusting away from primary production and exports in the course of its rapid economic growth, and labour-intensive textiles and clothing are rapidly expanding their contribution to Thailand's GDP, employment and net foreign exchange earnings. These structural changes have been helped by the Thai government's prudent macroeconomic policies and the removal of many of the disincentives to export-oriented industrialization. They were also helped initially by the opportunity to export textiles and clothing to high-priced markets subject to MFA quotas. Once the industry had expanded output beyond its quota limits under the MFA, however, it was forced to sell in non-MFA markets such as Saudi Arabia, United Arab Emirates and Singapore which are lower priced. In recent years, the industry's exports have been so large that only about half have gone to MFA-importing countries.

While the modelling results suggest that Thailand would now be better off in the absence of the MFA, an important lesson from the Thai experience is that it has been highly successful in its export-led industrial development and overall economic growth strategy, notwithstanding the MFA restrictions on its export earnings. Moreover, its rapid growth in clothing exports has occurred despite the dramatic increase in direct competition from China's exports after the reforms began there in 1978. A big help to both Thailand and China has been, of course, the reduced growth of textiles and clothing exports from the neighbouring East Asian NIEs as they structurally adjust towards more capital-intensive goods and services, just as Japan did for the NIEs in earlier decades (Anderson and Park 1989; Park and Anderson 1991).

Thai clothing and textile exports are expected to continue to grow rapidly for some time, providing prudent macroeconomic policies prevail and microeconomic intervention remains supportive. The market opportunities that continue to open up for clothing exports at the labour-intensive end of the industry appear to be considerable. Major textile and clothing exporters such as Korea, Taiwan and Hong Kong are expected to keep moving up-market, exporting higher-quality and more capital-intensive products. Current rapid rates of growth in these NIEs are putting upward pressure on real wages, making their labour-intensive products less competitive than Thailand's.

II
DEMAND FOR TEXTILE EXPORTS FROM NEWLY INDUSTRIALIZING ASIA

5

The Multi-fibre Arrangement and China's growth prospects

John Whalley*

How important is the removal of trade restrictions against exports of textiles and clothing under the Arrangement Regarding International Trade in Textiles, commonly known as the Multi-fibre Arrangement (MFA), for China's future growth prospects? This chapter tries to answer this question by posing three further questions.

The first is whether a textile export growth phase comparable to those experienced by rapidly growing developing countries which have preceded China must inevitably form part of Chinese growth and, if so, what are the implications? The experience of Japan, Korea and Taiwan underlies the view, held strongly in some quarters, that a period of rapid growth in both production and exports of labour-intensive manufactures such as textiles and clothing is an inevitable part of such a growth spurt.[1] China's growth to date has been dominated by strong productivity performance in the agricultural sector (McMillan, Whalley and Zhu 1989), and only now is China beginning to move towards significant attempts at reform and growth in the manufacturing sector.[2] How textiles and clothing exports fit into this picture, and what the potential is for China, are the issues.

* The author is grateful to Kym Anderson and other conference participants for comments. A considerable portion of the material in the paper draws on earlier joint work with Irene Trela on the global effects of trade restrictions on textiles and clothing reported in Trela and Whalley (1988a) and Trela and Whalley (1990), with emphasis placed here on the implications for China.

[1] See Anderson and Park (1989) for a discussion of the contribution of textile and clothing production and exports to China's recent growth, and Park and Anderson (1991) for these industries' contribution historically in Japan.

[2] There are, however, differences of view in the Western research community, with those who argue that recent strong Chinese growth has been accompanied by little or no improvement in productivity in the manufacturing sector (such as Lardy 1987), and those who argue that the productivity growth has been significant (such as Chen *et al.* 1988).

The second major question is: how severely is the MFA an impediment to GDP and export growth for China, given that Hong Kong, Korea and Taiwan all seem to have achieved substantial growth in textile and clothing exports despite the MFA's presence?[3] Unlike Taiwan and Korea, China may soon become large enough in both population and GDP terms for large increases in volumes of its textiles and clothing exports to cause major adjustments in importing countries. It may seem at first sight that a Chinese textile and clothing export-led growth phase can only occur with major dislocation on global markets, which, in turn, would intensify the existing pressures in advanced industrial economies for protection of textile and clothing industries. How large would such dislocations be in industrial countries? Is a major sustained export surge for a period of, say, ten or fifteen years accompanying high Chinese growth therefore a realistic scenario? And what are the prospects for the MFA? Is it likely to be weakened as a trade-restricting device in the near future, and could this possibly facilitate heightened Chinese growth?

The third major question is whether China's somewhat tenuous current position within the multilateral trading system as a non-contracting party to the GATT, along with the current uncertainties over how clear the trade rules in the system actually are, weakens the attractions of this route to higher growth for China. Concerns expressed by the industrial countries in the now-suspended GATT negotiations on a Chinese protocol of accession have focused on the threat of large import surges from China which might result from manipulation of domestic price controls and other policies. These would still remain outside of GATT disciplines after China had obtained the benefits of GATT membership (such as unconditional MFN).[4] While negotiations remain on hold on Chinese GATT accession, and without clear multilateral disciplines wihin the trading system which guarantee China's access to large export markets, it seems clear that, unlike the situation for smaller economies, the trade route to high growth for China may be substantially more difficult to follow.

With a much larger domestic market compared to other developing countries, it is equally less clear that the trade route is the most obvious one for China to follow for higher growth. China, therefore, is faced with a conflict in her policy choices in this area. She may have to take on additional international disciplines over her domestic policies in order to guarantee firmer rules of access for her exports to industrial country markets. But, in the process, China may be forgoing the use of precisely those policy instruments which may be necessary to propel the economy towards high levels of accumulation and, ultimately, income growth.

[3] See the more detailed discussion of how this has occurred in Trela and Whalley (1990).

[4] See the discussion by Lam (1989) and Author unknown (1988).

The picture which this chapter paints is thus somewhat clouded. The future form the MFA might take remains uncertain pending the outcome of the current GATT Uruguay Round. The prospects for Chinese accession to the GATT are now far from clear, and are made more problematic by the apparent insistence by industrial countries that China agree to the use of selective safeguards. Also, it is unclear to the present author that a period of dominance of textile and clothing exports in Chinese growth, comparable to that experienced in other smaller developing countries, is necessarily possible or even desirable.

With all these uncertainties, the chapter concludes that, in the present environment and facing trade restrictions abroad, Chinese policymakers may be unwise to assume that unlimited market access for textile and clothing exports would be theirs for the taking to fuel their economic growth. Nor may a policy that is heavily oriented towards trade and growing exports of labour-intensive textiles and clothing necessarily be the best policy for China to pursue.

Textiles and clothing exports in China's developmental process

The interrelationship between textile and clothing exports on the one hand, and economic growth on the other, has been much debated in recent literature. This follows the growth experiences of Japan, Korea and Taiwan in which rapid growth of textile and clothing exports characterized their initial growth surge, only to be followed subsequently by growth in exports of other manufactured commodities such as steel, consumer electronics, motor vehicles and higher technology products, and a relative decline in textile and clothing exports.

The special significance of textile and clothing products is that they are typically among the most labour-intensive, least technology-demanding manufactures for developing countries to produce. In an initial developmental phase involving large transfers of labour from the tradition-based farm sector to more modern manufacturing sectors, textiles and clothing production provides the opportunity to both employ and train large numbers of workers new to industrial activities. Increased exports of textiles and clothing accommodate increased production, which implies increased human capital accumulation and ultimately higher economic growth.

This link between increased textile and clothing exports on the one hand, and higher GDP growth on the other, is widely believed to be strong. Indeed, the OECD (1985) argues that 'the expansion of textile and clothing exports had become for the developing countries an increasingly important determinant of their economic development'.

Their view is that growth in textile and clothing exports is central to wider economic growth and social development. This, they argue, has been demonstrated in the growth experiences first of Japan, and then of Hong Kong, Korea and Taiwan. Implicitly, their argument is that in order to grow, developing countries need ever-expanding access to markets of the major industrial countries, and growth in exports of textiles and clothing are central to this process.

These arguments are, in turn, related to the famous sequence of stages that Rostow (1960a,b) believes countries pass through during the course of their development. He argues that, at any point in time, all countries typically are in one of five stages: traditional society, showing the preconditions for a growth take-off, at the take-off to sustained growth, showing a drive to maturity, or at a stage of high mass consumption.

Beginning with Rostow's traditional society, development starts with the reallocation of surplus agricultural workers, whose productivity is low, to industries where they become more productive. The precondition phase sees a build-up of infrastructure, notably in the form of ports, railways and roads, which are also important inputs for primary exports. Technological advance also occurs in agriculture, along with expanded markets, an expanded supply of funds to the modern sector, and a rise in the level of investment to at least 10 per cent of national income. This is accompanied by an expansion in imports, including capital imports, financed by the surplus generated in agriculture.

The take-off phase is characterized by a rise in investment to a level in excess of 10 per cent of national income, and rapid growth in a limited group of manufacturing sectors. In the nineteenth and early twentieth centuries these leading sectors ranged from textiles and clothing (Britain and New England, USA) to railways (the United States, France, Germany, Canada, Russia), to modern timber-cutting and railways (Sweden). Agricultural processing, oil, import-substitution industries, ship-building and rapid expansion in military production helped to provide the initial surge in other cases.

During the drive to maturity, Rostow saw growth proceeding through a changing sequence of leading sectors. There is, therefore, no need for the sequence of leading sectors in developing countries today to repeat the pattern of, say, Great Britain – that is, cotton, pig iron, steel, engineering, and so on. In fact, in the twentieth century some of the leading sectors have been petroleum (Arab nations), agriculture (Australia, Argentina, Ivory Coast), rubber, palm oil and timber (Malaysia), in addition to textiles and clothing (Japan, Korea, Hong Kong, Singapore, Sri Lanka and others).

Leading sectors, during the drive to maturity, are determined by the available pool of technology, as well as by natural or acquired resource endowments. They may also be determined by the policies of governments. Countries generally develop through structural change in response to shifts in comparative advantage – beginning with specialization in primary products and advancing to single-process, labour-intensive manufactures, capital- and technology-intensive goods, and finally to higher technology and knowledge-intensive products (Balassa 1979; Balassa and Bauwens 1988).

The issue, therefore, is how China's future growth pattern in manufactures will fit into this picture. Will it be dominated by rapid growth in both production and exports of textile and clothing products, with subsequent rotation to other leading sectors? Or will trade be less central because of China's size, with other leading sectors emerging?

China's recent growth record is shown in Table 5.1, with comparative data reported for other Asian developing countries.[5] The sharply elevated growth performance of China in the 1980s is clearly discernible.

Data on China's textile and clothing exports, reported in Table 5.2, show that the share of textile and clothing exports in total exports grew only slowly until the mid-1980s and were not greatly above the 20 per cent levels of the 1960s and early 1970s.[6] Taiwan's share of textile and clothing exports in total exports increased from 14 per cent in the mid-1960s to 30 per cent in the early 1970s, and fell to 22 per cent in the early 1980s. Korea's share similarly increased from 27 per cent in the mid-1960s to 39 per cent by the early 1970s, falling to 26 per cent by the early 1980s (Anderson and Park 1989: Table 2). Despite China's high GDP growth rate since 1978, growth of textile and clothing exports in proportional terms thus did not initially match that experienced by Taiwan, Korea and other rapid growers. In part this is because China's growth during the decade to the mid-1980s was so heavily agriculture-led.

Hence, exports of textiles and clothing are only just beginning to play the dominant role in China's growth that they have played in other smaller Asian economies, and as a result the seriousness of MFA restrictions remains a contentious matter for China's development. If textile and clothing industries *are* to play a key role in any future Chinese industrialization surge, then access to markets abroad is presumably crucial in allowing China to realize traditional gains from trade, and in speeding Chinese growth by moving through a sequential product line developmental process. This view of the growth process

5 See also the discussion of recent Chinese performance in the textiles and clothing sector in Guo (1987, 1988).

6 Anderson and Park (1989: Table 2) reported China's share of textile and clothing exports in all exports to be just under 20 per cent for 1965–69, up from 14 per cent for 1955–57.

Table 5.1: *Real GDP growth rates, China and other Asian developing countries, 1960 to 1986* (per cent, annual compound rates)

	1960–70	1970–80	1980–85	1986[a]
China	4.0	5.8	9.8	7.4
Asian NIEs				
Hong Kong	10.1	9.8	4.2	8.7
Korea	9.5	8.2	7.5	11.4
Singapore	9.2	9.3	6.0	1.9
Taiwan	9.6	9.7	6.1	9.9
ASEAN-4				
Indonesia	3.8	8.0	3.6	2.0
Malaysia	..	7.9	5.1	0.5
Philippines[b]	5.2	6.3	–0.9	0.1
Thailand	7.9	6.9	5.3	3.8
South Asia				
Bangladesh	..	5.8[c]	3.9	5.2
Burma	2.8	4.2	5.2	3.7
India	3.9	3.2	5.4	5.0
Nepal	2.2	2.0	3.9	4.2
Pakistan	..	5.6[c]	6.3	7.2
Sri Lanka	5.8	4.7	5.0	4.0

[a] 1986 preliminary estimates except for Bangladesh, Burma, China, Nepal and the Philippines.
[b] GNP.
[c] 1973–80.
Source: James *et al.* (1987: Table 1.3).

Table 5.2: *China's textile and clothing exports, by value and share of total exports, 1970 to 1986* (billion US dollars and per cent)

	Value of exports of:		Textile and clothing exports as % of total exports
	Textiles	Clothing	
1970–74	—	—	20.3
1975–79	—	—	21.8
1979	2.0	1.0	23.8
1980	2.4	1.7	23.2
1981	2.8	2.1	24.1
1982	2.6	2.4	26.7
1983	2.8	2.6	28.4
1984	3.6	3.3	26.0
1985	3.5	3.6	33.1
1986	4.6	5.7	33.6

Source: International Economic Data Bank, Trade Data Tapes, Australian National University, Canberra, 1990.

suggests that trade restrictions against textile and clothing exports may be important for China, even though some other countries, notably Hong Kong, Korea and Taiwan, have had remarkable growth rates despite increasingly restrictive quotas on their exports of textiles and clothing (Trela and Whalley 1990). But growth in China may not be so heavily trade-led as in other smaller countries because of the larger size of the internal market of that populous country.

One can also complicate matters by arguing that trade restrictions on textiles and clothing exports can actually be helpful by forcing certain types of developing countries to progress through stages more quickly, and hence grow more rapidly (Cable 1981). When combined with the observation that there are several successful growth experiences which appear not to have relied on an initial surge of production (and trade) in textiles and clothing, the significance of both textiles and clothing (and trade restrictions against exports) for the growth prospects of China becomes even more difficult to pin down.

The Multi-fibre Arrangement and export growth prospects for China

Beyond the question of how crucial textile and clothing exports may be to China's future growth, a further issue is whether the set of trade restrictions which China faces under the MFA could frustrate an export-led growth phase were it likely to occur.

MFA restrictions facing developing country exports are the outcome of bilateral negotiations between individual industrial and developing countries which cover exports of both textiles and clothing.[7] Restrictions are renegotiated every few years[8] in the GATT Committee on Textiles despite the fact that they are clearly inconsistent with several GATT articles (including Article 1 (non-discrimination) and Article 24 (bilateral trade agreements)). Their GATT incompatibility has never been tested through the dispute settlement procedures of the GATT. They involve export quotas typically administered by developing country governments and trade associations.

There are currently nine developed country participants in the MFA: Austria, Canada, the European Community, Finland, Japan, Norway, Sweden, Switzerland and the United States, although Japan and

[7] Since its inception, the MFA has dealt almost exclusively with exports from developing countries. Over the period, however, restraints have also been applied to Japanese and some East European exports.

[8] MFA I lasted from January 1974 to December 1977; MFA II from January 1978 to December 1981; MFA III from January 1982 to July 1986; and MFA IV was adopted in August 1986 and will run until July 1991.

Switzerland do not currently apply MFA restrictions on imports.[9] Developing country participants in the MFA are more numerous, numbering 33 in late 1987.[10]

Like the trade restrictions which preceded it in the 1960s, the MFA was intended to provide temporary protection for producers in industrial countries. At its inception, the main objective of the MFA was stated as 'achieving the expansion of trade, the reduction of barriers to such trade, and the progressive liberalization of world trade in textile products' (GATT 1975: 3–19). The aim was to allow advanced industrial countries time to adjust to foreign competition from developing countries, while at the same time giving exporters orderly access to industrial country markets. This was considered by developing countries as preferable to having their exports subjected to a series of more restrictive and *ad hoc* controls.

After 27 years of 'temporary' protection outside of GATT rules, however, there is little evidence that trade in textiles and clothing is currently any closer to a return to GATT disciplines.[11] Instead of liberalizing textile and clothing trade, successive bilateral agreements reached under the MFA appear to have grown progressively more restrictive.[12] Annual growth rates for quotas have generally been below 6 per cent; fibre coverage has been extended to include silk blends

[9] Other developed countries, including Australia and New Zealand and, for a period of time, Norway, rely on GATT compatible global import quotas (Article 19 measures) to restrict their imports of textiles and clothing. Australia participated in the earlier Long Term Agreement (LTA) and in the MFA until December 1974, when the Australian government imposed global 'tariff quotas' outside the MFA. New Zealand has never participated in these special arrangements, although throughout the period since 1961 imports of textiles and clothing have been subject to import licensing arrangements, the majority of which involve global quotas (see Lloyd 1989). Norway participated in the LTA and MFA I, but did not participate in MFA II. In 1979 Norway introduced global quotas, but these were phased out within one year after Norway accepted the 1981 Protocol of Extension to the MFA in July 1984.

[10] As of 30 September 1987 these were Argentina, Bangladesh, Brazil, Bulgaria, China, Czechoslovakia, Egypt, the German Democratic Republic, Hong Kong, Hungary, India, Indonesia, Macao, Malaysia, Malta, Maldives, Mauritius, Mexico, Nepal, North Korea, Pakistan, Peru, Philippines, Poland, Romania, Singapore, Republic of Korea, Sri Lanka, Thailand, Turkey, Uruguay, Vietnam and Yugoslavia. Japan is also a member of the MFA as an exporting country.

[11] In the negotiating group on textiles and clothing in the Uruguay Round there are, however, signs of a commitment to return the textiles and clothing sector eventually to GATT disciplines. The Montreal Mid-Term Review in December 1988 and the decisions which followed in April 1989 produced a commitment to engage in substantive negotiations until the end of the Round to find ways of returning textiles and clothing to conformity with GATT (Hamilton 1990). Some of the more active developing countries in this group are seeking a clear timetable for an unambiguous phase-out program for the MFA.

[12] The progressive expansion of the MFA in terms of fibre and country coverage has been cited by one leading authority as potentially the most important negative development in world trade in recent years (Corden 1987).

and other vegetable fibres; country coverage has been extended to include small suppliers; and flexibility provisions have been reduced. 'Anti-surge' mechanisms have also been included to limit full use of previously under-utilized quotas and to further protect industrial country markets from rapid increases in imports.

The importance of trade restrictions under the MFA for developing countries is immediately apparent once the country pattern of textile and clothing trade is understood. In 1986 world exports of textiles and clothing were US$128 billion[13] ($66 billion in textiles and $62 billion in clothing), of which exports by industrial market economies accounted for $71 billion (55 per cent), exports by developing countries for $43 billion (34 per cent), and exports by the East European trading area $14 billion (11 per cent). Worldwide, exports of all manufactured goods totalled $1430 billion in 1986, out of a total of $2120 billion for all merchandise exports. In other words, trade in textiles and clothing alone accounts for about one-tenth of world merchandise trade. Inter-industrial country trade (which includes intra-EC trade) still accounts for about half world trade in textiles and a little more than 40 per cent of trade in clothing. Even so, textiles and clothing exports are of major importance to developing countries, representing one-quarter of their exports of manufactured goods.

Textile and clothing exports are heavily concentrated geographically. Clothing exports are far more concentrated than textiles, with Korea, Hong Kong and Taiwan accounting for over 60 per cent of exports to industrial countries.

As Table 5.3 indicates, China has a rapidly growing share of the exports of textiles and clothing going from developing to industrial countries. Table 5.4, based on Cline (1987), shows that, over the period 1982–84, Chinese annual export growth to the United States averaged 73 per cent for textiles and 25 per cent for clothing (in square yard equivalent terms). Table 5.4 also shows that US imports of textiles from principal suppliers increased in physical quantity terms by 113 per cent between 1982 and 1984, while their value rose by 90 per cent. US imports of clothing from these countries also surged, but by far less than for textiles.

These rapidly growing import volumes in the US have, in recent years, led some to question the extent to which the MFA actually restricts textile and clothing exports of individual developing countries. Data for China from the World Bank database on the MFA, and reproduced here in Table 5.5, emphasize how sharp this debate is.

According to Table 5.5, quota utilization rates for China averaged, over a series of product categories covering both textiles and clothing, below 100 per cent. However, there are four instances in these data where imports under the quota system, due to the flexibility provisions

---

[13] The source for the data used in the next few paragraphs is GATT (1987: Table A12).

Table 5.3: *Share of textile and clothing consumption in industrial countries supplied by imports from China and other developing economies, 1970 to 1986*

| | Imports as a percentage of domestic consumption in industrial countries from: | | | | | |
	China	NE Asian NIEs	South Asia	Latin America and Caribbean	Other developing economies	All developing economies
Textiles (ISIC 321)						
1970–73	0.4	1.1	0.7	0.1	1.0	3.3
1974–77	0.4	1.5	0.7	0.2	1.4	4.2
1978–81	0.7	1.7	0.8	0.3	2.3	5.3
1982–85	1.1	2.2	0.9	0.2	1.8	6.2
1986	1.2	2.6	0.9	0.2	1.9	6.8
Clothing (ISIC 322)						
1970–73	0.1	3.4	0.1	0.0	0.8	4.4
1974–77	0.3	6.4	0.4	0.2	1.7	9.0
1978–81	0.7	8.7	0.8	0.2	2.8	13.2
1982–85	1.6	10.7	1.1	0.2	3.8	17.4
1986	2.3	10.9	1.4	0.2	5.1	19.9

Source: See Appendix to this volume.

in the MFA, exceeded the quotas granted. Furthermore, the rate of utilization differs across importing regions. For example, in 1987 China's utilization rate of Sweden's quota was 111 per cent, while for quota granted by Canada it was only 93 per cent. Utilization rates are also volatile over time and differ between products, reflecting the use by exporters of the flexibility provisions under the MFA to respond to changing market conditions and shifts in fashion.[14]

Unfortunately, these data provide far from conclusive evidence as to the degree of restrictiveness of MFA quotas against China, since there are many reasons why binding quotas can seem to be non-binding. One reason may be the way the quota is allocated among importers. Quotas in the EC, for instance, are in some cases allocated between importing countries on the basis of historical market shares, regardless of the distribution of demands within the EC. Hence, demand for, say, winter coats may be unmet in some EC countries with quotas binding, but quotas remain unused in other countries and are not allowed to be reallocated. Also, it can be the case that there are aggregate quotas for, say, shirts which are less than the sum of

[14] These flexibility provisions include a 'swing' provision which allows an exporting country to shift some portion of an under-utilized quota to a product category where the quota is binding, and allowance for a country to 'carry over' unfilled quota balances from the previous year's or to 'carry forward' from the following year's quota.

Table 5.4: *United States imports of textiles and clothing from China and other major suppliers, 1982 to 1984*[a]

	1982				Percentage increase over the period 1982–84			
	Textiles		Clothing		Textiles		Clothing	
	Value	Quantity	Value	Quantity	Value	Quantity	Value	Quantity
China	201	314	590	357	80	73	27	25
Hong Kong	107	153	1746	690	66	53	27	18
Taiwan	102	190	1408	748	387	240	38	25
Korea	154	188	1088	576	138	155	38	19
Japan	460	435	231	76	27	39	88	80
Sum of those 5 countries	1024	1280	5064	2447	94	96	35	23
India	767	60	149	73	64	105	78	80
Philippines	7	10	234	161	21	−24	57	46
Singapore	11	22	171	82	−50	−44	73	55
Thailand	33	64	93	53	49	65	129	101
Mexico	20	53	131	56	206	259	56	54
Sum of those 5 countries	148	209	778	425	69	110	73	61
Italy	171	195	138	14	82	132	209	302
United Kingdom	85	37	64	6	54	233	116	176
France	72	46	66	6	59	88	95	145
Germany	62	122	18	2	113	132	149	183
Canada	51	131	43	8	91	120	51	43
Sum of those 5 countries	441	531	329	37	78	132	144	191
Sum of all 15 countries	1613	2020	6171	2908	87	107	46	31
Other suppliers	429	533	940	474	100	138	96	92
World total	2042	2553	7111	3382	90	113	53	39

[a] MFA categories only. Values are in millions of current US dollars, quantity in square yard equivalents.
Source: Cline (1987: Table 7.2).

Table 5.5: *Average quota utilization rates for textiles and clothing exports by China to four importing countries, 1981 to 1987* (percentage utilization of annual quota quantity)

Importing country	1981	1982	1983	1984	1985	1986	1987
United States	95	71	99	96	87	99	94
EC	94	95	98	95	95	103	108
Canada	62	65	89	94	85	97	93
Sweden	65[a]	106[a]	89[a]	79[a]	83	95	111

[a] Quota imposed on value of shipments, not quantity.
Source: Calculated from World Bank Data Base on the MFA.

the sub-aggregate quotas for, say, particular types of shirts. Quotas may thus not appear to be binding at sub-aggregate levels, while they may be binding at the aggregate level.[15] Also, some quotas are issued on a monthly basis at an even rate throughout the year. Quotas in summer months for winter coats, for instance, can go unfilled, giving the appearance of unutilized quotas in annual data.

Much of the increase in imports into the United States in 1980–84, as Cline (1987) suggests, can be attributed to the flexible provisions for quota use within the structure of the MFA. These allowed exporters to take advantage of the overvalued dollar and the strong US recovery from recession in 1982. Hence, restrictive effects of the MFA can be partially offset through adjustments to basic quotas through MFA flexibility provisions.

Another way the restrictive effect of MFA trade restraints can be weakened is through product upgrading. Because the MFA involves physical quantity rather than value restrictions on trade (that is, by weight, number of pieces, or surface area), it encourages quality upgrading through changes in product mix. The principal reason for upgrading is that, when faced with a volume restriction on their exports, producers can expand their value of sales by moving up-market into higher-quality lines within quota categories. This has especially been true of Hong Kong, which has succeeded in establishing a reputation for quality fabrics and fashion sophistication.

Cline (1987: 83) provides evidence of product upgrading of quota-controlled products in the Chinese case, with an 18 per cent rise in real unit value of exports between 1982 and 1984. Diversification of trade to industrial country markets with no formal MFA restrictions (typically global import quotas), to minor suppliers and to product categories either uncontrolled or subject to loose 'consultation' controls, is another effect of the MFA. The latter dominated the increase

[15] Chaudhry and Hamid (1988), for example, found that in 1983 'the overall U.S. quota for Pakistan was less than the aggregate of category-wide quotas by 13 per cent. Thus, though a category-wide quota may be available, increased export sales may become impossible because of aggregate quota limitations'.

of clothing imports by the United States from China, when they rose by 94 per cent from 1982 to 1984 (ibid.).

Geographical diversification in the form of 'quota hopping' is yet another response to restraints. For example, the dramatic increase in foreign investment activities of Hong Kong clothing industries in lower-wage, less quota-restricted countries can be viewed as partly a response to Hong Kong quota limitations. Hong Kong investments occurred in Macao in the mid-1970s, Sri Lanka and Indonesia in the late 1970s, and more recently in the Maldives and, on a much larger scale, in China (see Young and Hood 1985). However, MFA IV has tightened restrictions against 'false declaration' of country of origin.

All of these features have, therefore, combined to allow for a sharp growth in imports of textiles and clothing by the United States in the mid-1980s. However, as a study by the Congressional Budget Office (1985) notes, further sharp growth in imports cannot continue because rising quota utilization rates eventually run their course as MFA quotas become exhausted, and swing provisions and inter-year quota adjustments provide only temporary flexibility. Evidence in Cline (1987) supports this point of view, showing that the growth in the physical volume of US textile imports fell dramatically from 54 per cent in 1984 to only 5 per cent in 1985, while the physical volume of clothing imports fell from 21 per cent to 9 per cent. Although the pace of import growth accelerated again in 1986 (21 per cent for textiles and 13 per cent for clothing), Cline (1987: 180) suggests 'the likelihood is that this rise was in response to the extreme overvaluation of the dollar in 1984–85, and perhaps pre-emptive purchasing ahead of feared tightening in view of both MFA renewal and the threatened veto override on the Textile and Clothing Trade Enforcement Bill'. There was also a sharp rise in import growth in the EC in 1985, but this was the result of a significant expansion in consumer demand following a delayed recovery from the recession.

The issue, therefore, is whether future restrictions on textile and clothing exports will continue only to slow the growth of Chinese and other developing country exports to major industrial country markets, or whether growth may be more sharply curtailed. While the conclusion from recent literature seems to be that protection under the MFA has thus far only slowed and obstructed rather than terminated the growth of textile and clothing exports by the smaller Asian NIEs, this result largely reflects the flexibility provisions within the MFA structure. Increasingly these are being exhausted, and when this happens, textile restrictions are likely to bite more fully. The implication for China would seem to be that relying on continued expansion of market access for textiles and clothing exports may be a tenuous basis on which to build a growth strategy. Only with fundamental reform, including the dismantling of the MFA, can such a strategy be effectively pursued with confidence.

One may be tempted to ask how China would fare under the elimination of the MFA. In recent work, Trela and Whalley (1988a), using data from Hamilton (1986), have estimated the welfare effects of eliminating both quota and tariff restrictions used by industrial countries towards imports of textiles and clothing. They use a global general equilibrium model which covers three major importers (Canada, the EC and the United States), thirty-four developing country exporters including China,[16] fourteen textile and clothing product categories, and one composite other good (residual GDP). The fourteen product categories reflect the constraints implied by generating a cross-country data set covering trade under the different MFA quota categories used by the major importing countries.

The model is used in counterfactual equilibrium mode involving calibration to an initial benchmark equilibrium analysis (see Shoven and Whalley 1984). Results using 1986 data clearly show that the vast majority of developing countries gain from the removal of trade restrictions on textiles and clothing, with China gaining around $1.6 billion per year and exports by China increasing by 327 per cent (Table 5.6).[17] This suggests that gains to China and other developing countries from improved access more than offset losses from forgone rent transfers as quotas and tariffs are abolished. This is even the case for relatively large holders of quotas such as Korea and Taiwan, which, it has always been argued, have a protected market niche against lower-cost competition under the MFA.

In the presence of quotas (and tariffs) they, along with China and other developing countries, are non-marginal suppliers to industrial country markets. Thus, rather than losing share to other developing countries under an MFA elimination, higher-income developing countries (including China and other lower-cost developing countries) gain market share due to growth in industrial country markets and to reduced inter-industrial country trade.

---

[16] These are Bangladesh, Brazil, Bulgaria, China, Colombia, Czechoslovakia, Costa Rica, Dominican Republic, Egypt, Guatemala, Haiti, Hong Kong, Hungary, India, Indonesia, Republic of Korea, Macao, Malaysia, Mexico, Nepal, Pakistan, Panama, Peru, Philippines, Poland, Romania, Singapore, Sri Lanka, Taiwan, Thailand, Turkey, Uruguay and Yugoslavia.

[17] The model results, however, have to be taken with some qualification, since there are a number of unstudied and unquantified factors which potentially complicate the picture, including the degree to which quotas are binding, effects on inter-developing country investment flows, and quality upgrading. Of particular importance is the non-inclusion of an activity called 'international textile and clothing marketing services', in which Hong Kong and to a lesser extent Macao have a very strong comparative advantage. Had such an activity been included in the model, these two economies undoubtedly would be gainers from MFA liberalization as the demands of these services from China increase, rather than losers as suggested by Table 5.6.

Table 5.6:   *Estimated general equilibrium welfare effects of removing bilateral MFA quotas and tariffs on textiles and clothing in all industrial countries, 1986*[a]
(1986 US $ millions)

Country	Welfare gain or loss	Country	Welfare gain or loss
Importing countries		*Exporting countries* (cont'd)	
United States	3478		
Canada	311	Indonesia	321
EC	3487	Korea	1562
		Macao	−5
Exporting countries		Malaysia	191
China	1640	Mauritius	30
		Mexico	101
Bangladesh	290	Nepal	18
Brazil	921	Pakistan	4
Bulgaria	2	Panama	1
Colombia	309	Peru	45
Czechoslovakia	81	Philippines	173
Costa Rica	7	Poland	131
Dominican Republic	5	Romania	104
Egypt	46	Singapore	16
Guatemala	5	Sri Lanka	53
Haiti	6	Taiwan	884
Hong Kong	−88	Thailand	17
Hungary	105	Turkey	629
India	74	Uruguay	3
		Yugoslavia	56
		All developing countries	7755
		All countries	15032

[a] See Trela and Whalley (1988a) for a more complete discussion of the model, the parameter values used and the sensitivity of results to changes in those parameter values. Welfare effects are calculated in terms of Hicksian equivalent variations for each country.
Source: Trela and Whalley (1988a).

GATT negotiations, MFA elimination and Chinese accession to the GATT

At the present time, global negotiations are under way in the GATT aimed at achieving major trade liberalization in the Uruguay Round. It is anticipated that these will conclude at the end of 1990. Among the fifteen negotiating groups is one on textiles and clothing which is explicitly taking up the question of trade restraints in this product area, including MFA restrictions. The issue for Chinese policymakers is in assessing what may result from these negotiations as far as textiles and clothing exports are concerned. Indeed, the Chinese position at the present time is made even more complicated by the fact that China is not a contracting party to the GATT, and has also been engaged in negotiations on a protocol of accession to the GATT.[18]

The negotiating group on textiles and clothing in the Round achieved little in its early phases, but following the decisions of the Mid-Term Review held in Montreal in December 1988, with negotiations left over in four groups (including textiles and clothing) until April 1989, a significant commitment has been made by industrial countries. They have said that between April 1989 and the conclusion of the Round they will negotiate with developing countries for a return of trade arrangements in textiles and clothing to regular GATT disciplines. These new arrangements are to come into place in July 1991 when the current MFA expires.

Clearly, then, these negotiations and their possible outcome are of substantial importance to China's growth prospects. If the MFA can indeed be eliminated, and if China can obtain significant improvement in her access to the large textile and clothing markets of the EC, United States, Canada and Japan, then export growth prospects, and hence GDP growth prospects, will increase markedly for China. The difficulty is that it is as yet unclear what the industrial countries have in mind when they talk of a return of trade restrictions affecting textiles and clothing to regular GATT disciplines.

The MFA is a voluntary arrangement, driven in large part by the threat of alternative trade actions being taken by industrial countries, and particularly global import quotas allowed under Article 19 of the GATT. What makes the MFA attractive to industrial countries is its use of country selective trade controls, which would be ruled out by a reversion to Article 19. Developing countries generally feel they have a more beneficial arrangement under the MFA than they would have under Article 19 actions which could be changed at any time. Uncertainties over the policy regime in this area, therefore, create problems in assessing China's growth prospects.

Moreover, China's influence over the outcome from this trade negotiating group is further constrained by the fact that China only has observer status in GATT. In addition to the issues surrounding the MFA and its impact on Chinese export prospects, there are, therefore, a series of further issues raised by China's participation in the GATT. China was one of the original signatories of the GATT

---

[18] Following the events of mid-1989 in China, these negotiations have been suspended by the contracting parties until the situation within China is clarified. See *Financial Times*, 6 July 1989, p. 6.

but left in 1949. In recent years there has been substantial interest in China resuming its status as a GATT Contracting Party. China joined the MFA in 1974 and in 1986 formally applied for restoration of GATT membership. A GATT working party has, until recently, been examining the question of China's membership, and China has been granted observer status during the GATT Uruguay Round. Substantial confusion has existed in this working party, however, over exactly how China's foreign trade system currently operates.[19]

China's objective of obtaining the status of a contracting party is a reflection of her wider concerns over her market access. There is a widespread belief in China that, in order to grow, China will eventually have to increase her trade volumes substantially. How significant this increase is likely to be depends on the growth strategy China follows, and in particular on how inward- or outward-oriented it is. But a scenario under which there would be a quadrupling of real income per capita in China between 1980 and the year 2000, one of the objectives stated by the State Council in China in the mid-1980s, would presumably produce at least a quadrupling in trade.

The empirical evidence for most economies suggests that trade growth typically exceeds GDP growth. Averaging over all industrial countries in the postwar period, trade growth has been about 4 per cent real per capita per year whereas GDP growth has been about 1.5 per cent in real terms (Kravis, Heston and Summers 1982).

This calculation therefore suggests that access to markets abroad is central to Chinese growth. And because China is becoming such a large economy, this access cannot be easily secured without importing countries undertaking significant amounts of adjustment. Growth through trade for a relatively small country such as Korea, with a population of approximately 40 million, is a different proposition to growth through trade for a country the size of China.

China, therefore, sees major advantages in becoming a GATT Contracting Party and receiving some of the benefits of the GATT system which accrue to contracting parties. For instance, under GATT rules MFN arrangements apply automatically. China cannot be discriminated against under any country's tariff if it is a GATT Contracting Party, whereas such discrimination is possible while China remains outside the GATT.

Perhaps more substantively, there is the question of Article 19 safeguard measures under the GATT. Current GATT rules require that any safeguard measure taken because of a problem with import surges be taken in a non-discriminatory manner. Selective safeguards are not allowable.

[19] See Author unknown (1988) which contains the responses of the Chinese government to over 800 questions posed by the working party as to how China's trade system functions. See also Lam (1989).

This is the heart of the GATT issue for China, as China's desire is to avoid selective trade actions being taken against her because of industrial country import surges which would follow from further substantial Chinese growth. Indeed, industrial countries in the GATT working party seemingly took the position that selective safeguards should be a condition for China receiving GATT membership. That is, China would be subject to selective trade actions until this particular provision was removed. This set of arrangements would in some ways have been similar to those which applied against Japan when Japan was admitted to the GATT in 1956.

China, therefore, faces something of a dilemma in her policymaking in this area. In order to comply with many of the concerns of industrial countries and to obtain GATT Contracting Party status, it may eventually be necessary for China to take on international disciplines over domestic policies in order to remove the perceived threat of policy-manipulated import surges. But this may limit China's ability to use domestic policies to stimulate capital accumulation and achieve higher growth.

On the other hand, from an industrial country point of view the benefit from China joining the GATT would be to provide a set of international disciplines over domestic Chinese policies which would otherwise restrict their access to the Chinese market. How these various considerations play out in the future, therefore, is central both to Chinese export growth prospects and to Chinese development more broadly.

Summary and conclusions

This chapter has discussed growth prospects for China in light of both her growing exports of textiles and trade restrictions under the MFA. It has suggested that, by the mid-1980s, the share of China's exports represented by textiles and clothing was not much greater than in the 1960s, and the sharp growth in their importance in exports, as occurred in Korea, Taiwan and Hong Kong, has only just begun to emerge. It has emphasized that the previous experience of earlier rapid-growing developing countries in Asia, for whom exports of textiles and clothing were crucial, occurred while MFA trade restrictions were in effect. At the same time, however, a textiles export phase comparable to that experienced in Japan and subsequently in Korea and Taiwan need not be inevitable in the Chinese case, in large part because of the size of the Chinese economy.

The chapter discussed how MFA restrictions work, and what some of their effects are. If growth of textiles and clothing exports is indeed central to Chinese development prospects, future Chinese growth may pose major adjustment problems for some producers in industrial market economies. MFA restrictions are intended to slow these adjustments by restricting market access for developing country exporters. A textile and clothing export-led growth phase for China will only worsen these problems, making the eventual phase-out of the MFA as part of the Uruguay Round negotiations that much more difficult.

Despite the difficulties that China has encountered with its negotiations on a protocol of accession for its entry into the GATT (even though these negotiations were suspended, following the events of mid-1989 in China), the fact remains that the system of international rules and disciplines represented by the GATT framework will be increasingly important to China in the years ahead. How to influence this system, and indeed how eventually to gain accession to the GATT, is an important issue for China.

In population terms, China is the world's largest economy. Industrial countries have always been fearful of the adjustment problems a rapidly growing Chinese economy might inflict on them. Whether recent political events in China will end the strong growth China has experienced since 1978, or whether growth will only slow temporarily, remains to be seen. But, whatever the outcome, the issues connecting trade, growth, and textiles and clothing will remain central to Chinese policy debates for some time to come.

6

International competition and Japan's domestic adjustments

Hideki Yamawaki*

The evolution of the Japanese textile industry in the past two decades is best characterized by its transition from maturity to decline. The industry's share of manufacturing employment fell from 13.4 per cent in 1965 to 6.1 per cent in 1983, and its share of manufacturing output declined from 8.8 per cent to 3.4 per cent. Over this period, imports of textiles rose from 26 billion yen in 1965 to more than 500 billion yen in 1985 (excluding clothing and synthetic fibres).

This relative decline of the textile industry is not peculiar to Japan. As shown in Chapter 2, the textile industry typically traces out a hill-shaped development pattern as a country industrializes, and Japan is no exception to that rule. The importance of textiles in the Japanese economy grew steadily from the 1890s to the 1930s, but it started declining after the 1950s (as shown in Table 2.1 in Chapter 2). The share of production exported in the Japanese textile and clothing industries peaked in the 1930s and has been declining thereafter, whereas the share of domestic sales supplied by imports started increasing from the late 1960s after the period of almost zero import dependence in the 1950s and the early 1960s (Table 2.2).

What *is* peculiar to Japan is the slowness of the relative decline of its textile industry as compared with other industrialized countries. Despite the record that portrays it as a declining industry, the Japanese textile industry remains a large gross exporter with exports of more than 1 trillion yen in 1985. In some product groups the share of production exported still exceeds 10 per cent. As well, the share of domestic sales supplied by imports in the Japanese textile and clothing market has been rather moderate compared with other industrial countries and was on average less than 10 per cent in 1985 (see also Table 2.9 above). Thus, in spite of the long-run tendency to decline,

* I am grateful to Kym Anderson, Richard Caves, Peter Drysdale, Yoko Sazanami and Ben Smith for helpful comments and suggestions. Any remaining errors are, of course, my own. An earlier version of this paper appeared as Yamawaki (1989).

the Japanese textile industry's international competitiveness appears
to have lingered more than might have been expected.

What accounts for the lingering comparative advantage of the textile
industry in Japan and the apparently moderate penetration of the
Japanese market by foreign textile producers? To what extent is the
slow import penetration linked to adjustments in Japan of its industrial
organization? Can it be explained by rationalization of production
capacities, adoption of new technologies, or specialization in some
specific products? Or is it simply due to rising tariff and non-tariff
import barriers? This chapter reviews forces underlying the lingering
comparative advantage and the relatively slow penetration of imports
into Japan's textile and clothing markets, and seeks to explain their
consequences.

The first section presents empirical data on the development of
Japan's imports and exports through the 1970s and the early 1980s.
The next describes the domestic adjustment process in the industry,
with particular attention to the forces underlying the increase in its
labour productivity. This section also analyses the scope for specialization and the role of government policies. The third section focuses
on another restructuring process, namely direct investment abroad,
and analyses the development of intra-industry and intra-firm trade.
The consequences of these restructuring efforts are assessed in the
fourth section using statistical models. The final section offers some
concluding remarks.

International competitiveness of Japan's textiles and clothing producers
Import competition

Imports of textiles and clothing into the Japanese market started to
increase during the 1960s and surged in the 1970s as other East Asian
countries improved their international competitiveness in these products. The significance of the flow of imports as a competitive force in
the domestic market is apparent from its market share. As Table 6.1
shows, import penetration by newly industrializing Asian economies
(NIEs) in particular was relatively high during the early 1970s in the
Japanese market as compared with other industrial country markets.
However, its growth through the late 1970s and the early 1980s was
much slower for Japan than for other industrial countries. The NIEs'
import penetration ratio for textiles into Japan was 3.2 per cent in
1970–73 but rose to only 4.4 per cent by 1982–86.

Of course the success of Japan's textile industry in defending its
domestic market against a surge of imports from newly industrializing

Table 6.1: *Import penetration by newly industrializing Asia into advanced industrial country markets for textiles and clothing, 1970 to 1986[a]*
(per cent)

Country	Textiles (ISIC 321)		Clothing (ISIC 322)	
	1970–73	1982–86	1970–73	1982–86
Japan	3.2	4.4	4.0	9.4
Australia	5.2	12.6	3.9	11.7
Canada	1.9	5.4	4.2	13.6
EC				
Belgium	1.0	4.1	1.8	3.4
France	0.5	1.8	0.4	3.6
West Germany	0.7	3.2	4.7	17.7
Italy	1.2	2.8	0.4	6.9
Netherlands	2.3	7.4	5.3	17.5
United Kingdom	1.9	3.9	7.0	14.7
Total	1.1	3.1	3.7	11.8
EFTA				
Finland	0.5	2.4	1.4	11.4
Norway	1.3	2.7	4.7	10.0
Sweden	2.1	4.8	7.7	20.8
Total	1.5	3.5	5.4	15.4
United States	1.0	3.5	3.5	16.6
All advanced industrial countries	1.6	3.8	3.7	14.1

[a] Imports as a percentage of domestic sales from all Northeast and Southeast Asian market economies excluding Japan, that is, from China, Hong Kong, Korea, Taiwan and ASEAN.
Source: See Appendix to this volume.

Asian economies has varied by product. Import penetration for silk yarns and for linen yarns and fabrics increased sharply during the late 1960s and the 1970s, and that for cotton yarns has risen rapidly since 1985. On the other hand, import penetration for man-made fibres and fabrics has grown only moderately.

For clothing the degree of increase in NIE import penetration has been faster, but during the 15 years to the mid-1980s it was still less than for other industrial countries (from 4.0 to 9.4 per cent for Japan compared with an increase from 3.7 to 14.1 per cent for all advanced industrial countries – see Table 6.1). In the mid-1980s, however, this import penetration ratio for clothing grew very rapidly: from 9 per cent in 1983 to 13 per cent in 1985 and to 22 per cent in 1987. As a result, the share of clothing in total imports of textiles and clothing has jumped. In fact it doubled between 1975 and 1987, from 22 per cent to 45 per cent.[1]

Export opportunities

An industry's international competitiveness can be judged not only by the extent of import competition but also by the extent to which its production is exported. Has the Japanese textile industry been reducing the share of its production that is exported? Not according to the data in Table 6.2 for the period 1970 to 1986 when it has remained close to 15 per cent. On the other hand, the share of Japan's clothing production that is exported declined sharply in the mid-1970s, but then it remained stable at around the 4 to 5 per cent level. During the same period, however, Japan's manufacturing sector as a whole became steadily more export oriented, both in gross terms and net of imports (see final two columns of Table 6.2). In relative terms, then, the textile and clothing industries have been slipping in competitiveness according to these indicators, even though Japan remains more competitive than the average advanced industrial economy (compare the upper and lower halves of Table 6.2).

The composition of Japan's textile and clothing exports has been changing substantially too. There have been declines in the relative importance of cotton, woollen and man-made rayon fabrics, and of apparel, while the importance of man-made rayon and synthetic fibres, and of synthetic yarns and fabrics, has increased. For example, the shares of total exports of textiles and clothing contributed by man-made rayon and synthetic products increased from 38 per cent in 1965 to 66 per cent in 1980, whereas yarns and fabrics made of natural fibres reduced their share from 41 per cent to 23 per cent during the same period.[2] In short, the Japanese textile industry through the late 1960s and 1970s concentrated its export growth on synthetic products and contracted its exports of products made of natural fibres, particularly cotton. This, together with parallel changes in the mix of imports of textiles and clothing, is consistent with the common belief that Japanese industry has moved upstream into the highly capital-intensive production of synthetic fibres, where its comparative advantage is strongest, and has been losing competitiveness in labour-intensive clothing production to the point where Japan is now a net importer of clothes.

[1] The estimate was made from the Ministry of International Trade and Industry's *sen'i tokeo nempo* [Annual Statistical Report on the Textile Industry].

[2] Based on the statistics obtained from Administrative Management Agency, *1965–1970–1975 Link Input–Output Tables* and *1970–1975–1980 Link Input–Output Tables*.

Table 6.2: *Trade orientation^a of textile and clothing industries, Japan and all advanced industrial countries, 1970 to 1986 (per cent)*

	Textiles (ISIC 321)			Clothing (ISIC 322)			All manufacturing (ISIC 3)		
	Import share		Export share	Import share		Export share	Import share		Export share
	gross	net		gross	net		gross	net	
Japan									
1970–73	7.1	–8.6	14.5	5.4	–5.4	10.3	4.5	–6.3	10.2
1974–77	7.7	–8.9	15.3	9.0	4.3	4.9	5.1	–9.5	13.3
1978–81	8.9	–6.4	14.3	11.4	7.8	3.9	5.3	–9.5	13.5
1982–86	9.1	–6.8	14.9	12.0	7.6	4.7	5.2	–11.2	14.7
All advanced industrial countries									
1970–73	14.5	–0.3	14.7	13.5	4.0	9.9	12.4	–2.3	14.4
1974–77	17.5	–0.2	17.7	20.9	8.7	13.3	15.1	–3.8	18.2
1978–81	20.6	0.8	20.0	27.6	12.8	17.0	17.0	–3.6	19.8
1982–86	21.2	2.3	19.3	31.9	17.5	17.4	17.7	–1.9	19.2

^a Japan's imports from the rest of the world (gross or net of exports) as a percentage of its domestic sales, and Japan's exports to the rest of the world as a percentage of its production, and similarly for all advanced industrial countries.
Source: See Appendix to this volume.

Domestic adjustments in the Japanese industries

Associated with the changing international competitiveness of Japanese industry were several important adjustment processes. The most important ones affecting textiles and clothing were the shedding of excess labour and capital equipment, the demise of small plants and adoption of modern, labour-saving equipment, investment in research and development, the already mentioned switch in production emphasis from labour-intensive to capital-intensive products, and changes in protection from imports. Each of these is discussed in turn.

The shedding of excess labour and capital equipment

A striking feature of Japan's textile and clothing industries is the extent to which they have shed labour. As a whole these industries employed almost 400,000 fewer workers in 1983 than in 1965. This occurred despite a substantial increase in employment in clothing production. For the other two parts (textiles and man-made fibres), the number employed fell by 600,000 or 43 per cent over this 18-year period (Table 6.3).

The large reduction in employment in the textiles and man-made fibres sectors was partly supported by laws on Temporary Measures For Those Unemployed in Specified Depressed Industries and in Specified Regions, which were implemented between 1978 and 1983.[3] Under these laws, the government implemented policy measures that provided subsidies to laid-off workers in the form of payments of extended employment insurance, subsidies to firms in the form of layoff allowances and training costs, and wage subsidies for transferred workers. The laws also promoted employment of laid-off workers in public enterprises, and employment retraining and guidance. Under these laws continuous nylon fibres, discontinuous acrylic fibres, continuous and discontinuous polyester fibres, cotton spinning, and worsted yarn spinning were designated as depressed industries.

As well as shedding labour, these industries have been reducing their excess production capacity. Since 1956 the government has implemented several controversial policy measures designed to rationalize and modernize production equipment.[4] A purchase-and-scrap

---

[3] For detailed accounts on these laws and associated policy measures, see Sekiguchi and Horiuchi (1988) and MITI (1989).

[4] For detailed discussions on these measures, see Yamazawa (1988), Sekiguchi and Horiuchi (1988), and MITI (1989).

Table 6.3: Total size of Japan's textile and clothing industries, 1965 and 1983

Industry	Number of employees ('000)		Number of establishments		Fixed assets (billion yen, 1965 prices)[a]	
	1965	1983	1965	1983	1965	1983
Textile mill products	1327	768	100157	99393	604	693
Spinning mills	277	93	2025	945	220	140
Cotton	113	36	1437	230	83	65
Man-made fibre	62	32	149	288	63	45
Wool	86	23	391	325	59	28
Silk	5	1	23	19	1	1
Linen	12	1	25	13	14	1
Twisted yarns	69	42	9295	9842	26	22
Woven fabric mills	471	209	54651	45422	132	146
Cotton and man-made staple	185	77	13874	11424	58	64
Silk and man-made filament	195	105	27004	27142	49	69
Wool	87	23	13513	6258	23	9
Linen	3	1	156	217	1	1
Knitting mills	174	190	12434	17873	64	115
Ropes and nets	25	16	990	1316	10	16
Lace and other products	36	21	3989	3798	13	15
Clothing	265	487	20629	40400	43	162
Man-made fibres	82	36	51	92	232	207
Rayon	31	6	17	13	53	26
Acetate	3	1	3	3	13	6
Synthetic	49	28	31	76	166	175
Total	1674	1291	120837	139885	879	1062

[a] Beginning-of-year fixed assets plus new acquisition of land, buildings and equipment minus elimination of these assets and depreciation.
Source: MITI, *Census of Manufacturers: Report by Industries,* Tokyo, various issues.

program for eliminating excess capacity was introduced in 1956 under the Law on Temporary Measures for Textile Industry Equipment (Old Textile Law, 1956–63). As well, a scrap-and-build program for installing one new machine for every two machines scrapped was introduced under the Law on Temporary Measures for Textile Industry Equipment and Related Equipment (New Textile Law, 1964–66). These programs have continued in the ensuing years along with additional laws which have provided government finances in the form of subsidies and low-interest loans to purchase and scrap excess capacity.[5] Over the period 1956 to 1981, 200,000 looms for cotton and staple fibres, 120,000 looms for silk and rayon, 22,000 looms for wool, and 5 million spindles were scrapped with the help of 360 billion yen in government subsidies and loans (Yamazawa 1988: Table II). These measures contributed to the 13 per cent increase in capacity utilization in these industries between 1965 and 1973. However, this gain was eroded subsequently and, according to MITI's index, capacity utilization by 1985 had fallen to 13 per cent *below* the 1965 level.

The scrapping of excess capacity was concentrated on equipment in the yarn and fabric stages, where the industry's international competitiveness was declining. However, production capacity for synthetic fibres quadrupled between 1965 and 1986, from 1150 to 5000 tons per day. The number of establishments in synthetic fibre production also increased, from 31 in 1965 to 76 in 1983.

Investment in new equipment and disappearance of small firms

In addition to shedding labour and scrapping excess capacity, rationalization of production can be achieved by installing new capital equipment and enlarging the size of those manufacturing establishments that are inefficiently small. The industry's efforts to adopt cost-reducing technologies have focused on introducing equipment that embodies automation and computerized techniques, thereby speeding up production processes.

The extent of investment in new capital equipment is shown in the final two columns of Table 6.3. Evaluated at 1965 prices, the annual growth rate of capital stock over this period varies from 8 per cent for clothing to –13 per cent for linen yarn. The overall increase in the

---

[5] These laws are the Law on Temporary Measures for the Structural Improvement of Specified Textile Industry (1967–73), the Law on Temporary Measures for the Structural Improvement of Textile Industry (1974–present), and the Law on Temporary Measures for the Adjustment of Industry Structure (1987–present). See MITI (1989).

capital stock during this 18-year period was 17 per cent, or less than 1 per cent per year.

A characteristic of the market structure of Japan's textile industry is the existence of a large number of inefficiently small manufacturing establishments, particularly in spinning, weaving and knitting mills.[6] Industrial policies implemented after 1967 emphasized the need to raise efficiency through enlarging the size of establishments. The policy measures under the Law on Temporary Measures for the Structural Improvement of Specified Textile Industry (1967–73 and 1974–present) provided manufacturing firms in spinning, weaving and knitting mills with government finances, in the form of low-interest loans, to rationalize production. As Table 6.3 shows, over the 1965–83 period the number of establishments changed greatly in many industries. In particular, it declined by more than 50 per cent in woollen weaving mills. On the other hand, the number of establishments increased in industries such as man-made fibre spinning mills, silk and man-made filament weaving mills, knitting mills, and synthetic fibres during the same period.

Associated with these changing numbers of firms were substantial changes in the average size and capital intensity of firms. Overall, the average size of textile and clothing firms doubled between 1965 and 1983, measured in terms of value added at constant (1965) prices, and cotton spinning mills increased their average size by a factor of six. However, the size of firms producing man-made fibres changed little (Table 6.4).

A traditional measure of the capital intensity of firms in these industries also nearly doubled over those two decades on average, though by different means for different industries. The increase in the (constant price) value of fixed assets per employee in clothing occurred despite a large increase in employees, whereas for textiles and man-made fibres labour-shedding accounts for virtually all of the increase in capital intensity (cf. Tables 6.3 and 6.4).

An alternative measure of capital intensity is value-added per employee (Lary 1968), a measure often used to indicate the productivity of labour. This indicator trebled in real terms for the sector between 1965 and 1983, increasing almost as rapidly for clothing as for textiles and man-made fibres (final columns of Table 6.4). The growth in this measure of labour productivity was among the highest in industries such as lace and textile products, silk yarns, man-made fibre yarns, acetate fibres and woollen fabrics, whereas it was among the lowest in silk and man-made filament fabrics, rayon fibres, apparel, woollen yarns and cotton yarns.

---

6 For example, the average size of Japanese spinning mill establishments was 60 per cent of the size of US spinning mills in 1983, measured as value added per establishment.

Table 6.4: *Average plant size, capital intensity, and labour productivity of Japan's textile and clothing industries, 1965 and 1983*

Industry	Average plant size (value-added per establishment, million yen, 1965 prices)		Capital intensity (fixed assets per employee, million yen, 1965 prices)		Labour productivity (value-added per employee, million yen, 1965 prices)	
	1965	1983	1965	1983	1965	1983
Textile mill products	9	16	0.46	0.90	0.58	2.08
Spinning mills	84	219	0.80	1.50	0.61	2.22
Cotton	46	296	0.74	1.81	0.58	1.90
Man-made fibre	234	338	1.01	1.40	0.56	3.05
Wool	154	155	0.69	1.24	0.70	2.24
Silk	91	175	0.29	1.02	0.46	2.51
Linen	268	190	1.19	0.86	0.58	1.91
Twisted yarns	3	8	0.38	0.52	0.45	1.83
Woven fabric mills	4	7	0.28	0.70	0.52	1.54
Cotton and man-made staple	6	14	0.31	0.83	0.48	2.07
Silk and man-made filament	4	4	0.25	1.49	0.49	1.06
Wool	4	11	0.26	0.41	0.65	3.02
Linen	12	12	0.36	0.66	0.52	1.85
Knitting mills	8	22	0.37	0.60	0.58	2.08
Ropes and nets	16	29	0.40	1.02	0.63	2.49
Lace and other products	5	18	0.36	0.70	0.50	3.32
Clothing	6	15	0.16	0.33	0.48	1.27
Man-made fibres	3322	3101	2.83	5.75	2.06	7.91
Rayon	2177	1392	1.73	4.17	1.20	2.88
Acetate	1777	4890	5.04	4.33	2.00	10.74
Synthetic	4100	4021	3.41	6.16	2.61	10.76
Total	9	18	0.53	0.82	0.64	1.93

Source: MITI, *Census of Manufacturers: Report by Industries*, Tokyo, various issues.

New technology and its diffusion

While production on a larger and more efficient scale and with more capital equipment per worker increases productivity, the growth of productivity in the textile sector also results from formal research efforts. Table 6.5 presents two measures of research and development (R&D) activity: R&D expenditure divided by sales and the number of engineers and scientists divided by total employment. These are shown for the textile sector and for total manufacturing between 1965 and 1986. The level of both measures is lower in the textile sector than in total manufacturing throughout this period. The expenditure measure has grown less rapidly but the proportion of scientists and engineers in total employment has grown more rapidly for textiles

Table 6.5: *Research and development activity in Japan's textile and other manufacturing industries, 1965 to 1986*
(per cent)

	R & D Expenditure/Sales		Engineers and Scientists/ Employment	
	Textiles[a]	All manufacturing	Textiles[a]	All manufacturing
1965	0.67	1.11	0.54	1.37
1966	0.58	1.11	0.77	1.55
1967	0.58	1.12	0.62	1.60
1968	0.59	1.22	0.90	1.80
1969	0.53	1.27	0.68	1.64
1970	0.55	1.36	0.80	1.80
1971	0.65	1.50	0.81	1.94
1972	0.62	1.54	0.83	2.10
1973	0.69	1.52	0.72	2.29
1974	0.77	1.58	1.19	2.46
1975	0.68	1.56	1.10	2.77
1976	0.65	1.59	1.04	2.58
1977	0.56	1.64	1.13	2.96
1978	0.75	1.75	0.78	3.01
1979	0.86	1.63	1.12	3.20
1980	0.81	1.63	1.77	3.23
1981	0.99	1.79	1.25	3.48
1982	0.94	2.01	1.45	3.59
1983	0.90	2.17	1.49	3.90
1984	1.03	2.22	1.59	4.21
1985	1.09	2.53	1.62	4.32
1986	1.19	2.90	2.13	4.68
1986/1965	1.78	2.61	3.94	3.42

[a] Not including man-made fibres.
Source: Management and Coordination Agency, Statistics Bureau, *Report on the Survey of Research and Development*, Tokyo, various issues.

than for other manufacturing. In fact, the latter grew at the annual rate of 7 per cent, quadrupling during the two decades.

Recent formal research efforts in the textile industry have aimed at developing new production processes that improve efficiency and provide flexible technologies that are capable of responding quickly to changes in demand.[7]

These new production processes have been used not only to boost the international competitiveness of Japan's textile industry, but also to earn foreign exchange directly through diffusing new technologies to foreign competitors. In 1987, for example, the industry exported 182 technologies and received more than 4 billion yen in royalties. More than 70 per cent of those technology exports were purchased by neighbouring Asian countries.[8] Although it is not easy to evaluate the long-term impact of such technological diffusion on Japan's international competitiveness, the comparative advantage that Japan holds currently may be short-lived if Asian countries such as Taiwan, Korea and Hong Kong are soon able to adopt similar new technologies.

Product specialization

In addition to rationalizing the production processes, the Japanese textile industry, as we have seen, has responded to changing market conditions by shifting its product mix to more technologically sophisticated items and by upgrading products. In particular, Japanese firms have concentrated on new synthetic materials and high-quality textiles.

Table 6.6 lists the products with the highest and lowest annual rates of growth of real output during the period 1967 to 1984. The full sample consists of 84 six-digit products (see note to table), and the annual growth rates range between 12 per cent and –22 per cent. As expected, production has increased most for newly developed and differentiated products such as polyester continuous filament and its fabrics, synthetic twisted yarn and thread, and polypropylene fabrics. Polyester and acrylic staples, and their products, are also among the items with the highest growth rates. The ones whose production has shrunk most include viscose fabrics, acetate fabrics and cotton fibres.

---

[7] For example, the government has supported research projects that have developed continuous and automatic production processes for polyester filament, and automatic cutting-sewing-pressing systems for clothing.

[8] Statistics Bureau, Management and Coordination Agency, *Report on the Survey of Research and Development*, Tokyo, 1987, Tables 12 and 14.

Table 6.6: *The textile products with the highest and lowest annual growth of output, Japan, 1967 to 1984*

Rank	Product	Average annual rate of growth of real output[a], 1967–84 (per cent)
1	Polyester yarn	11.7
2	Polyester continuous filament	11.6
3	Polypropylene fabrics	11.5
4	Synthetic twisted yarn	9.2
5	Polyester continuous filament fabrics	8.4
6	Acrylic fabrics	7.8
7	Cotton and synthetic blankets	7.5
8	Woollen twisted yarn	7.4
9	Polyester staple	7.3
10	Rayon continuous filament fabrics	7.1
11	Acrylic staple	6.6
12	Acrylic blended yarn	5.7
13	Linen fabrics	5.3
14	Synthetic tyre cord	5.1
15	Synthetic twisted thread	4.9
70	Silk twisted yarn	−6.1
71	Cotton unbleached muslin	−6.2
72	Vinylon yarn	−6.5
73	Nylon continuous filament fabrics	−6.9
74	Acetate continuous filament fabrics	−8.2
75	Jute fabrics	−8.8
76	Cotton fabrics made with indigenous technique	−9.1
77	Worsted fabrics for kimonos	−10.5
78	Cotton flannel	−10.6
79	Viscose rayon broad fabrics	−12.0
80	Viscose rayon narrow fabrics	−12.5
81	Vinylon blended yarn	−12.8
82	Acetate fabrics	−16.7
83	Man-made staple fibre blankets	−17.3
84	Viscose staple fibre narrowfabrics	−22.2

[a] The sample consists of 84 six-digit commodities from the following four-digit classifications: cotton yarn (SIC 2021), man-made fibre yarn (2022), woollen yarn (2023), silk yarn (2024), linen yarn (2025), twisted yarn (2031), cotton and man-made staple fabrics (2041), silk and man-made filament fabrics (2042), woollen fabrics (2043), linen fabrics (2044), and man-made fibres (264). Real output is defined as quantity shipped, and is measured by weight for yarn and fibres and by square metre for fabrics.

Source: MITI, *Census of Manufacturers: Report by Commodities*, Tokyo, various issues.

To find out if the Japanese industry has upgraded its products and shifted its production to more high-priced and thus to higher value-added areas, simple correlations between price in 1967 and real output growth for 1967–84 were calculated for four major product classes. If the Japanese textile industry has increased the production of high-priced specialty commodities, we should expect a positive correlation between the growth rate and the initial price level across commodities within the same product class. The statistically significant simple correlations in Table 6.7 confirm this for man-made fibre yarn, and cotton and man-made staple fabrics. The result for man-made fibres, although not statistically significant, also suggests the presence of such a relationship.

The simple correlation becomes insignificant in any of the four product classes when the latest 1984 price instead of the initial 1967 price is used as the price variable. This might suggest that the Japanese textile industry's response to the price level differentials in 1967 has increased the production of high-priced commodities in the ensuing years enough to compress the earlier differentials.

Protection from imports

After the conclusion of the Kennedy Round of multilateral trade negotiations under the GATT (1964–67), the Japanese government implemented several import liberalization measures as part of its trade liberalization policy.[9] Import tariffs on textiles were reduced under this program, and further lowered under the 1971 Generalized System of Preferences for developing countries. In addition, the government reduced tariffs in 1972. As Table 6.8 shows, the nominal tariff rates, measured as the ratio in tariff revenues to the value of imports on which tariffs were levied, declined over time between 1965 and 1975. The peak tariff was reduced from 50 to 13 per cent and the average tariff declined from 19 to 13 per cent over that period. There has been little change in these tariff rates since then, however (Deardorff and Stern 1984).

Although tariffs remain significant barriers to international trade, the policy measures used by importing countries such as the United States, Canada and the European Community to control imports of textiles and clothing are mainly bilateral agreements and import quotas under the framework of the MFA. Japan, however, does not currently apply any MFA restrictions to imports, although it participates in the

---

[9] For a historical overview and evaluations of the effects of these policy reforms, see Itoh and Kyono (1988) and Komiya and Itoh (1988).

Table 6.7: *Simple correlation for Japan's four-digit textile industries between unit price in 1967 and real output growth, 1967 to 1984*

	Number of observations	Correlation coefficient
Man-made fibre yarn	11	0.69[a]
Cotton and man-made staple fabrics	18	0.51[b]
Silk and man-made filament fabrics	10	−0.10
Man-made fibres	9	0.46

[a] Significant at the one per cent level.
[b] Significant at the five per cent level.

Table 6.8: *Tariffs on textile and clothing imports, Japan, 1965 to 1980*

	Nominal tariff rate (customs duties as % of dutiable imports)			
	1965	1970	1975	1980
Fibre:				
Man-made, rayon	27	11	7	5
Man-made, synthetic	18	14	8	9
Yarn:				
Silk	13	10	10	7
Cotton	1	7	3	3
Wool	1	1	—	—
Linen	50	15	8	8
Man-made, rayon	50	10	4	8
Man-made, synthetic	25	2	2	8
Fabric:				
Silk	19	15	8	10
Cotton	10	7	5	5
Wool	23	19	11	10
Linen	12	21	12	15
Man-made, rayon	16	12	7	6
Man-made, synthetic	18	13	6	5
Narrow	21	14	8	8
Knit	26	20	13	12
Finished textiles	22	16	9	7
Clothing	19	18	10	7
All textiles and clothing	19	18	13	14

Sources: Administrative Management Agency, *1965–1970–1975 Link Input–Output Tables* and *1970–1975–1980 Link Input–Output Tables*, Tokyo, 1980 and 1985.

Table 6.9: *Index of industrial countries' non-tariff barriers to textile imports from developing and industrial countries, 1983*[a]

	Imports from developing countries	Imports from industrial countries
Japan	13	11
European Community	68	16
Belgium-Luxembourg	44	30
Denmark	72	11
France	65	22
West Germany	72	9
Greece	34	4
Ireland	56	18
Italy	49	4
Netherlands	72	7
United Kingdom	79	26
Australia	29	28
Austria	15	—
Finland	63	24
Norway	60	40
Switzerland	46	69
United States	64	31
All industrial countries	57	23

[a] The extent to which imports are subject to non-tariff barriers, with a value of 100 per cent indicating that all actual imports were covered by NTBs.
Source: Adapted from Nogues, Olechowski and Winters (1986: Table 4c, p. 52).

MFA as an exporting country (Komiya and Itoh 1988). The extent of formal non-tariff barriers to imports in textiles estimated for sixteen major industrial countries by Nogues, Olechowski and Winters (1986) is given in Table 6.9. Their index uses the 1983 value of own-country imports as weights, and it covers quantitative import restrictions, voluntary export restraints, measures for the enforcement of decreed prices, tariff-type measures and monitoring measures. For imports from developing countries, Japan was the lowest in the extent of formal non-tariff barriers, while the EC and the United States were among the highest. For imports from industrial countries, Japan was not the least protectionist but it was well below the average for all industrial countries.

While Table 6.9 suggests the extent of formal non-tariff barriers to imports is low in Japan, both practitioners and researchers have pointed to the existence of various informal barriers to that trade.[10] Foremost among these informal trade barriers is the complex and fragmented organization of distribution channels. These may constitute important barriers to import penetration into Japanese textile

10 For a survey of these arguments, see Saxonhouse and Stern (1988).

and clothing markets. In textile fabrics and women's apparel, for example, the average sales of Japanese independent wholesalers are only half as large as the sales of the average wholesaler in the United States. Moreover, clothing import wholesalers tend to hold lower stocks than domestic wholesalers, putting the foreign producer who uses the import wholesaler at a disadvantage (Williamson and Yamawaki 1989).

The response of the government to the recent surge of imports from industrializing countries has so far been rather limited. The November 1988 Report (*Toshin*) of the Textile Industry Council (MITI 1988) recommended implementing temporary import restrictions such as anti-dumping and countervailing duties under the provisions of the GATT if a sharp increase in imports is due to unfair trade practices.[11] The report, however, was cautious about suggesting import restrictions be used under the provisions of the MFA, although it did not rule out the possibility of using MFA restrictions in particular products for a limited period as a last resort.

Changing patterns of Japan's trade in textiles and clothing

The analysis in the previous section focuses on the adjustments that have taken place in Japan's domestic market. This section turns to the international adjustments by Japan's producers in their direct investment abroad and its effects on intra-firm trade, as well as their participation in intra-industry trade.

Direct investment abroad

Towards the end of the 1960s, the Japanese textile and fibre firms started investing extensively in foreign countries and shifting production offshore (Tsurumi 1976). As Table 6.10 shows, the flow of direct investment increased through the late 1960s and early 1970s. During this period, Asia and South America received 90 per cent of Japan's direct foreign investment. This activity declined in the years immediately following the first oil crisis in 1973 but then increased again and reached its second peak in 1978. In contrast to the earlier period,

[11] Previous cases include the pleas by the Japan Spinners' Association in 1983 to impose anti-dumping duties on cotton yarn from Korea and countervailing duties on cotton yarn from Pakistan, and the plea by the Japan Knit Manufacturers Association in 1988 for anti-dumping duties on knit pullovers from Korea (Japan Tariff association 1989: 146–50).

Table 6.10:	*Foreign direct investment by Japanese textile producers,*[a]
by destination, 1965 to 1986
(million US dollars)

Year	North America	South America	Asia	Europe	Other	World Total
1965	—	2	3	—	1	6
1966	3	3	2	—	3	11
1967	—	5	11	—	1	17
1968	—	2	13	—	—	15
1969	—	5	25	—	4	34
1970	3	6	37	—	3	49
1971	1	11	53	—	—	65
1972	3	23	132	—	5	163
1973	28	93	191	4	10	326
1974	—	36	118	8	3	175
1975	4	17	71	4	2	98
1976	29	27	47	6	3	112
1977	27	34	83	13	1	158
1978	37	27	35	73	—	172
1979	22	15	34	17	1	89
1980	14	12	50	12	4	92
1981	26	10	43	13	—	92
1982	10	12	40	5	—	67
1983	11	17	132	14	—	174
1984	15	16	39	15	—	85
1985	1	11	8	8	—	28
1986	22	2	21	17	1	63

[a] Industries included are textiles (SIC 20), clothing (SIC 21), and man-made fibres (SIC 264).
Source: MITI (ed.), *Dai 16 kai wagakuni kigyo no kaigai jigyo katsudo* [The 16th Report on the Foreign Activity of Japanese Firms], Tokyo, Keibunshuppan, 1988.

more than 60 per cent of direct investment during the latter 1970s went to North America and Europe.

The flow of direct investment declined sharply again in 1979 when the second oil crisis occurred, and has been relatively stable since then except for the sharp increase that occurred in Asia in 1983. In 1986 the foreign subsidiaries of Japanese textile producers employed 122,000 employees in total, of which 80 per cent were in Asia and 11 per cent in South America. In total, 95 Japanese textile firms and 186 clothing firms had invested in Asia as of the end of 1986 (MITI 1989: 37).

How has the direct investment activity changed the trade pattern of the Japanese textile industry? Although it is not easy to answer the question directly because of insufficient data, some indication might be obtained by examining the pattern of intra-firm trade. According to survey statistics compiled by the Ministry of International Trade

Table 6.11: *The extent of Japanese intra-firm trade and the distribution of sales of overseas subsidiaries by destination, 1984* (per cent)

	Textile industries[a]	All manufacturing
Intra-firm trade:		
Exports to foreign subsidiaries/ Total exports of parent	3	30
Imports from foreign subsidiaries/ Total imports of parent	5	21
Distribution of subsidiary sales by destination:		
Sales in local market/ Total subsidiary sales	66	73
Exports to Japanese parent/ Total subsidiary sales	3	10
Exports to Japanese non-parents/ Total subsidiary sales	2	2
Exports to third-country markets/ Total subsidiary sales	29	15

[a] Textile industries are defined here as the aggregate of textiles (SIC 20), clothing (SIC 21), and man-made fibres (SIC 264).
Source: MITI (ed.), *kaigai toshi tokei soran* [Statistical Report on Foreign Investment], No. 2, Tokyo, Keibunshuppan, 1986.

and Industry, the extent of intra-firm trade in the textile industry has been much lower than that for manufacturing in total (MITI 1986: 242–63). The share of exports to subsidiaries in total exports of parent companies in 1984 was only 3 per cent in the textile industry, whereas it was 30 per cent for manufacturing as a whole. Likewise, the 1984 share of imports from subsidiaries in total imports of Japanese parents was 5 per cent for textiles compared with 21 per cent for manufacturing in total (Table 6.11).

The distribution of total subsidiary sales by destination indicates a similar pattern. The share of exports to parents in total subsidiary sales is 3 per cent for the textile industry, which is again much lower than the 10 per cent for manufacturing in total.

Notice from Table 6.11 that the share of total subsidiary sales going to local markets (66 per cent) is lower for the textile industry than for manufactures in total (73 per cent), but the share of exports to third-country markets in total subsidiary sales is higher for the textile industry (29 per cent) than for manufacturing in total (15 per cent). This suggests that the foreign subsidiaries of Japanese textile manufacturers export more than proportionately to third-country markets.

This pattern is consistent with the general pattern of the declining dependence of these firms on their exports from Japan as distinct from their exports from overseas subsidiaries.

While some firms choose to produce offshore, other firms choose to use arm's-length transactions with overseas producers. In particular, a relatively large proportion of Japan's clothing producers, wholesale trading companies and large retail stores import apparel that is produced under a contractual arrangement which specifies product design and quality. This type of transaction is more often used for low-grade apparel imports from NIEs. The apparel imports using this route have risen sharply in recent years, and are estimated to have accounted for about 80 per cent of total apparel imports from NIEs in the late 1980s (Mukaiyama 1989). High-grade apparel imports from Europe, by contrast, tend to use the conventional import wholesaler route.

Table 6.12:   *Index of intra-industry trade by Japanese textile industries, 1965 and 1980*

Industry	Intra-industry trade index[a]	
	1965	1980
Fibre:		
Man-made, rayon	0.007	0.024
Man-made, synthetic	0.040	0.273
Yarn:		
Silk	0.323	0.240
Cotton	0.376	0.482
Wool	0.495	0.675
Linen	0.018	0.136
Man-made, rayon	0.001	0.142
Man-made, synthetic	0.002	0.298
Fabric:		
Silk	0.087	0.279
Cotton	0.021	0.670
Wool	0.366	0.932
Linen	0.153	0.250
Man-made, rayon	0.117	0.271
Man-made, synthetic	0.019	0.108
Narrow	0.083	0.421
Knit	0.124	0.770
Finished textiles	0.155	0.909
Clothing	0.073	0.340

[a] The intra-industry trade index is defined as one minus the ratio of the modulus of exports minus imports to exports plus imports, so that it has the property of ranging from zero (no intra-industry trade) to one.
Sources: Administrative Management Agency, *1965–1970–1975 Link Input–Output Tables* and *1970–1975–1980 Link Input–Output Tables*, Tokyo, 1980 and 1985.

Development of intra-industry trade

The descriptive analysis so far has identified several forces which would contribute to the development of intra-industry trade in textiles. These include increases in import penetration, shifts in the product mix of exports, production specialization at the higher-priced and more capital-intensive end of the spectrum, reductions of import duties, and a trend towards offshore production.

In fact such a development has been taking place. Table 6.12 presents the index of intra-industry trade by product class for 1965 and 1980. This index varies between zero (no intra-industry trade) and one (exports equal imports).[12] The index has increased for virtually all product classes over this period, growing more rapidly for man-made yarns and cotton fabrics. The 1980 level of the index was highest for woollen fabrics, finished textiles, knit fabrics, woollen yarns and cotton fabrics, and was lowest for man-made rayon fibre, man-made synthetic fabrics, linen yarns, man-made rayon yarns, and silk yarns.

Statistical relationships between international competition and domestic adjustments
International competitiveness, industrial policy and R&D

The analysis in the preceding sections shows that Japanese textile industries have been relatively successful in retaining their international competitiveness, and that the government has been keen to assist by implementing several policy measures which have helped rationalize the industry. Furthermore, the industry has invested in formal research and development activities to improve its efficiency. Are there any causal relations between the slow decay in international competitiveness, formal research efforts, and industrial policy? In other words, did the increasing flow of imports and the declining growth of exports cause the implementation of policy measures to help rationalization and the growth of formal research activities, or did the rationalization measures and research efforts discourage imports and promote exports?

These hypotheses were tested statistically by using annual data for 1965 to 1986 on trade flows, industrial policy measures, and R & D

---

12 See Grubel and Lloyd (1975). The index is calculated based on exports to and imports from the rest of the world. Thus, no consideration is given to bilateral trade flows.

intensity. A vector autoregressive analysis is used, technical details and results of which are provided in the appendix to this chapter.

Some interesting causal relationships are identified by that statistical analysis. First, the government appears to have reacted to the decline in export opportunities for textile producers by increasing government finances for rationalization. Such policy measures have eventually contributed to improving the industry's international competitiveness and thus increasing its exports. Second, the Japanese textile industry has responded to the increase in imports by increasing its formal research efforts. The research activity appears to have helped the industry increase its exports. In other words, the industry's efforts to rationalize production, with the assistance of government finances, and to introduce new technology through augmented formal research efforts, seem to explain the lingering comparative advantage of the Japanese textile industry between the late 1960s and the early 1980s.

Productivity growth, domestic adjustments, and imports

While the vector autoregression analysis in the appendix has identified the time-series causal relationships among trade flows, industrial policy, and R&D intensity for Japan's textile industry, it fails to provide any specific evidence on the relationship between domestic structural adjustments and the shift in international competitiveness. How is the slow penetration of imports into the Japanese textile market linked to domestic adjustments? Did the rationalization of production increase labour productivity and contribute to maintaining international competitiveness? Did the industry react to the increase in import penetration by improving efficiency? Was the slow import penetration caused by tariff barriers?

A simultaneous-equation model to explain the growth of labour productivity and change in import penetration between 1965 and 1980 is estimated to help answer these questions. Using the sample of 20 textile products, the statistical analysis reported in the appendix finds that the growth of capital intensity and average plant size has increased the rate of labour productivity growth. This confirms the earlier conjecture that the increase in new capital investment, the contraction of employment and the increase in average firm size have raised labour productivity in the Japanese textile industry since the late 1960s.

While increasing import penetration was found to raise labour productivity, increasing productivity growth was found simultaneously to slow down import penetration. This finding completes the link between the industry's efforts for rationalization and its slow import penetration. The Japanese textile industry increased its labour productivity through rationalization, and this resulted in a slower decline in international competitiveness than would otherwise have been the case. Changes in tariffs, however, were found to be unimportant as barriers to imports in the Japanese textile industry for the period 1965 to 1980.

Summary and conclusions

The international competitive environment surrounding the Japanese textile industry has changed substantially since the mid-1960s. Companies in the industry have adjusted their production processes, investment strategies and products to the changing conditions in domestic and foreign markets. The adjustments have included shedding excess labour and capital equipment; closing inefficiently small plants; investing in new labour-saving equipment; undertaking more research and development; specializing in production of commodities with high value-added per worker; and shifting production abroad.

The statistical analyses have identified some links between these domestic adjustments and the changing pattern of international competitiveness. In particular, the time-series analysis found that increasing import flows and declining export flows have stimulated formal research efforts and led the government to finance rationalization in the industry. The cross-sectional analysis supports the hypothesis that increasing labour productivity growth has slowed import penetration. The growth of labour productivity is found to have been promoted by increases in capital intensity, average plant size, and import competition. Thus the lingering comparative advantage and the slow import penetration in the Japanese textile industry from the late 1960s to the early 1980s are partly accounted for by the structural adjustments that took place in the industry. In particular, the productivity-raising adjustments, rather than protection increases, were a major force in slowing the decline in Japan's international competitiveness.

More recently, however, textile and clothing imports into Japan have risen sharply, particularly of apparel from Japan's neighbours since 1985. In fact in 1987 Japan became a net importer of textiles and clothing as a product group. A relatively large proportion of these clothing imports from industrializing countries have tended to circumvent the complex wholesaler distribution channels because of the direct purchase method now being used increasingly by Japan's large-scale retailers and clothing firms. If the criticism that Japan's complex distribution system has been a major barrier to imports has been valid, then this recent development may well lead to a sustained growth in import penetration into the Japanese market in the future.

APPENDIX: statistical analysis
1. Time-series analysis of the relationships among trade flows, R&D intensity, and industrial policy

A vector autoregressive system (VAR)[13] for trade flows, R&D intensity, and industrial policy measures is estimated by using annual industry data for the period 1965 to 1986. The statistical model is represented by

$$Y_t = a_0 + \sum_{i=1}^{m} a_i Y_{t-i} + \sum_{j=1}^{n} b_j X_{t-j} + e_t. \qquad (1)$$

We use an F-test to test the hypothesis that $\sum_{j=1}^{n} b_j = 0$. When the hypothesis is rejected, we say that Y is Granger-caused by X (Granger 1969). In estimating equation (1), all variables are treated as endogenous. The variables used in estimation are defined as

X	=	total Japanese exports of textiles,
M	=	total Japanese imports of textiles,
NETX	=	net exports to total trade in textiles = $(X - M)/(X + M)$,
IP	=	total financing and leasing costs to rationalize industry under the Structural Improvement Programs, [14] and
RD	=	proportion of scientists and engineers in total employment.

To eliminate the trend from the time series, all the variables are transformed into logarithmic differences, and the transformed variables are denoted with prefix d. The three trade variables, X, M, NETX, are included separately in the system. Thus, a vector autoregressive system contains three endogenous variables, IP, RD, and one of the three trade variables.

Each autoregressive equation was estimated by the OLS method. To avoid bias due to the lag truncation and thus to choose the appropriate lag length, a likelihood ratio test was implemented for the three-variable autoregression system.[15] In all three specifications with different trade variables, consistent models were specified with

---

[13] Vector autoregressive systems and their rationale are discussed in Sims (1972, 1980). For applications in international trade, see Baldwin and Green (1988) and Marin (1989).

[14] Two programs were implemented during the years 1967 to 1981. See MITI (1989) and Yamazawa (1988: Table III). Government financing under these programs was provided in the form of low-interest loans.

[15] The test statistic is based on the covariance matrices and has a chi-squared distribution (Sims 1980).

one lag significant at the 10 per cent level. The causality test based on the autoregression is summarized in Table 6A.1.

To evaluate the causal relationship between net exports, industrial policy measures and research efforts, System 1 uses dNETX as the trade variable. In the estimated autoregressions, the lagged effect of dRD on dNETX is statistically significant and positive, and the lagged effect of dNETX on dRD is highly significant and negative. The test statistics in Table 6A.1 suggest that a decline in net exports causes an increase in research intensity, whereas this increase in research intensity causes an improvement of the net export position. On the other hand, industry policy measures are not caused by net exports, and they do not cause net exports.

Table 6A.1: *Tests of causality between trade flows, industrial policy, and R & D efforts, Japan, 1965 to 1986[a]*

Dependent variable	Regressors	Sign of the coefficient	Test statistic	Significance level
System 1				
dNETX	dIP	+	0.19	0.67
	dRD	+	4.40	0.05
dIP	dNETX	−	0.17	0.69
	dRD	+	5.68	0.03
dRD	dNETX	−	12.40	0.003
	dIP	+	0.55	0.47
System 2				
dX	dIP	+	3.46	0.08
	dRD	+	2.75	0.12
dIP	dX	−	3.38	0.09
	dRD	+	9.85	0.01
dRD	dX	−	1.30	0.27
	dIP	+	0.22	0.65
System 3				
dM	dIP	+	0.31	0.58
	dRD	−	1.21	0.29
dIP	dM	+	0.00	0.99
	dRD	+	5.44	0.03
dRD	dM	+	6.20	0.02
	dIP	−	0.06	0.82

[a] The test statistic is an F-ratio to test the null hypothesis that the lagged coefficients of each regressor are jointly equal to zero. A constant and the lagged dependent variables are also included in each regression. All the variables are transformed to logarithmic differences.

To separate the influences of exports and imports in net exports, System 2 and System 3 use dX and dM, respectively, as the trade variables. In System 2, the lagged effect of dIP on dX is statistically significant and positive, whereas the lagged effect of dX on dIP is significant and negative. On the other hand, the lagged effect of dRD on dX is not quite significant, although its causal direction is positive. The lagged effect of dX on dRD is also insignificant. Thus, as the results in Table 6A.1 indicate, a decline in exports causes an increase in government finances for rationalization, and an increase in government finances causes an increase in exports. An increase in research effort may also have caused an increase in exports.

In System 3, the lagged effects of dIP and dRD on dM are not statistically significant, whereas the lagged effect of dM on dRD is positive and statistically significant. The lagged effect of dM on dIP is insignificant. Thus, the test statistics in Table 6A.1 suggest that an increase in research intensity is caused by an increase in imports, but it does not cause a significant reduction of imports. On the other hand, government financial assistance and imports do not show any causal relationships.

To summarize, these findings suggest the following patterns of causality among trade flows, industry policy and research efforts: (1) declines in exports cause increases in government finances for rationalization; (2) increases in imports cause increases in research activity; (3) increases in government financial assistance, and to a lesser extent increases in research activity, cause increases in exports but do not cause a reduction in imports.

2. Cross-sectional analysis of the relationships among productivity growth, domestic adjustments, and import penetration

The analysis in the second section of this chapter shows that the Japanese textile industry has rationalized production by eliminating excess capacity and labour, installing new equipment, and enlarging the size of establishments. Such rationalizing measures should have increased labour productivity. Davies and Caves (1987: 17–20) have shown in a formal model that, under the assumption of a Cobb–Douglas production function, labour productivity for an industry that is expressed as the sum over its n plants is

$$Q/L = A(K/L)^a S^b \tag{2}$$

where Q is net output, L is labour input, K is capital input, and S is typical plant size expressed in terms of employment. Equation (2) shows that the industry's labour productivity is determined by capital intensity and plant size.

Based on this model, an appropriate equation to evaluate the effect of domestic adjustments on raising labour productivity is

$$dlPROD = a_0 + a_1 dlKL + a_2 dlPSZ + a_3 dNOT + a_4 dIMP + e \quad (3)$$

where e is the disturbance term, and the rest of the variables are defined as

dlPROD	=	change in the logarithm of labour productivity between 1965 and 1980, labour productivity being defined as value added (at 1965 prices) divided by employment,
dlKL	=	changes in the logarithm of the capital–labour ratio between 1965 and 1978, the capital–labour ratio being defined as fixed assets (at 1965 prices) divided by employment,
dlPSZ	=	change in the logarithm of average plant size between 1965 and 1978, average plant size being defined as value added (at 1965 prices) divided by employment,
dNOT	=	nominal tariffs in 1980 divided by nominal tariffs in 1965, nominal tariffs being defined as total import duties divided by total imports, and
dIMP	=	import penetration ratio in 1980 divided by import penetration ratio in 1965, that ratio being defined as imports/(total output – exports + imports).

To control for the effects of changes in competitive pressure, changes in nominal tariffs and import penetration are included in equation (3). If the Japanese producers were protected more from import competition, their needs to improve competitiveness and thus to raise productivity would be reduced. Therefore, we expect dNOT to have a negative coefficient. By the same token, increasing import penetration will inject more competitive pressure into the domestic market. Thus, dIMP is expected to have a positive coefficient.

While Japanese producers responded to the increasing import penetration by rationalizing their production processes, such rationalizing efforts may eventually have slowed down the increase in import penetration. If the share of the Japanese market that imports capture is a function of relative prices and thus relative production costs between Japan and foreign countries, an increase in labour productivity in the Japanese textile industry will lower its production costs and thus reduce import penetration. Thus, we expect labour productivity growth to have a negative relationship with import penetration. If this hypothesis is correct, the relationship between labour productivity growth and import penetration should be determined simultaneously.

To test this hypothesis, the following statistical model is proposed:

$$dIMP = b_0 + b_1 dPROD + b_2 dWAGE + b_3 dNOT + u, \qquad (4)$$

where u is the disturbance term. The variable dIMP is the growth of import penetration, dNOT is the growth of nominal tariffs, and dPROD is the growth of labour productivity (in natural numbers). The variable dWAGE is the growth of nominal wages per worker, and is expected to control for labour costs in total production costs. An increase in wages raises production costs and therefore accelerates import penetration, *ceteris paribus*.

To test if labour productivity is determined simultaneously with import penetration, a Wu–Hausman test was implemented on equation (4) – see Hausman (1978).[16] The null hypothesis that dPROD is statistically independent of the disturbance term of the dIMP equation is rejected at the 10 per cent level of significance, suggesting that dPROD needs to be considered as endogenous in the equation that explains dIMP, and that an equation to explain dPROD is needed. In addition, the exogeneity of import tariffs in the import share equation was tested given that labour productivity growth is endogenous. In this case, the Wu–Hausman test accepted the null hypothesis of exogeneity at the 10 per cent level of significance. Thus, dNOT can be treated as exogenous, but dPROD cannot.

The simultaneous equation system of labour productivity growth and import penetration growth is estimated using a sample of 20 textile products, and the result is presented in Table 6A.2. The two equations in Table 6A.2 are estimated by the 2SLS method treating dIMP in the dlPROD equation and dPROD in the dIMP equation as endogenous. For the dlPROD equation, all the coefficients for the regressors are statistically significant and have the expected signs. The variables dlKL and dlPSZ are positively related to dlPROD, suggesting that the growth of capital intensity and average plant size has increased the rate of labour productivity growth.[17]

The estimated coefficients for dIMP and dNOT indicate that the increase in import competition has raised labour productivity growth.[18] With the changes in capital intensity and average plant size

[16] The test was implemented assuming dKL, dPSZ, dWAGE are all exogenous. In addition to these variables, the import share in 1965, the change in export share, and a dummy variable identifying man-made fibres are used as instruments. Under this test, the residual from the OLS estimate of the full reduced form on dPROD was included in the dIMP equation, and its t-value was 1.92, given that dNOT is endogenous.

[17] This result is consistent with the previous finding on the determinants of labour productivity growth for a cross-section of Japanese manufacturing industries. See Caves and Uekusa (1976).

[18] This result is consistent with the previous finding on the effect of import competition on labour productivity growth. See Caves and Barton (1989), who also provide some theoretical considerations on this relationship.

Table 6A.2:   *2SLS estimation of labour productivity growth and import penetration growth in Japan's textile market,[a] 1965 to 1980*

Independent	Dependent variable	
	dlPROD	dIMP
Constant	−0.058 (0.329)	−23.198 (0.060)
dlKL	0.677 (4.841)**	
dlPSZ	0.564 (4.815)**	
dIMP	0.001 (2.900)**	
dNOT	−0.144 (2.102)*	−100.68 (0.851)
dPROD		−256.40 (1.891)*
dWAGE		194.71 (2.021)*

[a] All the equations are estimated by the 2SLS method treating dIMP and dPROD as endogenous. The number of observations is 20. Absolute values of t-statistics are in parentheses. The levels of significance at a one-tailed t-test are: **=1 per cent and *=5 per cent.

controlled for in the equation, the productivity-raising effect of import competition seems to be realized through its link to other forms of rationalization such as increasing formal research efforts[19], as well as through rationalizing product lines and specializing in more capital-intensive products.

While increasing import penetration raises labour productivity, increasing export opportunities may also play such a role. To examine this, the growth of export shares (exports/total shipments) for the period 1965 to 1980, dEXP, was included in the regression specification instead of dIMP. The coefficient of dEXP was positive and significant at the 5 per cent level. However, when both dIMP and dEXP were included in the equation, only the coefficient for dIMP was significant.

The result for the dIMP equation in Table 6A.2 shows that the coefficient for dPROD is negative and significant, suggesting that increasing productivity growth slows down import penetration. The coefficient on dWAGE is also significant and has a positive sign as expected, implying that increases in wages promote import penetration.

[19] The time-series analysis in this appendix confirmed this link.

Thus, changes in the components of production costs (unit labour costs) determine changes in import penetration, and declining costs discourage import penetration.

Finally, the coefficient for dNOT in the dIMP equation is insignificant, suggesting that changes in tariff barriers did not promote import penetration in the Japanese textile industry for the years 1965–80. Rather, increasing import competition resulted from rising labour costs.

7

The new silk road to Europe

Carl B. Hamilton*

There are two major developments taking place in Europe which will have implications for East Asia's trade with this region. First, the European Community (EC) is deepening the political and economic integration among its members through the creation of the so-called 'Internal Market' program to be concluded by 1992. Second, Eastern Europe is undergoing political and economic liberalization. From an economic point of view, and in the short run, the EC's 1992 program is the more important of the two developments. In the long run, however, provided the present economic and political liberalization is allowed to continue, the events in Eastern Europe could be more important economically, and certainly more important politically.

The first section provides some background information regarding clothing production historically in Western Europe, as well as more recent trade flows and apparent consumption of textiles and clothing. In the second section the EC's textile trade policy during the 1980s is analysed. New estimates are presented regarding the restrictiveness of EC voluntary export restraints (VERs) under the Multi-fibre Arrangement (MFA), as well as new estimates of selected countries' supply prices of clothing. Against this background, the third section discusses aspects of the EC's prospective future trade policy, particularly the changing role of its anti-dumping instrument, the emergence of new suppliers with preferential access, and an analysis of future conflicts of interest between 'sun-belt' protectionist EC countries and 'frost-belt' liberal members over the openness of the Community. The conclusions are summarized in the final section of the chapter.

From a commercial policy point of view, Europe at present is divided into three blocs: the European Community, the European Free Trade Association (EFTA) and Eastern Europe. The EC's twelve member

* The author has benefited from the assistance of Stig Blomskog, Edwin Dean, Refik Erzan, Paula Holmes, Robert Keller, Patrick Lau, Edda Liljenroth, P.L. Shin, Jan Urlings, Helen Wallace, Alan Winters, Peter Wise and Molly Akerlund.

states are Belgium, Denmark, Federal Republic of Germany, France, Greece, Ireland, Italy, Luxembourg, the Netherlands, Portugal, Spain and the United Kingdom.

EFTA consists of Austria, Finland, Iceland, Norway, Sweden and Switzerland. Of these, Sweden and Norway have unilaterally decided to dismantle all quantitative restrictions on textile product imports – including imports from Eastern Europe – when the present MFA IV expires in mid-1991.

Eastern Europe is defined here as Bulgaria, Czechoslovakia, Hungary, Poland, Romania and the Soviet Union.

The objective of creating the EC was primarily political, not economic, namely a wish to put an end to the recurrent wars that had plagued Europe and, through systems of alliances, other parts of the world as well. Economic integration in all its dimensions was (and still is) seen as one of the most important instruments for achieving the political objectives of peace and stability. Controls on how each participating country is allowed to exercise its sovereignty were institutionalized from the beginning. These included supranational arrangements for a common external trade policy, competition policy and – most important – a Community court of law. In negotiations in GATT and the MFA all twelve EC member countries have one representative only, whose instructions are the result of internal discussions and compromises in Brussels.

As Community integration deepens within the 1992 program, the supranational arrangements for external trade policy are becoming considerably stronger at the expense of remaining national trade policies. Since internal border controls will be abolished, member countries lose any remaining control over the domestic price of individual commodities.[1] More specifically, for imports under quantitative restrictions it will be impossible to enforce any national demarcation of quotas on trade. This is true regardless of whether the restriction is an import quota, an export restraint arrangement, an EC-wide restriction, a national one, a GATT 'legal' one (like the MFA), a GATT 'illegal' industry-to-industry arrangement, a 'grandfather' quota (based on past trade volumes), etc. The impossibility of demarcation follows from the elimination of border controls.[2]

With regard to the MFA, this means that after 1992 there will be no splitting of an overall EC quota into the national sub-quotas.

[1] On the 1992 program see, for example, Commission of the European Communities (1988), Padoa-Schioppa *et al.* (1987) and Pelkmans and Winters (1988). With the exception of agricultural products, today there are no tariffs or quantitative restrictions on trade in goods within the EC. There will be a reintroduction of free trade in agricultural products from 1992 when the Community's special Monetary Compensation Amounts (MCAs), which ensure prices for farm products differ between EC countries, are abolished.

[2] This conclusion can be drawn from the decision to make redundant the powers of Article 115 of the Rome Treaty.

A crucial issue will then be the member countries' reaction to these changes. Will they just accept them? Will they lobby in Brussels to stiffen EC external protection in order to 'compensate' for the internal liberalization? Will national governments and firms find new instruments to pursue old protectionist policies? An attempt is made later in this chapter to throw some light on these issues.

The EC has special trade relationships with a fringe of countries – a pyramid of privileges. At the top of this pyramid are the EFTA countries. Each EFTA country has its own national, external trade regime, and in GATT and the MFA negotiations each EFTA country negotiates on its own.[3] As an organization, EFTA has no long-term political aims. Its objective was limited to the administration and development of the EFTA countries' free-trade agreements in manufactures with the Community. These agreements include textile and clothing products.[4]

There are three 'associated' members of the EC, namely, Turkey, Cyprus and Malta. (From a legal point of view these associate members are more closely linked to the Community than the EFTA countries, but in practice this is not so.) Of these, Turkey has applied for full membership, and Cyprus is scheduled to become a member of the Community's common external trade policy (that is, to attain customs union membership).

In addition, almost all Arab countries located around the Mediterranean, and Israel, have trade and development agreements with the EC, which ensure relatively favourable treatment. The EC also has preferential trade and aid agreements with the so-called ACP countries (selected Asian, Caribbean and Pacific countries). As these countries become competitive in textiles and clothing, however, they typically see their exports quantitatively restricted, as happened, for example, to Mauritius.[5]

The EC's trade with East European countries has special features. The traditional approach of these countries – especially the Soviet Union, but even Czechoslovakia, Hungary and Poland – has been to

[3] This is why, for example, each EFTA country has its own system of MFA categories of textile and clothing products.

[4] EFTA is thus deliberately constructed to be an institutionally much weaker organization than the EC: the EC has a common external trade policy (unlike EFTA), a common competition policy (unlike EFTA), a common court of law for, among other issues, internal trade disputes (unlike EFTA), and supranational law making with direct effect in member countries (again unlike EFTA). During 1989 EFTA was given a new task, namely, to work for common EFTA positions in negotiations with the EC. After 1992, the present set of complex rules of origin which have hampered exports from EFTA to the EC will be simplified considerably. This non-tariff barrier has been estimated to be equivalent to a tariff in the range of 3 to 5 per cent of the value of the goods involved (Herin 1986).

[5] See Hine (1985) and, on Mauritius, Cable (1990). Pacific members are Fiji, Tonga and Western Samoa.

avoid interdependence with the industrial market economies of the West. This is now rapidly changing, but the stability and pace of the liberalization process is difficult to forecast. The East European countries' organization for economic cooperation – Comecon or SEV – is now in substance rapidly disintegrating, and for this reason is disregarded here. The EC's future trade relations with this and other groups of countries are discussed further in the third section of the chapter.

Europe's trade in comparative perspective

In the literature on development economics, a question that has attracted considerable attention is whether a country's economic progress can be described as a sequence of stages (Rostow 1960a,b). Part of that discussion concerns the role of textiles and clothing production in the development process. It has been noted that textiles and particularly clothing typically account for an important part of the production and exports of a newly industrializing country at the early stages of its economic development, and that subsequently, as that economy matures, these industries decline in relative importance (Anderson and Park 1989; Park and Anderson 1991; Trela and Whalley 1990; and Chapter 1 above).

Figures 7.1 and 7.2 show that the early experience of industrialization in Western Europe was consistent with this pattern. In so far as the number of cotton spindles per capita is a reliable index of production of textiles and clothing, it suggests that all of the European countries illustrated enjoyed an initial building-up phase with rapid growth until the 1860s–70s, followed by a slow-growth phase peaking in the 1930s (although Switzerland peaked as early as the 1870s), and then a third phase characterized by rapid decline. (The United Kingdom and Switzerland are on a higher level of production capacity per head than the others and so are included separately in Figure 7.1; for the sake of comparison Belgium is included in both Figure 7.1 and Figure 7.2.)

The declining relative importance of this industry is also clear from Figure 7.3 and Table 7.1, which show more recent cross-sectional and time-series evidence. The negative relationship between real income per capita and the share of clothing in total manufacturing output for the period 1970 to 1985 is clearly depicted in Figure 7.3. The changing structure of export specialization, summarized in Table 7.1, shows the relative decline of textiles and clothing and the growth of other manufactures in the exports of both the EC and EFTA as those countries continue to lose comparative advantage in primary products and labour-intensive manufactures. Even their export specialization

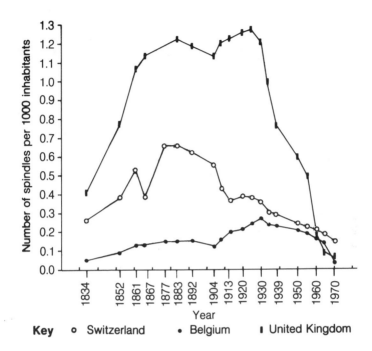

Figure 7.1: *Number of cotton spindles per thousand inhabitants, Belgium, Switzerland and the United Kingdom, 1834 to 1970*

Source: Derived from data reported in Mitchell (1978).

in capital-intensive synthetic fibres has been eroding somewhat with the increasing competitiveness of East Asian suppliers. Within the EC Italy and Portugal have retained the strongest comparative advantage in these products. Portugal's clothing export performance has been especially dramatic as it gradually takes full advantage of the protection from competition from non-EC countries provided by its recent joining of the protectionist European Community.

The effect of these developments on Western Europe's shares of world trade in fibres, textiles and clothing are summarized in Table 7.2. The EC-12 switched from being a net exporter to being a net importer of textiles and clothing in the 1970s, although Italy increased its share of world textile exports and Portugal's share of world clothing exports also increased. The declining importance of Western Europe's textile sector was accompanied by a fall in the region's share of world imports of natural fibres, again despite the growth in import demand by Italy and Portugal.

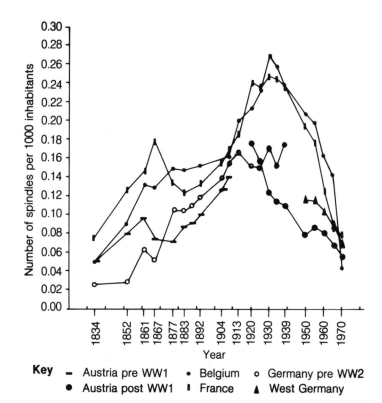

Figure 7.2: *Number of cotton spindles per thousand inhabitants,*
Austria, Belgium, France and Germany, 1834 to 1970

Source: Derived from data reported in Mitchell (1978).

The Community is a larger importer of textiles than the United
States even if intra-EC trade is excluded. The opposite is true for
clothing, however. In several other respects the two economies are
quite similar. The United States and the EC obtain the same shares of
their imports from developing countries, namely almost half their
textiles and just over three-quarters of their clothing (excluding intra-
EC trade: see Table 7.3). Shares of imports in apparent clothing
consumption are also similar. For several of the northern countries of
Western Europe, East Asia's developing economies in 1985 accounted
for about the same share of apparent consumption as in the United
States, namely one-sixth (Table 7.4). This is true of Germany, the UK,

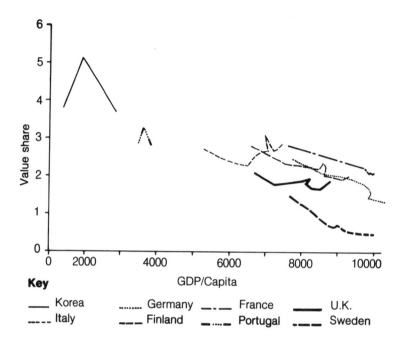

Figure 7.3:   *Relationship between real GDP per capita[a] and the
share of clothing in manufacturing output, selected European
countries and Korea, 1970 to 1985*

[a] Constant (1980) US dollars at purchasing power parity exchange rates.
Source: United Nations, *Industrial Statistics Yearbook*, New York, various issues; and
Summers and Heston (1988).

Denmark and Sweden.[6] Note that, while France is an exception, this
does not necessarily mean that the French government has been able
to protect (through VERs) its textile and clothing industry more
effectively against imports than other EC countries: free trade within
the EC-EFTA area ensures that the restrictive French import policy

[6] It is often pointed out that Western Europe imports a far larger share of its apparent
consumption of textiles and clothing than either Japan or the United States. However,
the data used to support such statements do not exclude intra-EC trade, and are hence
misleading in comparing the EC as a bloc with either Japan or the United States. In fact
two-thirds of the trade of EC member countries is intra-EC trade.

Table 7.1: *Importance of textiles, clothing and other manufactures in exports from EC-12, EFTA, Italy and Portugal, 1965 to 1987*[a]

	Share of total exports (%) from:			Index of export specialization[b] in:		
	Textiles	Clothing	Other manufactures	Textiles	Clothing	Synthetic fibres
EC-12						
1965–69	5.8	2.2	68.0	1.30	1.29	1.53
1970–74	5.2	2.4	69.2	1.32	1.19	1.41
1975–79	4.1	2.3	70.2	1.31	1.11	1.34
1980–84	3.5	2.3	67.2	1.27	1.03	1.23
1985–87	3.7	2.7	70.8	1.15	0.90	1.20
EFTA						
1965–69	4.0	1.7	68.0	0.89	0.97	1.47
1970–74	3.9	1.9	72.0	0.99	0.94	1.33
1975–79	3.2	1.8	73.9	1.03	0.88	1.56
1980–84	2.9	1.7	69.1	1.05	0.79	1.51
1985–87	2.8	1.6	74.5	0.89	0.54	1.24
Italy						
1965–69	7.8	6.2	66.7	1.75	3.60	2.20
1970–74	6.5	5.9	70.5	1.65	2.96	1.81
1975–79	5.7	5.8	72.1	1.81	2.81	1.58
1980–84	5.6	6.1	72.7	1.99	2.77	1.90
1985–87	6.1	7.5	74.0	1.91	2.46	2.65
Portugal						
1965–69	19.6	6.5	36.0	4.36	3.75	0.16
1970–74	17.5	10.2	39.8	4.43	5.07	0.12
1975–79	16.0	12.4	42.0	5.09	5.98	0.41
1980–84	12.8	14.9	44.9	4.57	6.76	0.63
1985–87	10.4	20.8	47.3	3.25	6.82	0.44

[a] Primary products cover SITC sections 0 to 4 plus division 68 (non-ferrous metals) less 266 (synthetic fibres); textiles and clothing cover SITC divisions 65 and 84.
[b] The index of export specialization is defined as the share of a product group in total exports of a country as a ratio of the share of that product group in world exports, following Balassa (1965).
Source: International Economic Data Bank, Trade Data Tapes, Australian National University, Canberra, 1990.

vis-à-vis countries outside of EC-EFTA simply results in increased imports to France of substitutes from within EC-EFTA, particularly from Italy and Portugal (Hamilton 1985, 1986).

Note also that consumers in west Germany and Sweden, two 'high-cost' countries, take only about 40 per cent of their apparent consumption from the 'low-cost' sources of Southern Europe (EC-5 which have free access) and East Asia, in spite of the fact that 80 to 90 per cent of their total consumption is imported (Table 7.4). That is, the world's low-cost producers only supply about half the clothing imports of these high-cost countries.[7]

The trends since 1970 in the shares of Europe's textile and clothing markets supplied by East Asian and other import suppliers are summarized in Table 7.5. The growth in East Asia's penetration has been only slightly lower into Western Europe than into North America, and faster than into Japan, despite the much higher level of other industrial countries' imports in West European markets. Incidentally, note from the final column of Table 7.5 the extent to which the EC is far more self-sufficient in clothing and especially textiles than are the Nordic countries of EFTA.

EC trade policy today

Three observations can be made when comparing EC and US barriers to textile and clothing imports. First, with regard to tariffs in Western Europe, both textile and clothing production is less protected than in the United States. In fact the post-Tokyo Round tariffs of the Community are lower at every stage of processing (Table 7.6).[8]

Second, when it comes to the effect of VERs under the MFA, a comparison is more difficult even though roughly the same set of exporting countries is subjected to the VERs. Both the United States and the EC protect clothing more than textiles, but there are no measures available of the restrictiveness of textiles protection in the form of estimated tariff equivalents of quotas. However, a crude indication of the extent of protection is available, namely the so-called trade coverage ratio or the share of restricted in total imports of textiles and clothing from developing countries. Table 7.7 suggests the EC may be more restrictive of textiles but less restrictive of clothing imports than the United States.[9]

Third, during the early part of the 1980s the combined trade barrier to imported clothing from Asia (tariffs combined with VERs) was less restrictive in Western Europe than in the United States. However, one should not interpret this statement to mean that the United States is more protectionist overall with respect to textile products from developing or other countries. The restrictiveness of a regime of bilateral

[7] On this point see also the discussion in Cable (1990).

[8] The tariff profiles of other industrialized countries are found in GATT (1984: Table 3.3).

[9] The trade coverage measure and its limitations are discussed in Nogues, Olechowski and Winters (1986). The World Bank data are described in Erzan, Goto and Holmes (1990: Appendix). Surprisingly there are no recent comparative studies of protection levels available: the most recent one seems to be 1962 (see GATT 1984: 67).

Table 7.2: *Importance of EC-12, EFTA, centrally-planned Europe, Italy and Portugal in world trade in fibres, textiles and clothing, 1965 to 1987[a]*
(per cent)

	Share of world exports of:				Share of world imports of:			
	Textiles	Clothing	Synthetic fibres	Natural fibres	Textiles	Clothing	Synthetic fibres	Natural fibres
EC-12								
1965–69	50	50	59	13	37	42	42	45
1970–74	51	46	55	12	40	47	46	39
1975–79	49	42	50	13	44	49	44	39
1980–84	44	35	42	13	39	42	35	36
1985–87	45	35	47	16	41	40	41	38
EFTA								
1965–69	6	6	10	—	9	13	7	3
1970–74	6	6	8	—	9	12	6	3
1975–79	6	5	9	—	8	11	4	3
1980–84	6	4	9	—	7	10	4	3
1985–87	6	3	8	—	7	10	4	3
Centrally-planned Europe[b]								
1965–69	6	8	3	8	8	6	19	14
1970–74	6	9	4	9	9	6	15	18
1975–79	5	9	6	11	8	4	14	17
1980–84	6	9	7	11	8	5	15	16
1985–87	5	8	6	8	6	3	11	13

Italy							
1965–69	8	16	10	—	2	1	6	8
1970–74	7	13	8	—	4	2	8	7
1975–79	8	12	7	—	4	1	9	9
1980–84	8	11	8	1	4	2	7	10
1985–87	9	12	13	1	5	2	9	12
Portugal							
1965–69	1.5	1.3	—	—	0.4	0.1	2.3	1.5
1970–74	1.4	1.6	—	—	0.5	0.2	2.4	1.8
1975–79	1.0	1.2	0.1	—	0.4	0.1	1.7	1.8
1980–84	1.1	1.7	0.2	0.1	0.5	0.1	1.0	2.2
1985–87	1.2	2.5	0.2	0.1	0.8	0.1	1.1	2.1

[a] SITC categories are as follows: textiles 65; clothing 84; synthetic fibres 266; natural fibres 26 less 266.
[b] Based on the trade of these non-reporting countries with reporting countries, and hence excluding trade within centrally-planned Europe.
Source: International Economic Data Bank, Trade Data Tapes, Australian National University, Canberra, 1990.

Table 7.3: *Value and sources of textile and clothing imports by the European Community (excluding intra-EC trade), the United States and Japan, 1985 to 1987*
(billion US dollars and per cent)

	Textiles			Clothing		
	1985	1986	1987	1985	1986	1987
Total imports (billion US$ per year)						
EC-12[a]	6.0	7.9	10.2	7.5	10.9	15.4
United States	4.5	5.3	5.9	14.8	17.2	20.2
Japan	1.6	1.7	2.5	1.7	2.5	4.0
Percentage of imports from:						
(a) Advanced industrial economies						
EC-12[a]	44	47	43	11	11	10
United States	50	49	45	14	13	11
Japan	33	38	36	17	17	16
(b) Developing economies						
EC-12[a]	45	43	47	77	78	78
United States	42	42	46	79	76	78
Japan	42	36	39	57	61	64
(c) China alone						
EC-12[a]	6	5	6	5	5	6
United States	8	9	9	7	11	10
Japan	24	25	25	26	22	20

[a] Excluding intra-EC trade. In 1987 intra-EC trade in both textiles and clothing accounted for about 65 per cent of the EC member countries' total imports.
Source: Calculated from the Appendix Tables in the GATT document COM.TEX/W/ 210, Geneva, 5 December 1988.

quotas is not just a function of the size of the quotas, but also of the level of economic activity in the importing country: a strong import demand results in a given quantitative restriction biting more, driving up the tariff equivalent of the quota. At the same time a strong import demand also stimulates increased imports of unrestricted substitutes in production and consumption, imports from unrestricted sources of supply, and also – in the case of VERs – increases in the rent transferred to exporters (especially when exporters are clever at pricing to market). For these reasons some established textile and clothing exporters such as South Korea seem to have done quite well out of the MFA.[10]

[10] In spite of a restrictive MFA regime, the volume of Korean exports of textiles and clothing to the United States increased by 203 per cent between 1982 and 1987, while Korea's exports of all products increased by 'only' 175 per cent over the same period. Korean exporters were clever at pricing to market and in this way increased their profits per exported unit very rapidly when the appreciation of the United States dollar so permitted. They also tried to take advantage of the strong demand in the United States market through foreign investment in the Caribbean which has a trade preference arrangement with the United States – the Caribbean Basin Initiative. See Hamilton and Kim (1990).

Table 7.4: *Shares of imports in apparent clothing consumption, by source, selected industrial countries, 1985*

Imports by:	Low-cost EC[a]	Developing East Asia						All countries
		Total	China	Hong Kong	Singapore	Korea	Taiwan	
Western Europe								
France	15.9	3.2	0.8	1.0	0.1	1.1	0.2	37.1
Sweden	21.4	18.3	1.9	10.9	0.7	4.5	0.3	93.0
United Kingdom	11.3	13.5	0.4	9.2	0.2	2.0	1.2	44.0
West Germany	25.4	16.4	2.2	7.6	0.3	4.2	2.1	79.5
Average of above	18.5	12.9	1.3	7.2	0.3	3.1	0.9	63.4
United States	1.7	17.7	1.9	6.3	0.6	4.4	4.5	28.9
Japan	0.2	10.1	1.1	3.6	0.4	2.5	2.6	16.5

Share (per cent by value) of consumption imported from:

[a] Greece, Ireland, Italy, Portugal and Spain.
Source: International Economic Data Bank, Market Penetration Tapes, Canberra, 1989.

Table 7.5: *Import penetration from East Asia and elsewhere into markets for textiles and clothing in the European Community and EFTA, 1970 to 1986*
(imports as a percentage of domestic production plus imports minus exports)

	East Asia					All developing countries	All countries	All countries (net of exports)[c]
	NE Asian NIEs	China	ASEAN	Japan	All E. Asia			
EC[a]								
Textiles								
1970–73	0.7	0.3	0.0	0.3	1.4	3.4	23.2	−4.1
1974–77	1.1	0.4	0.2	0.3	2.1	5.0	29.5	−2.2
1978–81	1.2	0.7	0.4	0.5	2.8	6.5	35.6	0.3
1982–85	1.5	1.1	0.5	0.7	3.8	7.9	40.7	−0.5
1986	1.6	1.1	0.5	0.9	4.2	7.6	41.0	−1.0
Clothing								
1970–73	3.6	0.1	0.4	0.2	3.9	4.5	25.0	2.1
1974–77	6.8	0.2	1.1	0.2	7.7	10.3	37.4	8.6
1978–81	8.3	0.5	2.3	0.2	10.3	14.5	47.1	12.4
1982–85	9.4	1.1	2.3	0.2	12.2	18.8	55.6	12.5
1986	8.9	1.4	2.3	0.3	12.0	20.5	60.7	12.4
EFTA[b]								
Textiles								
1970–73	1.1	0.4	0.0	1.0	2.5	2.9	43.0	29.3
1974–77	1.5	0.5	0.2	0.7	2.9	4.4	46.0	30.2
1978–81	1.7	0.7	0.4	0.5	3.3	5.2	52.6	33.1
1982–85	2.2	1.0	0.4	0.5	4.2	6.5	58.0	35.4
1986	1.9	0.9	0.3	0.5	3.6	5.9	56.5	34.8

Clothing

1970–73	5.2	0.3	0.4	0.2	6.2	7.1	44.1	20.6
1974–77	10.0	0.6	1.1	0.2	12.0	13.5	59.0	29.2
1978–81	10.0	1.1	2.3	0.6	14.0	15.9	73.8	35.9
1982–85	11.4	1.6	2.3	0.4	15.8	18.4	79.9	44.0
1986	10.9	2.5	2.3	0.3	16.1	19.7	90.3	58.4

[a] Belgium–Luxembourg, France, West Germany, Italy, the Netherlands and the United Kingdom only.
[b] Finland, Norway and Sweden only.
[c] Imports minus exports as a percentage of domestic availability (i.e. production plus exports minus imports).
Source: See Appendix to this volume.

Table 7.6:   *Post-Tokyo Round average tariff levels for textiles and clothing, European Community and the United States* (average percentages, weighted by MFN imports)

	Fibres	Yarns	Fabrics	Made-up articles	Clothing
European Community	0.5	7.0	10.5	7.5	13.5
United States	3.5	9.0	11.5	7.5	22.5

Source: GATT (1984: Table 3.3, p. 69).

Table 7.7:   *Share of restricted imports in total imports of textiles and clothing from developing countries (the trade coverage ratio), 1987* (per cent in value terms)

	Textiles	Clothing
European Community	33	46
United States	22	77

Sources: World Bank computer files on the MFA, Washington, DC, 1989; and United Nations Statistical Office, COMTRADE database, New York, 1989.

Estimates of the import tariff equivalent (MTE) of the bilateral VERs on clothing imported from Hong Kong, Korea and India to the EC and the US are presented in Table 7.8. The calculations for Hong Kong for 1980 to 1984 are based on Hamilton (1988) and for 1985 to 1988 on new information on export quota prices in the Hong Kong market. New estimates for Korea are made through a method described in Hamilton (1988) (the so-called indirect approach, using the supply prices of Korean clothing relative to those of Hong Kong from Table 7.9 below). The estimates for India are calculated from information in Kumar and Khanna (1990). Their estimates are based on prices at government quota auctions.[11]

During the 1980s the EC's MTE on imports from Hong Kong increased, from about 8 per cent in 1980 to at most 21 per cent in 1986. During 1986–88 the restrictiveness of the Community's VERs was higher than the average of the 1980s. Combined with an EC tariff of approximately 17 per cent in the late 1980s, this means an even more accentuated rise in the combined trade barrier, from about 30 per cent in 1983–85 to 37 per cent in 1986–88. Korea's low supply price (80 to 85 per cent of Hong Kong's) ensured the MTE of that country's exports to the Community was higher still, but declined in

---

11 More precisely, the 1988 VER rates in Table 7.8 are based on prices at quota auctions in January and June 1988 and January 1989, and thus could be said to cover also the market prospects in the first part of 1989.

Table 7.8: *Import tariff equivalent of VERs and tariffs on clothing imported from Hong Kong, Korea and India to the EC and the US, 1980 to 1988*

	1980[a]	1981	1982	1983	1984[b]	1985[c]	1986[c]	1987[d]	1988[d]	Average
Imports to EC from										
Hong Kong										
VERs	8[d]	18	7	9	13	12	21	16	14	13
VERs and tariffs[e]	26[d]	38	25	28	32	31	42	35	34	32
Korea										
VERs			31	18	41	42	48	25		34
VERs and tariffs			70	53	65	90	73	46		57
India										
VERs									35[f]	
VERs and tariffs									58[f]	
Imports to USA from										
Hong Kong										
VERs			9	37	47		(83)[g]	(58)[g]	(30)[g]	
VERs and tariffs			30	74	87					
Korea										
VERs			30	34	97					
VERs and tariffs			69	74	156					
India										
VERs										29

[a] Refers to 2nd half only.
[b] Refers to 1st half only, and EC is approximated by Germany, UK and France.
[c] Refers to Germany, UK, France, Italy and Denmark.
[d] Refers to Germany, UK, France, Italy and Denmark. A transport cost of 7 per cent is assumed to convert Kumar–Khanna's data into MTEs (see Hamilton 1986: footnote 7).
[e] EC tariff calculated to be 17 per cent during 1980–84, 14 per cent during 1985–88.
[f] Refers to January 1988–January 1989.
[g] Based on 'sweaters' only, i.e. categories 345, 445 and 645, and thus not comparable with earlier years, hence the parentheses.

Sources: Author's calculations for Hong Kong and Korea, based on information on Hong Kong quota prices supplied by the Federation of Hong Kong Garment Manufacturers, Inter-Coop Far East Ltd and, regarding USA 1986–88, calculated from data in Silberston (1989). Korean figures derived through the 'indirect approach' of Hamilton (1988) using the supply prices of Table 7.9 below. The estimates for India calculated from information in Kumar and Khanna (1990: Table 14).

a marked way in 1987. The MTE of sweater trade from Hong Kong
to the United States shows a clear declining trend between 1986 and
1988. After a wide discrepancy in restrictiveness in the mid-1980s,
the EC's and the United States' MTEs seem to converge during the
second half of the 1980s. It seems not too wild a guess to link this
with the fall of the high value of the US dollar. Such a convergence at
the end of the 1980s is indicated also by the MTEs facing Indian
exporters in 1988–89.

EC trade policy tomorrow

Looking towards the future trade policy of the European Community,
there are three potential problems to be faced by non-European
suppliers seeking to export to the EC: anti-dumping actions; privileged
access for Turkey and Eastern Europe to EC markets; and policy
responses to protectionist pressures from within the EC. However, it
is important to begin this section by balancing a discussion of problems
of access for non-European exporters with the observation that the
success of the 1992 internal market integration program and the
liberalization of Eastern Europe may well create a region with higher
incomes and more dynamic growth. Unless protectionism in both East
and West Europe increases very dramatically, it is difficult to see how
these developments cannot but be beneficial to all, including the
external countries trading with Europe. The benefits to the rest of the
world will simply be weakened by the three potential developments
discussed in this section.

Anti-dumping

Anti-dumping actions have become a popular protectionist instrument
against imports to the EC. According to Hindley (1989), during the
1980s the EC has developed a more forceful anti-dumping technique
than the United States. An important reason for this has been the EC
Commission's difficulty in obtaining authorization for Community-
wide VERs from liberal member-countries like Germany, the Netherlands, Denmark and the UK.

On examining the EC's history of anti-dumping cases which resulted
in some sort of protective measure during 1980–85, Messerlin (1989)
found the average tariff equivalent of the measures imposed by the
EC to be 23 per cent. Typically these measures were of a price-fixing
nature, and included specific and variable duties and price or quantitative agreements – 'undertakings' – between foreign and domestic

firms. The average tariff equivalent was higher in cases concerned with imports from the Asian NIEs and China, 32 and 36 per cent respectively, and lower for imports from Japan (17 per cent). These costs are calculated to be included in the import price, and hence a tariff comes on top of the tariff-equivalent-inclusive import price. In this way the anti-dumping cost has a multiplicative effect.[12] Messerlin also found that initiations of anti-dumping investigations in the Community had the effect of sharply reducing imported volumes: down by 18 per cent the first year after the initiation, further down to two-thirds after three years and to half after five years. The Asian NIEs, however, reduced their exports less than the average.

From an exporter's point of view, a price-fixing agreement in the form of an 'undertaking' has at least the advantage of distributing the rent from protection to the exporter, just as is the case with a VER. Has this rent transfer not been observed by the authorities at the importing end, that is, by the Community? Tharakan (1989) throws light on this question. In terminating anti-dumping proceedings he investigated the EC's choice between acceptance of undertakings and imposition of definite duties collected by the Community. He found that firms from countries with a trade surplus with the EC ran a significantly higher risk of being denied the softer option of undertakings than firms from other countries. This is disturbing – and not least for many East Asian exporters – because, as Tharakan points out, individual firms cannot affect the overall trade balance of their country.

So far, textile products have not been a prime target for the EC's anti-dumping actions. About 56 per cent of the cases initiated between 1980 and 1987 concerned chemical, pulp and paper, and steel products. Textile exports were the target in eleven cases only, out of a total of 263. In ten of these eleven cases the outcome was a restrictive one: four duties, one undertaking and five so-called 'mixed measures'.[13] During this period there were no cases which involved clothing exporters.

Can one find examples of anti-dumping actions used as a substitute for VERs, as suggested by Hindley? The answer is yes. Finger and Messerlin (1989) note that the Commission used anti-dumping actions against exporters of steel from a dozen countries not covered by the EC's umbrella of steel VERs.

The above describes EC policy up to 1987; what about the future? The trend to use anti-dumping as an additional measure of protection causes concern. The number of actual cases may not be very large,

[12] If the import price is 100, the tariff equivalent of the price-fixing measure is 30 and the tariff is 10 per cent, then the combined barrier is 43 per cent (1.1x1.3=1.43).

[13] Finger and Messerlin (1989: Table 6 and Annex Table 4). 'Mixed measures correspond to cases terminated by a mix of measures taken against the various firms and/or countries involved in the antidumping action' (Messerlin 1989).

but the real sting in anti-dumping actions is probably their connection with 'voluntary' export restraints and 'voluntary' price fixing on the part of exporting firms. 'Either the authorities or domestic producers are in a position to make credible threats to foreign producers that anti-dumping duties will be imposed upon their products unless they mend their ways and behave in a more co-operative and responsible manner – that is, accept a VER or raise their prices in the EC' (Hindley 1989).

But there is also one good sign. According to Hindley and other observers, there are indications that the intensity of EC anti-dumping action has lessened under the Commission that took office in January 1989. What one can hope for is not so much that the existing anti-dumping legislation is reversed in a more liberal direction, but rather that it is exploited in a less protectionist fashion in the years ahead.

New suppliers with privileged access

The Asian suppliers of textile products are close to the base of the EC's pyramid of privilege. Today their products would be highly competitive in the Community if they had been allowed free access. But Asian penetration into West European markets during the 1990s will depend critically on improved access being extended in a selective and guaranteed manner to new, non-Asian, suppliers.

In considering possible reshufflings within the Community's pyramid of privileges during the 1990s, it is helpful to look at Table 7.9. This shows an index of some selected exporting countries' supply prices of clothing, relative to the supply price of Hong Kong. The index was constructed in the following way: first, data were collected on 'compensation cost for production workers' involved in local clothing production. This labour cost to the firm was then adjusted for inter-country differences in labour productivity, by calculating the value of output per operator and hour.[14] Suppose we observe a narrowing of the gap between, say, Portugal and Hong Kong, as is the case in Table 7.9. How should one interpret such a development? The most obvious explanations are increases (decreases) in the Portuguese wages (labour productivity) relative to those of Hong Kong, but it can also be the result of a relatively faster upgrading of apparel quality in Portugal.

---

14 Our measure differs from the one used by Trela and Whalley (1988b, 1990) in that this measure refers to clothing only, account is taken of the fact that the number of hours per worker and year is quite different in different countries, and, thirdly, that the 'compensation cost' includes any social charges etc., which differ between countries and are more important in more developed economies.

Table 7.9: *Indexes of estimated relative costs of clothing*
production, selected countries, 1982 to 1987
(Hong Kong = 100)

	1982	1983	1984	1985	1986	1987	Average
Hong Kong	100	100	100	100	100	100	100
South Korea	80	89	73	79	82	93	83
Hungary	67	70	71	63	69	62	67
Portugal	100	107	94	87	93	111p	99
Spain	114	120	121	145	..	..	..
Turkey[a]	47	32	28	26	27p	27p	31

[a] Only in the case of Turkey is there a significant time trend, namely –3 points per year.
p = Preliminary figure.
Sources: US Department of Labor, Bureau of Labor Statistics, 'International comparisons of hourly compensation costs for production workers in manufacturing', Washington, DC, unpublished background data, 1987, except for Hungary, Turkey and Portugal which are calculated from UN, *Yearbook of Industrial Statistics*, New York, 1985, OECD, *Industrial Structure Statistics*, Paris, 1986, and from national statistics for 1986 and 1987.

The countries in Table 7.9 are of three kinds. The first is the established Asian exporters, Hong Kong and Korea, which are faced with both VERs and tariffs in the Community. Second, there are low-cost producers with guaranteed free access to the EC-EFTA market, namely, Portugal and Spain. Of these, Portugal is the more interesting country from the point of view of Asian competitors. In addition to being a competitive supplier during the 1980s, as indicated in Table 7.9, the Portuguese clothing industry may not have reached its full export potential yet, as the country has only been an EC member since 1985 and is still adjusting to new market opportunities made available by having joined.

Third, there are countries that are likely to be allowed better access for their textile exports to the Community during the 1990s, such as Turkey and the liberalizing countries of Eastern Europe. Today Turkey is quantitatively restricted in its textile and clothing exports to the EC, and also to several EFTA countries – restrictions that are not covered by the MFA.[15] Turkey has actively been seeking full and immediate membership in the Community, but for a variety of political and economic reasons in 1989 it was denied and put on hold for the time being. One important reason for the delay is fear of a large inflow of migrants from Turkey.[16] To say 'no' to Turkey's application for

15 The United States, by contrast, does restrict imports from Turkey under the MFA.

16 Turkey has about 50 million inhabitants, and Italy, the United Kingdom, France and Germany each have between 55 and 61 million. GNP in Turkey is $1110 as compared with $8500–$12,000 in the above-mentioned EC countries (in 1986 US dollars).

membership is an awkward decision politically for the Community, because when it was granted 'associate' membership there was mention of full membership to be considered for the year 1997. Because of this, and since the Community (particularly Germany) finds it unacceptable to have a free inflow of Turkish citizens, it is fairly safe to forecast that the EC during the 1990s will at least allow a free inflow of Turkish goods, including textile and clothing products. Judging from Table 7.9, Turkey will be a formidable competitor with Asian producers in the EC market. Even if one is sceptical about the exact magnitude of the Turkish cost advantage, indications regarding its competitiveness are also revealed by Turkish production and export figures. From 1978 to 1985 the volume of Turkish clothing production increased over tenfold, from 4.8 to 54 billion Turkish liras (in 1978 prices). Exports of clothing took off in the early 1980s, and between 1981 and 1987 the volume of clothing exports increased by 574 per cent. Of total clothing exports in 1987, 77 per cent were destined for the EC.

The second potential new source of competing imports will be from the countries of Eastern Europe. There are very strong motives behind the West European countries' support of political and economic liberalization in Eastern Europe. These developments have already been enhanced by trade preferences. All the East European countries are negotiating and implementing new and more liberal institutional trade arrangements with the EC and, in some cases, with GATT. Beginning in 1995 at the very latest, manufactured imports by the EC at least from Hungary, Czechoslovakia and Poland will be freed from all of today's quantitative restrictions, including those on textile products. There will be free trade in 1990 for those textile and clothing products which are not covered by the MFA classification. All the East European countries have asked for a quicker implementation of the liberalization. Eastern Germany is in an exceptional position, since it has had a history of enjoying free access to former West Germany for its goods.[17] (Also, West German textile firms used to have labour-intensive offshore processing in former East Germany.) Former East Germany's privileged access will be extended step by step during the next few years to the rest of the Community and will have been abolished in 1992. In any case, eastern Germany will be the East European economy with the best preconditions for increased textile and clothing exports to the EC-EFTA countries, as a consequence of

[17] The reason for this was political, of course. The formal basis for the arrangement was that both East and West Germany were regarded as being within the 1938 German customs union (*Zollverein*) and common market. The integration has occurred spontaneously and very rapidly so that this old agreement is now irrelevant.

likely substantial financial and technological support from the western part of Germany.[18]

Of the East European countries, it was possible to estimate only Hungary's supply price for Table 7.9 because of the difficulty of finding realistic exchange rates for the other countries. Clearly, if the supply-side constraints are removed in Hungary, it could become a competitive exporter in the EC-EFTA market.

Finally, with enhanced domestic supply-side policies, countries like Egypt, Morocco, Tunisia and Israel also have the potential to increase exports of textile products, provided the Community continues to treat them in a relatively favourable way. However, such treatment certainly cannot be taken for granted.

Protectionist pressures from within the EC

What external trade policy will the EC pursue on completion of its 1992 integration program? As we have seen from Table 7.9, some of the low-cost producers in the 'sun belt' of the EC, like Portugal, have supply prices that are close to those of major Asian exporters. These low-cost producers within the EC have an incentive to lobby Brussels to keep out textile products from all external sources of supply, including Asia.

It is unlikely that the 'sun-belt' protectionists (France, Italy, Portugal and Spain) would be able to hamper significantly an opening towards Eastern Europe. The political costs to them would be large. It would involve a clash with Germany in a policy area of very high priority, and also with the other 'frost-belt' liberals (Denmark, Netherlands, Luxembourg and the UK). Moreover, especially for countries like Italy and Greece where the overall benefits from enhanced economic and political liberalization in Eastern Europe are so large, the domestic political costs of increased imports of textile products from Eastern Europe relative to the non-economic benefits would be minor in the overall calculation.

The Rome Treaty was amended by the Single European Act in 1987, the most important innovation being the widespread adoption of qualified majority voting (Wolf 1989: 13). Whereas before the Single Act there had to be formal consensus among EC member countries, since 1987 only a qualified majority is needed on a vast number of issues, for example on issues related to external trade policy

18 This capital inflow is likely to be at the expense of German capital going to other parts of the Community, e.g. Spain and Portugal. The import policies of the EFTA countries *vis-à-vis* Eastern Europe are at least as liberal as those of the EC, and in some cases more liberal – especially the policy of Finland.

and the common agricultural policy and on how the 1992 program is to be implemented (excluding issues related to taxation).[19] Before the Single Act, voting was rare. Now it is used to an increasing degree, and even when explicit voting does not take place, countries are adopting diplomatic behavioural norms to that effect as a method to reach decisions.

> Thus negotiations over the Common Agricultural Policy and the external trade policy of the EC now regularly rely on the possibility and practice of voting . . . Under the Dutch presidency in the first semester of 1986, over forty decisions were reached by voting, and over fifty during the subsequent British presidency. Though formally only ministers vote, in practice committees of senior officials often implicitly anticipate them . . . [So] the language of the negotiations is now the language of voting. Officials and even occasionally ministers are prepared to use the vocabulary of majorities and minorities. Thus, for example, in the debate about how open or closed the external trade stance of the EC is likely to be, there are 'blocking minorities' both protectionists and liberals, with outcomes thus depending on the attitudes of the median group, individual issue by individual issue (Wallace 1989: 37).

With the present membership of twelve countries, a qualified majority means 71 per cent of the votes.[20] Together there are in total 76 votes: Belgium 5, Denmark 3, West Germany 10, Greece 5, Spain 8, France 10, Ireland 3, Italy 10, Luxembourg 2, the Netherlands 5, Portugal 5, and the United Kingdom 10.

To get an indication of the relative strength of the 'frost-belt' liberals and the 'sun-belt' protectionists, three voting procedures on the question of external textile trade policy are simulated. Naturally, a simulated voting procedure rests on important simplifications. First, each member country's position reflects that of its government,which could be a strong national coalition or a weak one. Second, one may wonder whether it is reasonable to assume that an external trade policy issue can be analysed in isolation from other issues. Is it not the case that negotiators package their deals? An important reason for not seeking a package deal in the first instance is that once a member country starts to widen the menu of issues in a negotiation it also takes a risk: it must weigh the benefit of hoping to reach a good package deal against the cost of losing some – or all – control over the agenda of issues in the continued negotiations. The other party's menu of reaction possibilities increases dramatically when new issues are thrown into a negotiation. However, in recent years package deals

[19] The body in which voting can take place is the EC's lawmaking body, the Council of Ministers, where member countries' ministers represent national governments.

[20] In principle, member countries have votes in relation to their population, but with the very important modification that all smaller countries have more votes per capita. In Denmark there are 1.7 million citizens per EC-vote, in Belgium 2.0 and in the Netherlands 2.9, compared with 6.1 in West Germany, 5.5 in France, and 5.7 in the UK.

in the EC have become more common and 'there is formidable evidence now accumulated that it is common for bargains to take place across issue areas and on the basis of future expectations' (Wallace 1989: 5). For this reason, the discussion below allows for the possibility of so-called side payments.

To investigate the future conflicts of interest over the EC's external trade policy, the following procedure is used. First, the countries' positions on external openness and support for multilateral free trade generally are identified (Table 7.10). Next, the countries' positions are investigated with regard to imports of clothing from countries with no preferential status, such as those in Asia and the Americas (Table 7.11). In each one of the simulations the EC countries are identified as either 'For', 'Against', or 'Unclear' in their position. In the third simulation, the issue of external trade policy is investigated under the assumption that some EFTA countries become members of the Community during the 1990s (Table 7.12).

In the left-hand column of Table 7.10 one can see that, on the issue of external openness, five countries have been classified as 'For', namely, Denmark (DK), West Germany (D), Luxembourg (L), the Netherlands (NL), and the United Kingdom (UK). The countries judged to be clearly 'Against' are France (F), Spain (E), Italy (I) and Portugal (P). In a first phase of the negotiations Ireland (IRL), Belgium (B) and Greece (GR) are regarded as 'Unclear'. This label has no deeper meaning than that these countries have been difficult to classify.

The allocation of countries into slots has been made from the literature on EC trade policy and from unstructured interviews with diplomats, political scientists, correspondents in Brussels, and observers of EC politics in Copenhagen. In fact, the classification of countries into 'For' and 'Against' proved to be a fairly uncontroversial task, especially since differences of opinion over a country's position resulted in the country being put among the 'Unclear' ones. The tables also show the countries' shares of total GNP of the EC. This information serves as an indication of a coalition's capacity to pay side payments to 'Unclear' countries or to countries with an opposite view.

From the first simulation it can be seen that a first round of voting (phase I) produces a qualified majority of neither 'For' nor 'Against', both sides reaching blocking minority positions. In phase II it is assumed that, through side payments, the support from the 'Unclear' countries goes to 'For' (an assumption biased, of course, in favour of external openness of the Community). Nevertheless, even with this assumption, the two blocking minorities remain, and the margins required to reach any qualified majority are wide. To outsiders such as the Asian countries and the United States, this result significantly implies that there is a pro-openness minority that can block increased protection against the rest of the world, but it cannot enforce increased external openness of the EC.

Table 7.10: *Conflicts of interests over EC external openness*

	Phase I				Phase II		
	Share of GNP	Votes	Qualified majority[a]	Blocking minority[b]	'Unclear' to 'For'	Qualified majority[a]	Blocking minority[b]
'For' (DK,D,L,NL,UK)	51	30	No	Yes	43	No	Yes
'Unclear' (IRL,B,GR)	5	13		}			
'Against' (F,E,I,P)	44	33	No	Yes	33	No	Yes
	100	76					

Source: Author's simulation of voting behaviour.

[a] For a qualified majority, 54 votes are required.
[b] For a blocking minority, 23 votes are required.

Table 7.11: *Conflicts of interests over liberalization of EC clothing imports from non-preferential areas*

	Phase I				Phase II			Phase III		
	Share of GNP	Votes	Qualified majority[a]	Blocking minority[b]	B,E,F to 'For'	Qualified majority[a]	Blocking minority[b]	Either IRL,P, or GR to 'For'	Qualified majority[a]	Blocking minority[b]
'For' (DK,D,L,NL,UK)	51	30	No	Yes	53	No	Yes	54<	Yes	Yes
'Unclear' (B,E,F)	29	23								
'Against' (I,IRL,P,GR)	20	23	No	Yes	23	No	Yes	<23	No	No
	100	76								

Source: Author's simulation of voting behaviour.

[a] For a qualified majority, 54 votes are required.
[b] For a blocking minority, 23 votes are required.

Table 7.12: *Consequences of including EFTA members in the EC for conflicts of interests over external openness of an enlarged EC-16[a]*

	Phase I				Phase II		
	Share of GNP	Votes	Qualified majority	Blocking minority	'Unclear' to 'For'	Qualified majority	Blocking minority
'For' (DK,D,L,NL,UK,A,IC,N,S)	54	44	No	Yes ⎫	57	No	Yes
'Unclear' (IRL,B,GR)	5	13		⎬			
'Against' (F,E,I,P)	$\frac{41}{100}$	$\frac{33}{90}$	No	No	33	No	Yes

[a] Assumed votes of new members:

Norway (N)   3
Austria (A)   4
Sweden (S)   5
Iceland (IC) 2
              ‾‾
             14

Total number of votes is therefore 76 + 14 = 90. Thus a qualified majority of 71 per cent is 64 votes and a blocking minority requires 27 votes.

Source: Author's simulation of voting behaviour.

The next simulation (Table 7.11) involves liberalization of clothing imports to the Community. As above, even if all 'Unclear' countries (Belgium, Spain, France) are brought over to 'For' in Phase II there is still no qualified majority for liberalization. However, the margin is the smallest possible, one vote only, and if in Phase III side payments are used to bring over one of Ireland, Greece or Portugal there would be a qualified majority for liberalized imports of clothing. Clearly transfers from the 'frost-belt' liberals, and the stance of France, would be crucial in this situation.

In the third simulation (Table 7.12) it is assumed that the coalition of liberal countries is augmented through new membership of all EFTA countries except Finland and Switzerland. The total number of votes is increased to 90 and so a qualified majority, which is still assumed to require 71 per cent of the total vote, means at least 64 votes.[21] Despite the inclusion of the liberal EFTA countries, the result from the first simulation basically remains intact: neither party masters a qualified majority, and there are two blocking minorities. But for the 'frost-belt' liberals the distance to a qualified majority is now considerably shorter. France will again have the power to swing the outcome either way. In fact, an important insight gained from the last two simulations is the power of France over the Community's future external trade policy.

Conclusions

Important changes are taking place in Europe which have implications also for countries outside the Community. First, in so far as the EC's 1992 integration program and the post-1989 liberalizations of Eastern Europe succeed, this will mean higher incomes and more dynamism in the economies of Europe. Unless Europe becomes significantly more protectionist – which would be against the trend of the East European countries, and not in the interest of the blocking minority of the 'frost-belt' liberal EC countries – these developments will result in higher European demand for textiles and clothing and possibly more competitive European export supplies of these products. The former could benefit non-European textile exporters, while the latter would benefit non-European consumers but only to the extent that the governments of external countries allow enhanced European competitiveness to be reflected in lower prices to their consumers.

---

21 The new members' number of votes is derived from comparisons of population and income size with present members. Norway is assumed to receive the same number of votes, 3, as it negotiated in 1971, Austria and Sweden are assumed to receive 4 and 5 votes, respectively, through comparisons with Belgium, the Netherlands and Spain, and Iceland is assumed to receive 2, the same number as Luxembourg.

Second, for non-European exporters three 'threats' have been analysed. One is that, during the 1980s, the Community's anti-dumping legislation was used to an increasing extent as a protectionist instrument against the rest of the world, and as a substitute for Community-wide VERs. The second is that textile exporters in Asia, America and elsewhere will probably have to cope with favourable discrimination towards Turkey and the East European countries through improved access to the EC for their products. Finally, an analysis of future conflicts of interest, between the Community's 'frost-belt' liberals and 'sun-belt' protectionists, suggests there will be a blocking minority to prevent increased external protection, and that the position of France could be crucial in the formulation of the EC's external trade policy. During the 1990s, free-trade lobbyists may find they have to be as active in Paris as they are in Brussels.

8

The redirection of United States imports

Joseph Pelzman*

Since its establishment as a temporary trade measure on 1 January 1974 the MFA has gone through four refinements. The latest extension, referred to as MFA IV, became effective on 1 August 1986 and is scheduled to expire on 31 July 1991. This extension expanded the coverage of the MFA from textiles and clothing of cotton, wool and man-made fibres to include products of silk blends and of non-cotton vegetable fibres. As of 16 December 1988, MFA IV had been signed by 39 countries, including the US, and the EC as a single signatory.

During 1988 the United States had bilateral textile agreements with 43 countries and 2 US possessions. All but 15 per cent of the volume of US textile and clothing imports were from MFA signatories. Of the countries with which the United States had bilateral agreements, the leading suppliers were China, Taiwan, Korea and Hong Kong. Together these four accounted for 41 per cent of all US imports of textiles and clothing. In the same year the GATT reached the mid-point of the Uruguay Round, the eighth round of multilateral trade negotiations conducted since its inception. Much of the work related to trade in textiles in the GATT during 1988 focused on reviewing proposals to establish 'techniques and modalities' which would permit integrating the sector into the GATT. These discussions are expected to continue for some time with minimal results. This pessimistic conclusion is based on the recent record of the US in monitoring and controlling textile and clothing imports from all suppliers, and especially from its leading suppliers.

This chapter deals with three central issues concerning US imports of textiles and apparel from East Asia. The first is the positive question regarding the effects of the MFA on the direction and composition of East Asian textile and clothing exports to the United States. This requires focusing predominantly on the role of the bilateral agreements

* This is a revised version of a CIES Seminar Paper (Pelzman 1989c).

as instruments affecting East Asian exports. The second is the normative question concerning the costs of this restrictive system of trade quotas. And the third issue is a policy one concerning the future of this trade instrument in the context of recent discussions on establishing 'techniques and modalities' which would permit the integration of this sector into the GATT.

The chapter is planned so that the first section summarizes the development process of the US bilateral control system up to the current 1984–88 bilateral agreements, and the complexity of the US textile trade agreements are discussed in the second. The performance of each of the Asian textile exporters over the 1976–88 period are then analysed in the third section. The prospects for liberalized textile and clothing trade, following the mid-term review of the Uruguay Round, are discussed in the final section which also presents recent estimates of the welfare costs of the US bilateral restraint program.

Major provisions of the current Multi-fibre Arrangement

The MFA authorizes contracting importing countries to limit textile imports through unilateral restraints and permits the negotiation of bilateral restraint agreements. In effect, these agreements sanction country-by-country discriminatory trade restraints, unlike the GATT's unconditional most-favoured-nation principle. Furthermore, all of these agreements grant semi-permanent quotas rather than the temporary quotas provided for in GATT safeguard mechanisms.[1]

The MFA provides a framework for the negotiation of bilateral agreements between importing and exporting countries (Article 4), or for unilateral action by importing countries in the absence of an agreement (Article 3), to control textile and clothing trade among its signatories and prevent market disruption. On 31 July 1986, negotiators from major textile-importing and textile-exporting countries agreed to a protocol extending the MFA for a fourth time, through to 31 July 1991.

The 1986 protocol expands the product coverage of the MFA to include silk, linen, ramie and jute, and further expands the right of

[1] The history of the MFA and its predecessor agreements have been sufficiently documented in the literature and need not be repeated here. A chronology of these agreements includes: 1957 – Japanese voluntary export controls on cotton products; 1961–62 – Short Term Cotton Arrangement (STA); 1962–73 – Long Term Arrangement on Cotton Textiles (LTA); 1974–77 – Multifibre Arrangement (MFA I); 1978–81 – MFA II; 1982–86 – MFA III; 1986–91 – MFA IV. Those unfamiliar with this history might consult Keesing and Wolf (1980) or USITC (1978).

importing countries to restrict imports. With the inclusion of silk and vegetable fibres, the United States has temporarily eliminated the possibility of having trade diverted into non-MFA fibres. The 1986 protocol also includes statements of principles or guidelines to be used in administering the Arrangement. These relate to appropriate measures of market disruption, imposition of unilateral restraints, levels of growth and flexibility, under-utilized quotas, special treatment for certain countries such as new suppliers, circumvention of quotas, and other areas of concern to participants.

The mechanism most used by the United States to control imports of textiles and clothing under the provisions of the MFA is the negotiation of bilateral agreements with exporting countries under Article 4. These bilateral agreements have increased in number since the MFA was established in 1974 and have become more detailed and comprehensive in terms of setting specific limits on individual product categories. In late 1977 the United States had agreements limiting imports with 18 countries, in mid-1984 there were agreements with 28 countries, and by 1988 there were agreements with more than 40 countries.

Some agreements set limits on both specific categories and groups of categories. Most agreements provide that the United States may request consultations on additional categories if imports of these products are disrupting the domestic market and may unilaterally limit imports in the 'called' category during negotiations. The MFA specifies that unilateral limits shall not be less than actual imports in a recent 12-month period and that, other than in exceptional cases, an annual increase of 6 per cent shall be allowed. However, bilateral agreements may specify growth rates other than 6 per cent and recent US bilateral agreements with major suppliers such as Hong Kong, Korea and Taiwan provide for growth rates that are substantially less than 6 per cent.

Currently, 147 individual categories have been established for purposes of setting restraint levels for US imports. These categories comprise groupings of numbers in the tariff schedule of the US and in the annotated Harmonized Tariff Schedules (HTS) which became effective on 1 January 1989. The number of categories under restraint varies widely from country to country: some large suppliers may have as many as 100 categories under restraint but some new or smaller suppliers may have fewer than a dozen categories.[2]

Overall, MFA IV has met the official US objectives in that the

[2] Given the nature of the MFA bilateral agreements, the textile categories referred to are fibre-based rather than industry-based. As a result of the unique nature of the MFA, there is a problem in matching the textile categories used to monitor and restrict textile and clothing imports with the Standard Industrial Classification nomenclature used to measure output. Given the weakness of the domestic output data, summary information concerning import penetration rates is suspect and therefore not provided here.

current textile agreement has (i) provided for controls on products made of fibres not covered in the existing MFA (silk and non-cotton vegetable fibres), (ii) included provisions preventing 'surges' in imports, and (iii) lowered the growth rates for major suppliers. Nevertheless, some US textile interests in industry and in the Congress continue to press for more stringent measures such as limiting total imports of textiles and clothing to a growth rate equal to the growth in the domestic market, allowing reductions or 'roll-backs' of imports from predominant suppliers, and allowing strong unilateral action against countries that circumvent quotas.

Bilateral US textile agreements

The bilateral agreements negotiated by the United States are in general very comprehensive. These agreements restrain textile and clothing imports under a variety of quota instruments, varying by degree of restrictiveness. At the most restrictive end there are specific limits, which are upper-bound quotas, and at the least restrictive end are consultation levels which serve as trigger boundaries in anticipation of damage. In between these two extremes there are designated consultation levels, minimum consultation levels, agreed limits, restraint limits, 'export' type consultation provisions applicable to Hong Kong, Taiwan and Korea, guaranteed access levels, and other miscellaneous limits. Over time, the US bilateral agreements have evolved to include a larger number of specific limits and fewer consultation provisions. In 1989, specific limits affected 61 per cent of all US textile and clothing imports.

During the 1984–88 period, apart from the specific limits imposed on the new categories, the addition of a growing list of partial and combined categories could also be observed. The preponderance of partial and combined categories, in effect, converts the system of controls from 147 individual categories to a total of 706 categories. While the number of controlled items does not by itself designate the degree of restrictiveness, it is nevertheless a sign of the growing specificity of US bilateral agreements. The majority of these restrictions apply to clothing where imports are notable. For cotton, 59 categories cover textile products while 199 cover clothing; for wool, 9 categories cover textiles and 44 clothing; for man-made fibres, 83 categories cover textiles and 228 clothing. Given that the textile monitoring program is by nature *ex post*, the distribution of quota categories signifies that the US is protecting its current list of non-competitive domestic apparel manufacturers.

Table 8.1 provides a summary of the bilateral agreements of Hong

Table 8.1: *Textile and clothing import quotas, United States, 1984 to 1988* (million square yard equivalents and per cent)

	Northeast Asian NIEs						Share of total (%) for		
	China	Hong Kong	Korea	Taiwan	Japan	Total	China	Northeast Asian NIEs	Japan
1984									
Cotton and man-made yarn textiles	—	—	—	—	—	—	—	—	—
Cotton and man-made yarn clothing	—	—	—	—	—	—	—	—	—
Cotton textiles	234	146	142	201	—	1422	16	34	—
Cotton clothing	178	483	44	111	74	1986	9	32	4
Wool textiles	2	—	4	—	15	28	7	16	53
Wool clothing	8	40	15	5	4	105	8	57	4
Man-made fibre textiles	24	3	144	45	279	644	4	30	43
Man-made fibre clothing	178	318	645	1501	5	4075	4	60	—
Silk blend, linen and ramie textiles	—	—	—	—	—	—	—	—	—
Silk blend, linen and ramie clothing	—	—	—	—	—	—	—	—	—
1985									
Cotton and man-made yarn textiles	—	—	—	—	—	—	—	—	—
Cotton and man-made yarn clothing	—	—	—	—	—	—	—	—	—
Cotton textiles	266	149	151	209	25	1714	15	30	1
Cotton clothing	257	489	72	166	58	2098	12	35	3
Wool textiles	4	—	5	7	15	32	13	14	47
Wool clothing	9	40	15	7	3	111	8	56	3
Man-made fibre textiles	27	3	159	61	255	689	4	33	37
Man-made fibre clothing	250	305	649	1005	20	3768	7	52	1
Silk blend, linen and ramie textiles	—	—	—	—	—	—	—	—	—
Silk blend, linen and ramie clothing	—	—	—	—	—	—	—	—	—

1986

Cotton and man-made yarn textiles	—	—	—	—	—	—	—	—	—
Cotton and man-made yarn clothing	—	—	—	—	—	—	—	—	—
Cotton textiles	276	167	153	215	96	2022	14	26	5
Cotton clothing	317	496	71	169	77	2373	13	23	3
Wool textiles	2	—	5	—	11	27	8	17	40
Wool clothing	10	41	15	7	3	119	9	53	3
Man-made fibre textiles	31	3	155	64	282	795	4	32	35
Man-made fibre clothing	351	330	663	1030	26	3910	9	52	1
Silk blend, linen and ramie textiles	—	—	—	—	—	—	—	—	—
Silk blend, linen and ramie clothing	38	79	105	17	—	354	11	57	—

1987

Cotton and man-made yarn textiles	—	—	—	—	—	—	—	—	—
Cotton and man-made yarn clothing	—	—	—	—	—	—	—	—	—
Cotton textiles	305	170	157	214	91	2013	15	27	5
Cotton clothing	343	498	75	166	78	2556	13	29	3
Wool textiles	2	—	4	—	10	26	8	18	40
Wool clothing	10	41	15	7	3	118	8	53	3
Man-made fibre textiles	32	3	159	61	260	744	4	30	35
Man-made fibre clothing	388	334	668	1056	27	4098	9	50	1
Silk blend, linen and ramie textiles	—	—	—	—	—	—	—	—	—
Silk blend, linen and ramie clothing	53	190	188	42	—	492	11	85	—

1988

Cotton and man-made yarn textiles	28	160	43	106	35	1060	3	29	3
Cotton and man-made yarn clothing	13	31	0	18	3	110	12	45	3
Cotton textiles	313	26	144	151	90	2268	14	14	4
Cotton clothing	385	477	78	170	80	3316	12	22	2
Wool textiles	2	—	5	—	11	39	6	12	28
Wool clothing	13	41	15	7	3	124	10	52	3
Man-made fibre textiles	64	2	140	40	257	1040	6	18	25
Man-made fibre clothing	419	339	774	1103	22	4855	9	46	—
Silk blend, linen and ramie textiles	—	—	—	—	—	5	—	—	—
Silk blend, linen and ramie clothing	121	174	200	42	—	705	17	59	—

(cont'd)

Table 8.1: *(cont'd)*

		Northeast Asian NIEs				Total	Share of total (%) for		
	China	Hong Kong	Korea	Taiwan	Japan		China	Northeast Asian NIEs	Japan
1986–88 average									
Textiles									
man-made fibre	42	3	151	55	266	860	5	24	31
wool	2	—	5	—	11	30	7	16	36
other	307	174	166	229	92	2459	12	23	4
total	351	177	322	284	369	3349	10	23	11
Clothing									
man-made fibre	386	334	702	1063	25	4288	9	50	1
wool	11	41	15	7	3	120	9	53	3
other	424	648	239	206	78	3302	13	33	2
total	821	1023	956	1276	106	7710	11	42	1

Source: Office of Textiles and Apparel, International Trade Administration, US Department of Commerce, Washington, DC.

Kong, Korea, China, Taiwan and Japan, aggregated by major product groupings. The first observation to be made from the data is that East Asia's developing economies are dominant quota holders, with one-third of the textile quotas and half the clothing quotas. As well, Japan holds a third of the quotas for capital-intensive man-made and wool textiles (see bottom of Table 8.1). However, as noted elsewhere in this volume, the predominant position of Japan and East Asia's NIEs has been declining somewhat in all product groups while China's shares have been increasing.

A review of bilateral US–Hong Kong textile agreements to date demonstrates that the degree of flexibility has been substantially reduced with MFA IV. Furthermore, with the signing of the 1986 agreement a number of silk items were added, to be followed in 1988 by a number of combined yarn items. Overall, with the exception of the new series where growth in limits was tangible, the other categories had limits growing at rates substantially less than 6 per cent. According to 1988 US Customs data, Hong Kong was within 5 per cent of filling most of its quotas. This contrasts with Japan where, in 1988, fulfilment levels in broadcloth, sateens, art fabric and polyester fabric were above 80 per cent but its level of fulfilment in the other categories was substantially below 50 per cent.

Korea is the third largest textile exporter to the United States. Its bilateral agreements are much more extensive both in coverage and in their limited growth rate. In addition to specific limits the current Korean bilateral agreement includes group limits on miscellaneous yarn and fabric, clothing, silk sweaters, silk blends and luggage of all fibres. This agreement controls 9 cotton and 13 man-made textile categories as well as 21 cotton, 15 wool and 32 man-made clothing categories. In the majority of categories under restriction in 1988, over 90 per cent of the quotas were filled.

During the 1984–88 period the Korean quotas increased by an average of 5 per cent per year. (This average may be somewhat misleading given the varied flexibility in each of the categories.) Quotas for Hong Kong grew at 6 per cent and those for China at 12 per cent. By way of contrast, the Japanese quotas actually declined by an average of 3 per cent over the same period.

Given the now predominant position of China as the biggest textile and clothing exporter to the United States it is not surprising to find the large number of categories under specific limits. The United States current agreement with China is the third to be signed since 1980. It limits the export of 18 fibre and fabric categories, 5 yarn categories, 10 new silk categories and 83 clothing categories. In the majority of categories covered by specific limits, China completely filled its quota. Moreover, following the 12 per cent growth rate of China's quotas over the 1984–88 period, the degree of flexibility in 1988 was severely restricted. This was in large measure due to industry pressure in the US to limit exports from China.

Taiwan has the honour of being the second-largest textile and clothing exporter to the United States despite a highly restrictive agreement. Of the total items covered in the current agreement, 16 encompass textile fabrics and fibres, 8 cover new yarn categories and 2 cover new silk-blend clothing. Of the remaining controls, 63 categories cover clothing exports. Taiwan typically fills more than 95 per cent of its quotas.

Trends in East Asian textile exports to the United States

The discussion thus far has focused on the trend in the bilateral textile agreements of each of the five East Asian exporters. One could conclude from this discussion that the bilateral agreements under MFA IV are far more restrictive than the agreements under MFA I, MFA II and MFA III. Nevertheless, despite these more restrictive bilaterals, imports of textiles and clothing have been increasing, at least until 1988 when more restrictive restraints and currency realignments slowed the growth in the volume of textile and clothing imports.

Table 8.2 summarizes the trend in US textile and clothing imports from Northeast Asia and elsewhere over the 1976–88 period. As one might expect, Japan's import volume and share have been declining rapidly, the volumes of imports from East Asia's NIEs have been rising but their shares of total US imports have been falling slightly, while China's volume and share have been rising extremely rapidly. The growth in the volume of US imports from China averaged 20 per cent per year between 1976 and 1988, which boosted China's volume share of US imports from 3 per cent in 1976 to 12.5 per cent by 1988. The share of US import volume from the rest of the world grew also, but at the much more moderate rate of 2.6 per cent per year compared with 12 per cent for China.

Also shown in Table 8.2 are the import shares in terms of dollar values. Notice that the rate of decline in the value share is the same as for the volume share for Japan but is slower for the Asian NIEs. Moreover, the rate of increase in the value share is much faster than the increase in the volume share for China while for the rest of the world it is slower. This comparison suggests that, relative to the rest of the world, the Asian NIEs and especially China have been improving the quality (as reflected in price per square yard equivalent) of their exports to the United States.

Table 8.2:   *Volume and share of US imports of textiles and clothing from Northeast Asia and the world, 1976 to 1988*

	1976[a]	1979	1982	1985	1988	Growth rate (% p.a.)
Volume (million square yard equivalents)						
China	152	231	670	1049	1607	19.9
Hong Kong	851	812	843	1296	1074	1.8
Korea	590	503	764	1285	1210	5.7
Taiwan	597	612	938	1646	1385	6.7
Japan	747	492	511	732	430	−4.2
Rest of world	2050	1998	2209	5412	7144	11.0
World total	4987	4648	5935	11420	12850	7.6
Share (% of volume of total US textile and clothing imports)						
China	3.0	5.0	11.3	9.2	12.5	11.5
Hong Kong	17.1	17.5	14.2	11.4	8.4	−5.3
Korea	11.8	10.8	12.9	11.3	9.4	−1.7
Taiwan	12.0	13.2	15.8	14.4	10.8	−0.8
Japan	15.0	10.6	8.6	6.4	3.3	−10.9
Rest of world	41.1	43.0	37.2	47.4	55.6	2.6
World total	100.0	100.0	100.0	100.0	100.0	
Share (% of value of total US textile and clothing imports)						
China	1.1	1.8	8.6	7.4	9.6	21.8
Hong Kong	23.0	21.5	20.2	18.7	14.3	−4.3
Korea	12.0	11.3	13.6	12.3	11.4	−0.4
Taiwan	13.8	14.0	16.5	14.3	12.7	−0.7
Japan	11.5	10.9	7.6	6.0	3.2	−10.9
Rest of world	38.6	40.5	33.5	41.2	48.8	2.3
World total	100.0	100.0	100.0	100.0	100.0	

[a] The value shares in column 1 refer to 1978, not 1976.
Source: Office of Textiles and Apparel, International Trade Administration, US Department of Commerce, Washington, DC.

Clearly the aggregate share of US imports of textiles and clothing from Northeast Asia fell over the decade to 1988. China's dramatic entry into this market was not enough to offset the decline in the Asian NIEs' shares as well as Japan's. In 1982 Northeast Asia supplied two-thirds of the value of US imports of textiles and clothing, but by 1988 this was down to just over half.

The increase in the share of imports from China at the expense of the Asian NIEs and Japan is very largely due to the changing bilateral arrangements discussed above. The data in Table 8.2 point to the limited effectiveness of the US quota system in controlling imports from the Asian suppliers. Despite the rigorous controls imposed on the leading exporters, the exports of textiles and clothing have not declined. They have, however, been diverted to a small extent both in value and quality terms to the next generation of exporters, the most notable being China.

Table 8.3: *Import penetration from East Asia and elsewhere into markets for textiles, clothing and all manufactures in the United States and all industrial economies, 1970 to 1986 (imports as a percentage of domestic consumption)*

	Share of United States sales from:							Share of all industrial market economies' sales from:						
	NE Asian NIEs	China	ASEAN	Japan	All East Asia	All developing countries	All developing countries	NE Asian NIEs	China	ASEAN	Japan	All East Asia	All developing countries	All developing countries
Textiles														
1970–73	0.9	—	0.1	1.2	2.2	2.3	5.5	1.1	0.4	0.2	0.8	2.4	3.3	14.5
1974–77	1.1	0.1	0.2	0.9	2.2	2.6	5.2	1.5	0.4	0.2	0.7	2.8	4.2	17.5
1978–81	1.4	0.3	0.2	0.9	2.8	3.4	6.3	1.7	0.7	0.3	0.7	3.5	5.3	20.6
1982–85	2.2	0.6	0.3	1.0	4.2	4.6	8.1	2.2	1.1	0.4	0.9	4.5	6.2	20.8
1986	3.3	1.0	0.5	1.3	6.1	6.6	11.2	2.6	1.2	0.5	0.9	5.2	6.8	22.5
Clothing														
1970–73	3.1	—	0.4	1.1	4.6	4.1	6.8	3.4	0.1	0.1	0.7	4.4	4.4	13.5
1974–77	6.0	0.1	0.6	0.6	7.2	8.2	10.0	6.4	0.3	0.5	0.4	7.6	9.0	20.9
1978–81	9.7	0.6	1.2	0.6	12.0	13.8	15.8	8.7	0.7	1.1	0.4	10.9	13.2	27.6
1982–85	12.3	1.6	2.0	0.7	16.6	18.9	21.9	10.7	1.6	1.6	0.5	14.3	17.4	30.6
1986	13.9	2.9	2.7	0.8	20.2	24.2	28.9	10.9	2.3	1.8	0.5	15.5	19.9	35.9
All manufactures														
1970–73	0.4	—	0.1	1.1	1.6	1.3	6.1	0.3	—	0.1	0.8	1.3	1.5	12.4
1974–77	0.6	—	0.2	1.3	2.2	2.1	7.4	0.5	0.1	0.3	1.0	1.8	2.1	15.1
1978–81	0.9	0.1	0.3	1.9	3.2	2.7	9.0	0.8	0.1	0.4	1.3	2.5	2.6	17.0
1982–85	1.4	0.1	0.4	2.5	4.4	3.5	11.0	1.0	0.2	0.4	1.7	3.4	3.1	17.7
1986	1.6	0.2	0.4	3.2	5.4	3.6	12.2	1.1	0.2	0.4	2.1	3.7	2.9	17.6

Source: See Appendix to this volume.

It should not be inferred from these import share data that East Asia is doing relatively poorly in penetrating the United States markets, however. On the contrary, the evidence in Table 8.3 shows that the increase in import penetration by East Asia has been considerably more rapid into the United States than into other advanced industrial countries, particularly since the late 1970s. During the decade to 1986, developing East Asia's share of US textiles and clothing markets increased from 3 to 11 per cent (cf from 4 to 9 per cent for other light manufactures – see Appendix Table A1.5). By contrast, developing East Asia's share of these product markets for industrial countries as a whole rose from 4 to only 8 per cent during the same 10-year period. Clearly, the United States has been redirecting the source of its imports of textiles and clothing (and of other manufactures – see the bottom of Table 8.3) to developing East Asia even more rapidly than have other industrial countries.

The data presented thus far demonstrate that the shifts originating from the imposition of MFA quantitative restrictions are far more complex than expected from a simple quota system. Since most of these quantitative restrictions are product and country specific, as long as there are new untapped sources of exports, the intended reduction in trade can be partially offset (Yoffie 1983; Bhagwati 1988).

There are two major offsetting shifts in response to these MFA restrictions. First, the restricted country may shift its exports to unrestricted markets. In effect the trade restrictions imposed by the US or Europe will divert exports to a free market. Second, the composition of exports to a particular market may change as a result of the uneven sector and product coverage of the quota system.

Sector-specific measures can lead to major changes in effective rates of protection along the production process. These trade restrictions may induce offsetting shifts in the degree of processing of traded products, where restricted exports of finished products will be replaced by unrestricted exports of components and vice versa.

In the second place, the degrees of restrictiveness usually vary by product categories. One would, therefore, expect that exporting countries would shift the composition of their exports to those sectors with the least restrictions. Consequently, one may find the total volume of exports from a restricted country will increase as the exporting country adjusts to the quota system.

The compositional changes which are induced by the trade restrictions are accentuated by the incentives those quantitative restrictions create for exporting countries to move among the restricted categories from those with lower to those with higher value added per worker, and from those with higher to lower elasticities of demand. The extent of these offsetting changes is partially dependent on the inherent 'restrictiveness' of the quota system in terms of the leeway it provides for compositional shifts and in the ability of the exporting country to shift across product categories. The latter is a function of the complementarity in the technology used across product categories.

Activities which depend on complex technology, capital intensity or static and dynamic scale economies display substantial barriers to entry and exit and thus limit product substitution. By way of contrast, in highly labour-intensive activities, such as in the textile and clothing industries of China, variable costs dominate the cost structure and the sunk costs required to initiate a new product are relatively low. In these industries a large and persistent cost differential separates China's textile and clothing suppliers from other Asian suppliers. Therefore, despite the threat that quotas will be extended to new products, discriminatory quota controls can be offset by the emergence of new products. This diversion across product categories can be seen in the detailed trade of each of the East Asian exporters. The greatest diversion is observed in the case of China.

New 'modalities' for the 1990s

A great deal of time and effort has been devoted to a discussion of possible future scenarios for the textiles and clothing trade. Within GATT, while a number of countries have tabled proposals as part of the Uruguay Round of multilateral trade negotiations, as of 1989 the group as a whole had not agreed on a common negotiating plan.

Some of the proposals that have been made include: (i) a phase-out of MFA restrictions beginning on the expiration of the present MFA protocol (31 July 1991), (ii) a freeze on further restrictions under the MFA, and (iii) a commitment by all participants to contribute towards liberalization of the textiles and clothing trade.[3] The United States opposes the suggestion of a freeze on existing textile restraints.[4] Some developing countries want liberalization of trade in textiles, including the application of GATT principles. Two possibilities repeatedly raised are: the conversion of MFA quotas to tariffs, and/or the use of GATT article XIX as a safeguards mechanism instead of the differential quotas as under the MFA (Cable 1987).

With respect to the first of these two reform options, what are the tariff equivalents of MFA quotas? Estimates for the 1978–87 period are reported in Table 8.4, based on an econometric methodology developed in Pelzman (1988b). The tariff equivalents of the quotas represent the difference between the price paid and the hypothetical

---

[3] See 'News of the Uruguay Round of Multilateral Trade Negotiations', Information and Media Relations of the General Agreement on Tariffs and Trade, NUR 023, 14 December 1988.

[4] See 'Accord Sighted in 4 Key Areas', *The Journal of Commerce*, 5 April 1989, p. 1.

Table 8.4: *Tariffs and tariff equivalents of MFA quotas,*
United States, 1987
(percentages and million US dollars)

	Tariff rate (%)	Quota rate (%)	Tariff on uncontrolled imports	Tariff on controlled imports	Quota on controlled imports
			Revenue from:		
TEXTILES					
300 Carded yarn	7.2	19.3	1.7	6.6	17.8
301 Combed yarn	10.4	21.0	0.4	3.7	7.4
310 Gingham fabric	14.2	21.4	0.7	2.0	3.1
311 Velveteen fabric	20.2	27.9	—	0.5	0.7
312 Corduroy fabric	25.4	39.0	0.2	1.8	2.7
313 Cotton sheeting	7.9	13.9	5.3	20.6	36.6
314 Poplin, broadcloth	11.1	16.5	0.6	8.1	12.1
315 Cotton printcloth	9.0	12.9	1.7	14.6	20.9
316 Cotton shirting	14.4	18.2	0.1	0.7	0.9
317 Twill and sateen	8.2	13.8	4.2	16.7	28.0
318 Other yarn-dyed fabric	13.2	14.9	2.7	5.5	6.2
319 Duck	6.9	14.6	0.3	5.6	11.7
320 Other woven fabric	11.9	15.4	12.8	17.2	22.3
410 Woollen and worsted	32.1	35.9	30.2	25.8	28.8
411 Apstry, upholstery	7.5	—	3.1	0.2	—
425 Wool knit fabric	19.9	28.5	1.0	0.4	0.5
429 Other wool fabric	9.4	18.8	0.5	—	—
600 Textured yarns	9.6	—	6.4	6.0	—
601 Cellular filament yarn	11.1	13.0	1.9	0.5	0.6
602 Other filament yarns	10.8	23.8	5.0	3.4	7.5
603 Spun cellular yarns	11.5	—	0.2	0.3	—
604 Other spun yarns	11.9	20.3	3.9	4.4	7.5
605 Other M-MF yarns	13.9	15.8	4.2	3.7	4.3
610 Wov of cell. fila	18.7	99.5	2.2	2.8	14.9
611 Wov of spun cell	17.3	45.6	7.0	7.3	19.4
612 Wov of oth. filay	18.4	20.3	9.1	67.1	74.0
613 Wov of oth. spuny	17.0	—	3.2	15.3	—
614 Oth. woven fabrics	17.0	—	27.6	18.8	—
625 Knit fabrics	17.0	21.8	3.4	2.3	3.0
626 Pile, tufted fabrics	17.0	—	1.0	1.4	—
627 Specialty fabric	17.0	92.0	21.5	11.8	63.6
Average and sum:	14.1	22.1	162.2	275.2	394.4
CLOTHING					
330 Handkerchiefs	12.0	13.2	0.1	1.2	1.3
331 Cotton gloves	23.7	42.2	0.4	11.2	19.9

(cont'd)

Table 8.4: *(cont'd)*

332	Cotton hosiery	18.7	38.4	0.9	1.2	2.5
333	Suit-typ coat, MB	10.5	14.6	0.4	2.7	3.7
334	Oth. coats, MB	10.1	15.5	2.0	23.5	36.1
335	Coats, WGI	9.8	—	3.8	32.1	—
336	Cotton dresses	13.5	—	6.5	21.8	—
337	Cotton playsuits	9.5	—	0.9	9.1	—
338	Knit shirts, MB	21.0	25.0	8.4	127.0	150.8
339	Knit blouses, WGI	20.9	32.9	27.0	126.2	198.3
340	N-knit shirts, MB	20.9	33.7	15.3	154.8	249.6
341	N-K blouses, WGI	16.5	23.9	7.7	119.3	173.1
342	Cotton skirts	8.9	17.8	6.2	30.0	60.1
345	Cotton sweaters	20.8	44.2	17.7	39.2	83.5
347	Trousers, MB	16.9	22.9	8.3	128.8	174.5
348	Trousers, WGI	16.9	19.5	14.2	169.5	195.7
349	Brassieres, etc.	21.9	34.8	0.2	1.6	2.5
350	Dressing gowns	8.8	41.8	1.0	5.8	27.4
351	Cotton nightwear	10.6	14.2	0.9	14.2	19.0
352	Cotton underwear	10.6	13.2	2.2	10.0	12.5
353	Down-filled, MB	4.7	13.8	—	1.0	2.9
354	Down-filled, WGI	4.7	17.4	—	1.1	4.0
359	Oth. CWM clothing	9.1	63.0	3.1	36.9	255.8
431	Wool gloves	9.4	—	0.1	0.8	—
432	Wool hosiery	12.2	53.4	0.7	0.3	1.3
433	Suit-type, MB	22.5	31.0	8.1	8.3	11.4
434	Oth. coats, MB	24.0	48.3	8.9	7.6	15.3
435	Wool coats, WGI	22.9	31.1	14.2	21.4	29.2
436	Wool dresses	18.4	—	4.2	5.6	—
438	K shirts, blouses	18.4	48.7	1.7	15.4	40.8
440	NK shirts, blouses	22.7	26.6	1.3	3.9	4.5
442	Wool skirts	17.2	19.1	8.9	9.2	10.2
443	Wool suits, MB	22.7	39.3	26.5	16.0	27.8
444	Wool suits, WGI	17.8	26.8	3.7	6.0	9.0
445	Wool sweaters, MB	16.4	23.0	15.9	16.3	23.0
446	Sweaters, WGI	17.0	25.4	18.6	37.6	56.0
447	Trousers, MB	22.4	31.7	7.6	8.1	11.4
448	Trousers, WGI	17.3	25.0	4.0	6.1	8.8
459	Oth. wool clothing	12.5	27.2	7.3	5.2	11.3
630	Handkerchiefs	14.6	23.6	—	0.3	0.5
631	M-MF gloves	19.6	25.6	0.1	14.1	18.4
632	M-MF hosiery	20.5	22.6	3.4	8.9	9.8
633	Suit-type, MB	25.2	46.3	1.7	18.5	34.1
634	Other coats, MB	24.7	25.5	1.7	80.8	83.4
635	M-MF coats, WGI	27.3	51.9	5.8	121.3	230.6
636	M-MF dresses	21.4	35.3	5.9	66.5	109.7
637	M-MF playsuits	20.6	28.1	0.4	8.9	12.2
638	Knit shirts, MB	34.5	35.2	1.4	161.4	164.4
639	Knit blouses, WGI	34.5	43.6	2.2	315.1	398.5
640	N-K shirts, MB	29.2	42.5	1.7	164.6	239.8
641	N-K blouses, WGI	29.2	34.1	7.1	162.7	190.1
642	M-MF skirts	18.0	28.0	5.5	42.0	65.2

Table 8.4:   *(cont'd)*

643 M-MF suits, MB	27.5	33.5	0.8	17.0	20.7
644 M-MF Suits, WGI	27.9	31.7	4.2	30.9	35.0
645 M-MF sweaters, MB	34.1	48.8	3.5	67.5	96.6
646 Sweaters, WGI	34.4	53.3	5.3	246.7	381.5
647 Trousers, MB	29.2	52.0	2.8	141.3	251.2
648 Trousers, WGI	29.8	51.7	5.0	156.6	271.5
649 Brassieres, etc.	27.6	29.1	7.1	59.6	62.9
650 Dressing gowns	20.3	—	0.3	5.9	—
651 M-MF nightwear	20.6	26.7	0.4	21.4	27.7
652 M-MF underwear	21.9	32.7	2.2	18.8	28.0
653 Down-filled, MB	4.7	10.4	—	1.9	4.3
654 Down-filled, WGI	4.7	5.4	—	1.2	1.4
659 Oth. M-MF app.	16.7	22.2	12.5	71.8	95.7
Average % and sum	19.0	28.3	339.8	3241.3	4766.4
Grand total	17.4	26.3	502.0	3516.6	5160.8

Source: Pelzman (1989a).

price that would have been charged had the MFA quotas not been in effect during 1987. In most cases the MFA quotas were binding with an *ad valorem* equivalent exceeding that of the tariff by at least 10 per cent. On average, the tariff rate on cotton textiles and clothing was 13 per cent while the estimated tariff equivalent of the quota was 22 per cent. For wool textiles and clothing, the average tariff rate was 18 per cent with the quota rate of 27 per cent, while for man-made fibre textiles and clothing the tariff rate was 21 per cent and the quota rate was 30 per cent. Aggregated in terms of textiles versus clothing products, the data in Table 8.4 confirm the generally accepted expectation that tariffs and quotas are higher in the clothing industry: the average tariff and quota rates for textiles were 14 and 22 per cent, while for clothing the rates were 19 and 28 per cent.[5]

The tariff revenue for imports controlled and uncontrolled by quotas as well as the quota rent applicable to controlled imports are also presented in Table 8.4. Total estimated textile and clothing quota rent in 1987 was US $5.2 billion. Of that total over 92 per cent, or $4.8 billion, was charged on clothing imports. Tariffs collected on controlled imports equalled $3.5 billion while those from uncontrolled imports equalled $0.5 billion.

[5] Hufbauer *et al.* (1986) assume that for MFA III, textile tariffs were equal to 14 per cent while quotas introduced an additional *ad valorem* rate of 7 per cent. For clothing they assume that the tariff was equal to 25 per cent with the quota adding an additional 14 per cent. Cline (1987) assumes that, for 1986, tariffs on textiles were equal to 12 per cent and on clothing were equal to 23 per cent. Protection attributable to the quota was assumed to equal 16 per cent on textiles and 32 per cent on clothing.

The proportional changes in the controlled and uncontrolled import prices that would result from a full elimination of tariffs and quotas have been estimated by Pelzman (1989a) to equal 18 per cent for controlled textile imports and 12 per cent for uncontrolled textile imports. The change in domestic textile prices is estimated to range from 0.5 to 2 per cent, but for clothing the elimination of tariffs and quotas would result in a 22 per cent decline in the prices of controlled imports, a 16 per cent decline in uncontrolled import prices, and a 5 to 29 per cent decline in comparable domestic clothing prices.

The partial-equilibrium estimates of the traditional net welfare cost to the United States of its current tariffs and quotas on textiles and clothing for 1987 range from US $2.3 to $2.6 billion, depending on the domestic supply elasticity assumed. As expected, most of these costs are in the clothing industry ($2.2 to $2.4 billion), and the majority are due to quotas. Removing this protection would displace between 29 and 36 per cent of clothing producers and 2 to 4 per cent of textile producers (Pelzman 1989a).

It is clear from these estimates of the tariff equivalents of the MFA quotas that converting the quotas to tariffs would highlight the enormous costs associated with this trade program, something the domestic industry would be very keen to avoid.

The second reform option, namely converting the MFA to GATT safeguards provisions, has been discussed in Cable (1987). Given the lack of progress at the Montreal mid-term review of the Uruguay Round in December 1988, a number of issues need to be re-stated. Primary among them is the fact that, despite universal agreement on the need for a safeguards code, wide disagreement persists over two of the fundamental concepts involved, namely selectivity and grey area measures. It should not be surprising, therefore, that although many elements of the current 'safeguards' text were not controversial, a few points of disagreement remained. Many developing countries sought an agreement in which safeguard actions should have time limits; in which these actions should be non-discriminatory rather than selective;[6] and in which 'grey area' measures – usually safeguard-like actions taken without following GATT safeguard rules and applied selectively – should be eliminated. These are all stumbling blocks that have been encountered for years.

Although no consensus emerged in 1989, negotiators envision an agreement that will reinforce the discipline of the GATT and elaborate

[6] Some countries have long argued that GATT safeguards provisions would be more effective and better adhered to if the measures could be taken selectively against those countries mainly responsible for import surges. This concept, known as 'selectivity', is not currently allowed under GATT article XIX, which requires non-discriminatory, global restraints. See GATT, *News of the Uruguay Round of Multilateral Trade Negotiations*, Press Release No. NUR 005, 3 July 1987.

on transparency, criteria for action such as serious injury, digressiveness (or the progressive reduction of measures), structural adjustment, compensation and retaliation, and procedures for notification, consultation, surveillance and dispute settlement. The United States would like to see such an agreement deal with so-called 'grey area' measures, or safeguard-type actions that are implemented without using GATT procedures and that are currently outside multilateral control. Other GATT member countries would like to see the negotiations allow 'grey area' measures to be subject to multilateral scrutiny, while others would like to see them eliminated. Because of the remaining differences, approval for the plan for safeguards negotiations was gained only with the understanding that it did not bind participants to any specific positions regarding the final outcome on major negotiating issues.

Any movement within the GATT on textiles and clothing negotiations will have to wait for a resolution of the broader 'safeguards' issue. To date, the agreements reached on textiles have been more in the domain of ceremony and less in the realm of substance. First, GATT members agreed on the importance of the textiles and clothing sectors for the economies of many countries, notably many developing countries. Second, they agreed that textiles and clothing negotiations are 'one of the key elements' of the Uruguay Round negotiations, and that negotiations in this sector should contribute to further trade liberalization. Third, the GATT representatives agreed on certain points for achieving 'substantive results' in textiles and clothing, including the following: agreement to begin 'substantive negotiations' in April 1989 to allow parties to reach agreement by December 1990 on modalities for the integration of the sector into the GATT; agreement that such modalities for the integration process of the sector into the GATT should include phasing out current restrictions on textiles and clothing trade under the MFA and other forms of restriction not consistent with GATT rules and disciplines; agreement to invite participants to table additional proposals by 30 June 1989 on how to meet these goals; and agreement that the least-developed countries should be accorded special treatment. [7]

Given the record of the bilateral arrangements for controlling textile and clothing exports to the United States, plus the costs of these restrictions along with the vested interest they create, it is extremely difficult to anticipate the nature of a post-MFA IV textile agreement. Even if the current GATT negotiations convert the MFA system of controls to the 'safeguards' provisions, the passage of the Omnibus Trade and Competitiveness Act of 1988 changes the basic injury standard, making the 'safeguards' clause even less attractive to domestic petitioners. The Act provides that, following an affirmative injury

---

[7] A review of the Montreal meetings is presented in *GATT Focus* No. 61, May 1989.

determination by the International Trade Commission (USITC), the President is to take action that will 'facilitate efforts by the domestic industry to make a positive adjustment to import competition and provide greater economic and social benefits than costs'. The Act states that such positive adjustment may include the transfer of labour and capital to other 'productive pursuits'. A petitioner may submit a 'plan to facilitate positive adjustment to import competition'. During 1988 only two section 201 cases were initiated at the USITC. This is a reflection of the disfavour that 'escape clause' cases have among petitioners. It is, therefore, highly unlikely that domestic US interests would favour the transfer of MFA controls to the 'safeguards' provision. Given the shakiness of the domestic output data this position is not difficult to understand.

In conclusion, the US experience of relatively rapid increases in import penetration from East Asia, despite the presence of MFA limitations and of rapid growth in imports from the European Community, suggests the MFA is somewhat porous. Indeed the market penetration data in Appendix Table A1.5 show developing East Asia has penetrated the US textile, clothing and footwear market even more rapidly than the US market for other less restricted labour-intensive products. Developing countries seeking to follow the Asian example of embarking on rapid industrialization and economic growth based on exports of labour-intensive manufactures should find some encouragement in the US case study. Even though access to the American market is limited by import-restrictive policies, sales growth there is still clearly possible provided enough is invested in finding ways around the apparent fortress of the MFA restrictions.

9

Structural adjustments in Australia and New Zealand

Peter J. Lloyd*

As a group the textiles and clothing industries in Australia and New Zealand have a number of features in common with each other and with other advanced industrial countries. One is that they are heavily protected by government policies. Another is that they have been facing increasing competition from Asia's newly industrialized economies (NIEs) and more recently from the People's Republic of China. Despite high protection, they have been declining in relative terms as contributors to their national economies in terms of both output and employment. The Australian and New Zealand experiences provide interesting case studies because, notwithstanding these similarities, some other trends and behaviour within this group of industries differ markedly both between Australia and New Zealand and between these two countries and other advanced industrial economies.

The first section of this chapter looks at the patterns of trade and production specialization in Australia and New Zealand and compares these patterns with those in other advanced industrial countries. The second and third sections examine these two country cases in greater detail, while the fourth analyses these stylized facts in terms of an adaptation of a model, developed by Dixit and Grossman (1982), of intra-industry production and trade for goods-in-process. This model can be used to interpret the trends in the region in relation to trends in the global industry.

Patterns of trade and production specialization

Most advanced industrial countries are net importers of textiles and clothing commodities as a group and most developing countries are net exporters. (Australia conforms to this pattern but New Zealand

* This chapter is based on a CIES Seminar Paper (Lloyd 1989).

is a rare exception to it.) Economic commentators in the industrial countries frequently refer to these industries as import-competing. However, this characterization is inadequate because it masks a surprising variation within the group. An examination of the statistics on exports and imports of textiles and clothing reveals that in all countries there is simultaneous exporting and importing of the products of virtually all textile and clothing industries, that is, there is significant intra-industry trade. To explain the pattern of net imports and the trends in import shares it is important to consider the intra-industry pattern of trade and production specialization. It is necessary also to consider trade in fibres, because the cost of domestic production or importation of fibres is a major determinant of the pattern of trade in textiles and clothing.

Consider the trade of an individual country in the three commodity groups 'fibres', 'textiles' and 'clothing'. One can classify the pattern of trade by considering the sign of the net export trade (exports-imports) of each of these commodity groups. Let X_i and M_i respectively denote a country's exports and imports of commodity group i for i = 1,2,3 where 1 = Fibres, 2 = Textiles and 3 = Clothing. Net exports for each group are thus $(X_i - M_i)$, which is positive (negative) if the country is a net exporter (importer). Since the sign of net exports in one group may be associated with either net exports or net imports in each of the other two groups, there are eight possible sign patterns. For example, (+,+,+) signifies that the country is a net exporter of each of the three groups and (–,–,–) signifies that it is a net importer of each of the three groups. There are six mixed sign patterns such as (+,–,–) which signifies that the country is a net exporter of 'fibres' and a net importer of 'textiles' and of 'clothing'.

These sign patterns can be quantified by using measures of intra- and inter-group trade. For each commodity group the absolute value of this difference, $|X_i - M_i|$, is known as the 'inter-industry' trade in the products of this group or industry, and $(X_i + M_i)$ is then the sum of two components, inter-industry trade and intra-industry trade. That is,

$$X_i + M_i = |X_i - M_i| + [(X_i + M_i) - |X_i - M_i|]$$

Each of these two components can then be expressed as a percentage of total trade for the group to obtain indexes of inter- and intra-industry trade, respectively (Grubel and Lloyd 1975). These percentages, when graphed, give a convenient picture of the pattern of trade, including the relative size of the total trade and the intra- and inter-industry trade in each of the three commodity groups. Figure 9.1 shows such graphs for the advanced industrial countries of the Pacific rim for the year 1979. (This is a convenient year since it is near the middle of the period 1970 to 1986, the period which is used for the

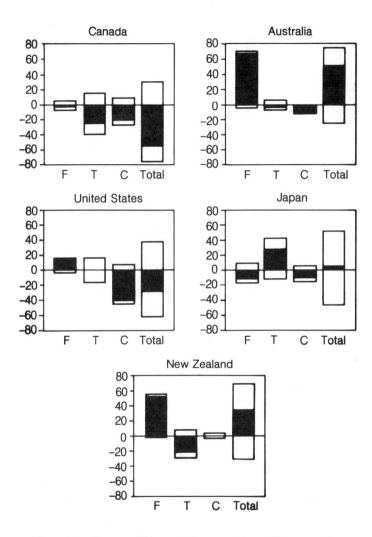

Figure 9.1:   *Inter- and intra-industry trade in fibres, textiles and clothing for Australia, Canada, Japan, New Zealand and the United States, 1979*

F = fibres (SITC 26), T = textiles (SITC 65), and C = clothing (SITC 84). Exports are shown above the 0 line, imports below. All figures are expressed as a percentage of total trade (exports plus imports). The shaded part within each block is the trade balance (exports minus imports as a percentage of total trade) for that product group.
Source: OECD, *Textile and Clothing Industries: Structural Problems and Policies in OECD Countries*, Paris, OECD, 1983, p. 57.

Table 9.1:   *Fibre, textile and clothing trade sign patterns, selected industrial countries, 1979*

Country	Sign pattern[a]
Turkey	(+,+,+)
United States	(+,+,−)
New Zealand	(+,−,+)
Australia	(+,−,−)
Italy	(−,+,+)
Finland	(−,−,+)
Japan	(−,+,−)
Canada	(−,−,−)

[a] The three signs refer to the net trade situation in fibres (SITC 26), textiles (SITC 65) and clothing (SITC 84), respectively. A positive sign indicates exports exceed imports and conversely for a negative sign.
Source: From data reported in OECD, *Textile and Clothing Industries: Structural Problems and Policies in OECD Countries*, Paris, OECD, 1983, pp. 50–1.

detailed analysis of the Australian and New Zealand experiences in the sections below.)

Table 9.1 sets out the sign patterns of the net trade in each of the three commodity groups for Pacific rim and other industrial countries. The table illustrates the diversity in the trade patterns among industrial countries, as all eight possible sign patterns are represented. This belies the common belief that the textile and clothing industries are simply import-competing industries in these countries.

Among the Pacific basin countries, Australia is a net exporter of fibres and a net importer of both textiles and clothing. There was no other industrial country with that pattern of trade in 1979. Indeed, there are only a few OECD countries which are net exporters of fibres, namely, Australia, Turkey, New Zealand and the USA. The cases of Australia and New Zealand are explained by the natural endowments of land and climate which are suitable for wool production whereas the USA case is partly explained by the natural endowments which favour cotton production and partly by large-scale production and exports of synthetic fibres. Turkey is similarly an exporter of both wool and synthetic fibres. New Zealand was a net importer of textiles[1] and a net exporter of clothing and the USA was a net exporter of textiles and an importer of clothing. Japan is an example of a country which is a net exporter of textiles and a net importer of fibres and clothing, a pattern which no other OECD country had in 1979. It reflects the strength of the Japanese synthetic yarn production

[1] The statistics in Table 9.4 below show that New Zealand is a net exporter of textiles as well as of clothing products. This discrepancy is explained by the fact that for Table 9.1 the OECD uses the SITC classification which excludes wool scouring and some other manufacturing activities from the textile group whereas these activities are classified as 'textiles' in the ISIC data in Table 9.4.

industry at that time. Canada was a net importer of all three commodity groups. This pattern is more typical of the other industrial countries, including the UK, West Germany and France.

The fact that all eight patterns are represented among these industrial countries reveals two basic and important facts concerning these groups of industries. One is that the full spectrum of commodities from fibres to finished textile products involves tradable commodities. The other is that, with few exceptions, the technologies required for production are not 'high' technologies. This combination of trade and technology characteristics means that any country can specialize in the production of a subset of these commodities at some stage of production, using readily available importable inputs and technologies. The clothing and textile industries as a group are ubiquitous industries: every country has some textile and/or clothing production. Indeed, the world output of these industries is perhaps more evenly spread among all the countries of the world than the output of any other manufacturing industry. It is this freedom of production, as it were, which makes the industry group truly global and unusually competitive.

The sign patterns shown in Table 9.1 are not constant over time. Net imports of both textiles and clothing have increased steadily in most advanced industrial countries since the sample year 1979. This has changed the sign pattern of some countries as well as the level of net imports. For example, Japan and the United States have moved since 1979 from being net exporters of textiles to net importers of this commodity group, and Belgium, which was a net exporter of clothing, has become a net importer. Details of the changes between 1970 and 1986 are provided in Table A2 of the Appendix to this volume.

The structure of Australia's textile and clothing industries

The period from 1970 to 1986 gives a sufficiently long view of the Australian industries to identify their behaviour and their problems, and the data for this period are readily available from the Australian Bureau of Statistics and from the International Economic Data Bank (IEDB) of the Australian National University. The latter data set is of particular value as it presents the data on a common basis for Australia and New Zealand and other industrial countries. It contains annual series for production, apparent consumption, and exports and imports for the textile and clothing industries at the four-digit level of the International Standard Industrial Classification (ISIC) since 1970.

Consider first the IEDB series for the most recent available year, 1986. These give an overall picture of the industries at the end of the sample period. It was noted above that the Australian textile and clothing industries are both net importers. The four-digit ISIC classification disaggregates the textile industry into six sub-industries: 'spinning, weaving and finishing textiles', 'man-made textile goods excluding wearing apparel', 'knitting mills', 'carpets', 'cordage, rope and twine industries' and the 'manufacture of textiles, not elsewhere classified (nec)'. Table 9.2 shows that Australia was a substantial net importer in all of the six sub-industries in 1986. Hence, in the Australian case, the textile industry is unambiguously an import-competing industry in terms of net trade flows in all sub-industries.

This pattern is notable in view of the fact that Australia is a large net exporter of fibres, chiefly wool and to a lesser extent cotton. Historically the Australian wool industry has not provided a basis for a substantial textile and clothing industry specializing in materials derived from wool fibres. Around 75 per cent of the annual production of wool is exported greasy and only 5 per cent is processed within Australia into final textile products. Similarly, only about 10 per cent of the annual production of raw cotton is processed into final textile products within Australia (chiefly denims and bed linen). Thus fibres continue to provide more than 10 per cent of Australia's exports (more than a quarter before the 1970s) while textiles and clothing contribute less than 1 per cent of export earnings (Table 9.3).

Australia's experience is in sharp contrast to that of most other major natural fibre producers. Historically, the great expansion of the textile and clothing industries of England from the Middle Ages

Table 9.2: *Net imports of textiles and clothing as a share of apparent consumption,*[a] *Australia, 1970, 1979 and 1986* (per cent)

ISIC code	Industry	1970	1979	1986
3211	Spinning, weaving and finishing textiles	19.0	24.1	18.3
3212	Made-up textiles, except wearing apparel	20.7	34.1	37.9
3213	Knitting mills	6.0	13.2	11.1
3214	Manufacture of carpets and rugs	26.5	22.6	13.5
3215	Cordage, rope and twine	4.7	27.3	26.9
3219	Manufacture of textiles, nec	22.1	11.7	13.2
321	All textiles	17.1	21.7	17.8
322	Clothing	4.8	13.9	16.0

[a] Imports minus exports divided by production plus imports minus exports.
Source: International Economic Data Bank, Market Penetration Tapes, Australian National University, Canberra, 1989, based on data compiled by the OECD Secretariat. See Appendix to this volume for details.

Table 9.3: *Importance of natural fibres, textiles, clothing and all manufactures^a in exports of Australia, New Zealand and all industrial economies, 1965 to 1987*

	Share of total exports (%) from:				Index of export specialization^b in:				Net exports as a percentage of exports plus imports of:	
	Natural fibres	Textiles	Clothing	All manufactures	Natural fibres	Textiles	Clothing	All manufactures	Textiles	Clothing
Australia										
1965–69	26.3	0.4	0.2	14.8	11.1	0.1	0.1	0.3	–91	–66
1970–74	15.3	0.4	0.2	19.5	10.7	0.1	0.1	0.3	–89	–78
1975–79	10.6	0.4	0.1	19.7	11.4	0.1	0.1	0.3	–87	–90
1980–84	9.2	0.6	0.1	19.6	12.8	0.2	—	0.3	–78	–92
1985–87	11.4	0.7	0.1	17.5	17.9	0.2	—	0.3	–77	–91
New Zealand										
1965–69	24.1	0.5	0.1	6.9	10.2	0.1	—	0.1	–91	–73
1970–74	19.8	1.3	0.2	10.8	13.9	0.3	0.1	0.2	–77	–25
1975–79	18.9	1.7	0.7	17.1	20.4	0.6	0.3	0.3	–62	41
1980–84	14.5	1.9	0.8	20.5	20.2	0.7	0.4	0.4	–54	25
1985–87	13.2	2.2	0.7	22.1	20.7	0.7	0.2	0.3	–46	3
All industrial market economies										
1965–69	1.5	4.6	1.7	71	0.6	1.0	1.0	1.2	8	–6
1970–74	0.9	4.1	1.7	73	0.7	1.0	0.8	1.2	5	–20
1975–79	0.7	3.3	1.5	74	0.7	1.0	0.7	1.3	4	–30
1980–84	0.6	2.8	1.4	73	0.8	1.0	0.6	1.3	4	–35
1985–87	0.5	2.8	1.6	68	0.8	0.9	0.5	1.1	–2	–42

^a Natural fibres are SITC 26 less 266; textiles are SITC 65; clothing is SITC 84; all manufactures includes SITC 5 to 8 less 68 plus 266.
^b The index of export specialization is defined as the share of a product group in total exports of a country as a ratio of the share of that product group in world exports, following Balassa (1965).
Source: International Economic Data Bank, Trade Data Tapes, Australian National University, Canberra, 1990.

through to the nineteenth century was founded on homegrown supplies of wool, and the growth of the American textile and clothing industries in the nineteenth century was based largely on cheap supplies of domestic cotton. Today, Japan and the United States, for example, are major fibre producers (silk and man-made fibres in Japan's case) and are also major textile manufacturers.

The lack of development of a woollen and worsted textile industry is surprising in a country which is a low-cost and large-scale producer of wool fibre. The explanation is that wool is long staple, and its end-uses in clothing are in areas where Australia is a high-cost producer; also the hot Australian climate which is eminently suitable for growing wool ensures a small home demand for woollen clothing. However, these factors do not inhibit Australia as an exporter of other processed products. The latter climatic factor would seem to have favoured cotton textile production as the Australian climate is suitable for the wearing of cotton textile products. Yet the rapid expansion of cotton growing in Australia after 1964 has been accompanied by little expansion of textiles based on domestic cotton production and in most years between 60 and 80 per cent of the annual cotton output has been exported.

The primary explanation seems to be the relative costs of manufacturing production. The consistent net import pattern across all sub-industries and over time (see also the final column of Table 9.3) indicates that the Australian textile and clothing industries are high-cost producers. One should note too that the wool-scouring and top-making producers have received in recent years no effective assistance and the cotton ginners have received negative effective protection in Australia (Industries Assistance Commission 1989: 133). This is in sharp contrast to the high rates of assistance for all other segments of the textile and especially clothing industries, and must have contributed to the situation in which the country exports raw wool and cotton and reimports processed fabrics and products made from these fibres.

In terms of the country source of imports, other advanced industrial countries, chiefly Japan, the EC and the United States have traditionally been the main sources of textile imports, supplying just under 20 per cent of domestic sales in the 1970s and 1980s. However, all of the growth in textile import penetration into Australia has been from developing East Asian economies. Protection increases have ensured there has been somewhat less growth in clothing import penetration into Australia since the mid-1970s, although again the increased imports of clothing have come predominantly from developing countries in East Asia, chiefly the Asian NIEs and increasingly from China (Table 9.4). Indeed the percentage of imports of clothing from China increased so rapidly during the 1980s that China became the principal source of imports of clothing products in the late 1980s. This partly reflects the increasing competitiveness of Chinese products, but it is

Table 9.4: *Import penetration from East Asia and elsewhere into markets for textiles, clothing and all manufactures in Australia and all industrial market economies, 1970 to 1986* (imports as a percentage of production plus imports minus exports)

	Share of Australian sales from:							Share of all industrial market economies' sales from:						
	NE Asian NIEs	China	ASEAN	Japan	All East Asia	All developing countries	All countries	NE Asian NIEs	China	ASEAN	Japan	All East Asia	All developing countries	All countries
Textiles														
1970–73	3.4	1.7	0.4	7.0	12.7	7.7	25.6	1.1	0.4	0.2	0.8	2.4	3.3	14.5
1974–77	5.3	1.8	0.8	6.3	14.2	10.1	29.6	1.5	0.4	0.2	0.7	2.8	4.2	17.5
1978–81	6.6	2.4	1.3	5.2	15.6	13.0	32.7	1.7	0.7	0.3	0.7	3.5	5.3	20.6
1982–85	8.3	2.6	1.5	6.1	18.5	14.8	34.1	2.2	1.1	0.4	0.9	4.5	6.2	20.8
1986	9.0	2.6	2.0	5.1	18.6	15.9	33.9	2.6	1.2	0.5	0.9	5.2	6.8	22.5
Clothing														
1970–73	3.1	0.7	0.1	0.3	4.2	4.3	7.3	3.4	0.1	0.1	0.7	4.4	4.4	13.5
1974–77	7.8	1.1	0.8	0.4	10.2	10.8	14.8	6.4	0.3	0.5	0.4	7.6	9.0	20.9
1978–81	7.8	1.8	1.3	0.3	11.2	11.9	15.4	8.7	0.7	1.1	0.4	10.9	13.2	27.6
1982–85	8.6	2.4	1.0	0.3	12.4	13.3	16.9	10.7	1.6	1.6	0.5	14.3	17.4	30.6
1986	6.9	2.8	0.9	0.4	10.9	12.2	16.8	10.9	2.3	1.8	0.5	15.5	19.9	35.9
All manufactures														
1970–73	0.5	0.2	0.3	2.6	3.5	1.5	15.2	0.3	—	0.1	0.8	1.3	1.5	12.4
1974–77	1.0	0.2	0.6	3.9	5.7	3.0	18.5	0.5	0.1	0.3	1.0	1.8	2.1	15.1
1978–81	1.3	0.2	0.9	4.1	6.6	3.7	20.2	0.8	0.1	0.4	1.3	2.5	2.6	17.0
1982–85	1.7	0.3	0.9	5.4	8.3	4.2	22.0	1.0	0.2	0.4	1.7	3.4	3.1	17.7
1986	2.0	0.3	1.0	5.8	9.1	4.3	24.5	1.1	0.2	0.4	2.1	3.7	2.9	17.6

Source: See Appendix to this volume.

also due in part to the change in Australian importing arrangements under which more broadly based quota categories, and tendering for a greater proportion of the quota entitlements to import, have encouraged imports of lower unit values.

It is noteworthy that, despite Australia's proximity to East Asia, and its strong comparative disadvantage in manufacturing (see column (8) of Table 9.3), the share of domestic sales of clothing supplied by imports from East Asia is not high by the standards of other high-income countries, while that for textiles is relatively high (Table 9.4). A considerable part of the explanation for this has to do with the structure of protection: effective assistance to knitting mills and other clothing producers has been two or three times as high as assistance to textile producers (final column of Table 9.5).

As a group, the output of textiles and clothing has been declining continuously since 1970 as a proportion of value added of the manufacturing sector, which in turn has declined relative to the rest of the Australian economy (Industries Assistance Commission 1986a, especially Table 1.3.13). However, the distribution of output valued at current prices combines changes in both quantities and prices.

Table 9.5 provides basic statistics for Australia's textile and clothing industries. One should note that the statistics of enterprises and of employment understate the true total since they do not record 'outworkers' and outwork production. In recent years the Australian Council of Trade Unions (ACTU) has led a union drive to have outworkers registered and covered by wage awards. However, these awards and the conditions for outworkers are difficult to enforce. It is believed that recently the outwork production has come to be dominated by enterprises in Melbourne and Sydney which are owned by Vietnamese immigrants.

Real output in Table 9.5 is measured in terms of value added at constant prices. Where the data for the period after 1976 are available they have been recorded to bring the series to the most recent date. The classification of industries in this table differs from that above as it is based upon the Australian Standard Industrial Classification. In the ASIC, 'knitting mills' are recorded as a separate 3-digit item which is grouped along with 'clothing', instead of being included in 'textiles' as in the ISIC. (Since knitting mills are a distinct group of fabric producers, the statistics for this group are recorded separately.) The table shows that the real output of these industries was virtually constant over the period 1970 to 1988, apart from an increase in textiles output in the mid-1980s.

To explain this constancy of real output one must consider the trends in imports, exports and domestic consumption. Table 9.2 shows that net imports have increased since 1970 as a percentage of apparent consumption in four of the six ISIC 4-digit groups. The only two exceptions are 'spinning, weaving and finishing textiles' (which

Table 9.5:   *Details of Australia's textile and clothing industries, 1973 to 1989*

Year ending June	Number of establish-ments	Employment (000s)	Value added at constant prices ($m)		Average effective rate of assistance (%)
			In 1974–75 prices	In 1984–85 prices[a]	
Textiles (ASIC 234 + 235)					
1973	871	54	463	..	45
1974	897	55	512	..	35
1975	847	44	409	..	37
1976	880	44	457	..	39
1977	869	40	438	..	51
1978	851	38	419	..	52
1979	849	37	454	769	52
1980	874	38	450	787	55
1981	872	37	452	784	61
1982	907	36	458	800	54
1983	881	33	..	738	68
1984	630	33	..	769	69
1985	656	34	..	848	75
1986	..	33	..	946	72
1987	661	34	..	886	66
1988	731	35	..	1067	68
1989p	..	..	..	..	74
Knitting mills (ASIC 244)					
1973	417	19	154	..	87
1974	419	19	158	..	67
1975	390	16	134	..	74
1976	377	16	156	..	103
1977	377	16	153	..	135
1978	365	16	153	..	142
1979	342	14	152	1315	152
1980	327	13	149	1355	135
1981	319	13	163	1381	150
1982	323	13	161	1376	159
1983	318	12	..	1287	181
1984	266	13	..	1386	177
1985	265	13	..	1433	222
1986	..	..	..	1422	189
1987	257	13	..	1424	192
1988	251	12	..	1328	192
1989p	..	..	..	..	168
Clothing (ASIC 245)					
1973	2394	74	466	..	97
1974	2443	73	503	..	70
1975	2294	61	439	..	87
1976	2248	60	442	..	96
1977	2147	56	419	..	148
1978	2014	53	413	..	140

(cont'd)

Table 9.5: *(cont'd)*

Year ending June	Number of establish-ments	Employment (000s)	Value added at constant prices ($m)		Average effective rate of assistance (%)
			In 1974–75 prices	In 1984–85 prices[a]	
1979	1965	54	443	1315	140
1980	1996	55	461	1355	137
1981	1024	53	462	1381	133
1982	2032	53	468	1376	213
1983	1984	47	..	1287	189
1984	1474	47	..	1386	222
1985	1544	49	..	1433	243
1986	..	..	..	1422	136
1987	1613	49	..	1424	167
1988	1865	51	..	1328	167
1989p	..	..	..	..	158

[a] The series in 1984–85 prices for Knitting Mills (ASIC 244) and for Clothing (ASIC 245) is the same series, and refers to the aggregated group Clothing and Footwear (ASIC 244 + 245 + 246).

p = Preliminary figure.

Sources: Australian Bureau of Statistics, *Manufacturing Establishments, Details of Operations by Industry Class,* ABS Catalogue No. 8203, Canberra, various annual issues and *Australian National Accounts, Gross Product, Employment and Hours Worked,* ABS Catalogue No. 5211, Canberra, various annual issues; Industries Assistance Commission, *Annual Reports,* Canberra, various issues.

includes wool scouring and top making) and 'manufacture of textiles, nec'. Thus, apart from the areas of production based on the limited processing of Australian wool fibres and specialized areas, the textile and clothing industry in Australia has become steadily less competitive with imports on local markets. This conclusion is supported by the measures of price competitiveness of the Australian textile and clothing industry group which the IAC compiled in its last major study of the industries (Industries Assistance Commission 1986b). After adjusting for the changes in exchange rates, the price competitiveness of Australian goods relative to similar goods produced by Italy, Taiwan, China, Korea and the United States clearly declined between 1968 and 1983, the last year in the IAC's study.

However, this increase in gross and net import shares of domestic sales is only part of the story. One must also consider the levels of protection given to the local producers. The last column in Table 9.5 tabulates the average effective rates of assistance received by these industry groups from 1973 to 1989. These rates have been estimated for individual 4-digit ASIC codes by the Industries Assistance Commission and they include the estimated effects on sale prices of all quotas and tariff quotas applying to commodity groups within these industries. Australia began to introduce tariff quotas on selected knitwear products in 1972 and 1973 but the main increase in protection started in December 1974 with the introduction of country quotas and voluntary export restraints.[2] The range of clothing and textile commodities subject to quantitative restrictions steadily expanded in the decade of the 1970s. By 1979 about 90 per cent of Australia's clothing production and 30 per cent of textile production was protected by quotas. These increases in levels of protection have been made possible because Australia has chosen not to be a signatory of the MFA.

These series show that the effective rates of assistance to the 'textiles', 'knitting mills' and 'clothing' groups of commodities have all risen quite substantially since 1974.[3] Over this period the effective rates of assistance going to other manufacturing producers have, by contrast, trended downwards. In 1988–89 the average effective rate of assistance for the whole manufacturing industry in Australia was 17 per cent, half the level of the early 1970s, while the effective rates for textiles and clothing have doubled since 1973. That is, the group of commodities produced by the textile and clothing industries, along with footwear, stand out as by far the most highly protected group within the manufacturing sector in Australia, and to a much greater extent than they did fifteen years or so ago. The only other commodity group receiving high levels of assistance is 'motor vehicles and parts', which received an average rate of assistance of 70 per cent in 1988–89, down from twice that level in 1984–85 (IAC 1989: Table A7.7).

These increases in the levels of assistance to textiles and clothing have boosted aggregate output of these industries substantially compared with what their output would have been in the absence of this change. In general, in international trade models in which there are multiple commodities, one cannot be certain that an increase in effective protection for a commodity group will necessarily increase aggregate output of the group. This is partly because the volume of output in existing activities may decline when the range of outputs is increased, and partly because in a multi-stage production process assistance to upstream activities by means of quotas or tariffs lowers the effective protection of downstream activities (see next section).

2 Textile importers in Australia were struck in 1972 and 1973 by a combination of major shocks which worsened their position. In addition to the increasing competitiveness of overseas suppliers, there were two substantial appreciations of the Australian dollar in 1972 and 1973, an across-the-board unilateral reduction of all import tariffs in 1973, and the introduction of large wage increases for female employees because of the introduction of equal pay in 1973. For more details see, for example, Anderson and Garnaut (1987: 82–6).

3 Since 1982 an increasing fraction of the import quotas has been allocated by tenders. The tender premiums provide an accurate measure of the *ad valorem* nominal rate of protection implied by quotas, and the IAC has used these premiums as well as direct price comparisons and other methods to estimate the nominal rates of assistance. The estimates of the structure of assistance for this group in Australia are probably as detailed and as reliable as those of any country.

However, in the Australian case the quotas on individual categories of imported commodities at different stages were each manipulated where necessary to ensure that the gross outputs of commodity groups were maintained. In this situation the increased protection would also have reduced the share of total imports and the net share of imports in apparent consumption above what they would have been in the absence of protection.

While the increase in protection for many textile and clothing commodities did enable the industry to maintain roughly the same level of aggregate output during a period when the competitiveness of the industry was declining, it did not prevent a substantial decline, of about one-third, in the level of employment in the industry (Table 9.5).

Lloyd (1985) carried out a decomposition analysis of the change in employment in these industries based on the identity between real output and real (apparent) consumption less net imports. Over the period 1968–69 to 1978–79 the trend level of employment declined by 44 and 41 per cent in the textiles and clothing industries, respectively. In the case of textiles, the increase in imports accounted, statistically speaking, for 35 per cent of the reduction in employment while the increase in consumption itself accounted for an increase in employment equal to 45 per cent of the actual decrease in employment. Similarly, in the clothing industry the increase in imports accounted for 145 per cent of the decrease in employment while the change in consumption accounted for an increase in employment equal to 140 per cent of the actual decrease of employment. Labour inputs per unit of output decreased and these decreases accounted for 106 and 96 per cent of the decrease in total employment in the textile and clothing industries. The author concluded that 'For employment, the long-term problem is one of substitution of capital for labour rather than the substitution of imported supplies for domestic supplies' (Lloyd 1985: 513).

While any analysis of the trends in employment in the industry must include an analysis of the downward trend in the use of labour per unit of output, it is also true that the reduced competitiveness of the Australian industry threatened employment in these industries. Thus the labour employed was subject to reduced demand both because of capital intensification in the industries and because of import substitution.

In extending the system of quantitative restrictions on textile and clothing industry products, the government has since 1977 administered assistance to the industries by means of a series of textile, clothing and footwear plans. (There are sectoral plans for some other industries also, most notably for steel and passenger motor vehicles.) The avowed objectives of these plans has been to control the levels of employment in segments of the industries subject to intense import competition and 'to preserve an efficient industry'. The effects on employment in these industries have undoubtedly been positive compared to what the situation would have been without them.[4]

It is difficult to estimate how many jobs have been protected in the absence of detailed knowledge of the production technology of the industry. The interpretation of the facts listed above – the constancy of real output and declining employment – and other features such as the substantial increase in real wages relative to capital rentals in the industries, depends on such features as the degree of capital specificity versus labour specificity and the extent to which wage rates in the industry are determined exogenously to the industry. (See the discussion of Lloyd's paper in Jungenfelt and Hague (1985: 523–32). In particular, one should note that there was a wage explosion in the industry after 1974, partly associated with an acceleration in the rate of increase in wages in the economy as a whole and partly due to the introduction of wage parity for female wage earners following the 1972 equal pay decision of the Arbitration Commission. For the four years 1973–74 to 1977–78 the average industry wage rose by 20–25 per cent per year, which was considerably higher than the average increase for the economy as a whole. Thus changes in the structure of wages have compounded the reduced demand for labour due to declining competitiveness associated with the growth of new trading partners (the Asian NIEs and more recently China) and exogenous labour-reducing improvements in technology.

In relation to the second objective – to maintain an efficient industry – the sectoral plans have failed miserably. The industry plans have really been designed to provide relief from import competition by means of border protection. The government has not introduced measures to modernize technologies by scrapping obsolete plants or by plant conversions or mergers or other means of improving factor productivities, as have Japan, the UK and some other advanced industrial countries. The current plan has only very limited provisions for facilitating structural adjustment, mainly relating to retraining and relocation of retrenched workers.

The combination of high nominal and effective rates of assistance

---

[4] One should, however, look at aggregate employment in all industries and consider the general equilibrium effects. Simulations with the ORANI general equilibrium model (see Dixon *et al.* 1982) demonstrate that increases in the level of protection for the textile and clothing industries have a detrimental effect on aggregate economy-wide employment. This is partly due to increasing costs to other industries but primarily because they increase the price level for consumers, and a macro policy of maintaining real wages increases the production costs and reduces the competitiveness of the export sector. See, for example, Higgs, Parmenter and Powell (1984).

and of reliance on quantitative restrictions has created numerous distortions. The Industries Assistance Commission has done an outstanding job in measuring the levels of assistance implied by various government assistance measures and in identifying and estimating the resulting distortions. These have been reported in the major reviews of textiles, clothing and footwear policies which were carried out in the late 1970s and 1980s (IAC 1980, 1986b) and in a series of special appendices in the IAC's annual reports in 1975, 1980, 1981 and 1987. These distortions include intra-industry distortions due to the complexity and instability of the pattern of assistance that has resulted from a complex set of quotas applied to individual commodity categories. Since these effects are now well known they will not be discussed here.

The Australian government has slowly acknowledged the deficiencies of the industry plan for the textiles, clothing and footwear group. The Seven Year Plan which began in 1982 included a number of reforms such as the increase in tariffs on within-quota imports to capture rents accruing to importers, the widening of categories to give greater uniformity of levels of assistance, the increase in quota levels, the elimination of anomalies and the introduction of tendering as a means of allocating valuable property rights. These changes improved the structure of assistance, mainly by reducing the dispersion of rates within the industries.

The central feature of the latest post-1988 plan, as amended, is the gradual phasing out of quota assistance and its replacement by tariffs of either 55, 45 or 40 per cent in 1995. This plan adopted some of the recommendations of the 1986 IAC Report, including the phasing-out of tariff quotas and the extension of tendering during the phase-out to all quota imports by 1 March 1992 and reductions in 'out of quota' duty rates. However, it weakened the recommendations of the IAC in a number of respects, for example by adopting a slower annual increase in the volume of quota imports and higher base tariff rates. While the rates of tariffs are still very high these changes in import arrangements will result in a substantial reduction in levels of assistance to producers in the industries. The Textiles, Clothing and Footwear Authority, the body which administers the current plan, is seeking to promote greater specialization, as well as further raw materials processing and more export orientation in the industries. Recently the Australian Industry Development Corporation, in association with the Authority, hired an international management consultant company based in Belgium to examine the potential for more processing of the wool clip and the cotton crop by downstream industries within Australia (Werner Associates, Inc. 1988a,b). Altogether these features of the current plan reflect a somewhat tougher and less protectionist attitude of the government towards the industry.

Nevertheless, the textile, clothing and footwear industries continue to be regarded as a group that requires special treatment. For example, the outputs of these industries were subject to separate reductions in the program of tariff reductions announced in the 1988 May Statement by the Treasurer. In its last report on the group of textile, clothing and footwear industries in 1986, the IAC noted that there had been some 500 separate reports to Australian governments since the 1920s on assistance to these industries.

The structure of the New Zealand textile and clothing industries

In New Zealand the structure of the industries and the recent trends parallel those of Australia in some respects but in other respects the New Zealand pattern and trends are unique among the advanced industrial countries. Textile and clothing industries in New Zealand are problem ones which have been subject to exceptionally high rates of protection. Since July 1980 the governments' interventions have been coordinated by means of a Textile Industry Development Plan. This plan has been concerned until recently with import relief rather than fostering adjustment to changes in the global industry. Throughout the period almost all production of clothing and much production of textiles has been protected by means of quantitative restrictions as a part of New Zealand's comprehensive system of import licensing. In these respects the New Zealand experience resembles that in Australia and in several other advanced industrial countries.

However, the structure of the industry and trends in output and employment exhibit a distinctly different pattern. In the first place, the import–export pattern in New Zealand is unique. As observed in the first section to this chapter, New Zealand was in 1979 a net exporter of fibres, a net importer of textiles and a net exporter of clothing. Table 9.6, however, suggests that in 1979 New Zealand was a net exporter of both textiles and clothing commodities. The differences between the New Zealand data in Figure 9.1 and Tables 9.1 and 9.3, and those in Table 9.6, arise because the former use the SITC and the latter the ISIC. In the ISIC 'spinning, weaving and finishing textiles' includes woollen scouring and other output of the New Zealand woollen mills which are an important part of the New Zealand output and some of which is classified as 'fibres' in the SITC. The New Zealand textile industry has closer links with wool fibre production than its Australian counterpart. Only about three-quarters of New Zealand's production of wool is exported whereas for Australia the share is about 90 per cent. In particular, the substantial amount

Table 9.6: *Net exports of textiles and clothing, New Zealand,*
1970, 1979 and 1987
(US$ million)

ISIC code	Industry	1970	1979	1987
3211	Spinning, weaving and finishing textiles	−12815	+216832	+347161
3212	Made-up textiles, except wearing apparel	−6955	−15381	−13739
3213	Knitting mills	−5415	−21353	−26435
3214	Manufacture of carpets and rugs	+7869	+24269	+34588
3215	Cordage, rope and twine	−149	−580	+172
3219	Manufacture of textiles, nec	−4076	−14340	−32330
321	All textiles	−21541	+189447	+309417
322	Clothing	−232	+15157	+3297
	Total of above	−21773	+204604	+312714

Source: International Economic Data Bank, Trade Data Tapes, Australian National University, Canberra, 1990.

of manufacture and export of carpets in New Zealand is based on the domestic production of coarse wool fibres, hence the greater importance of textiles in New Zealand's as compared with Australia's exports (Table 9.3 above).

New Zealand's exports have grown steadily in value terms throughout the period, particularly in the 'spinning, weaving and finishing textiles' group, but there has also been strong export growth in carpets and clothing commodities. These statistics relate to trade in current prices and New Zealand has had a relatively high rate of inflation. Unfortunately, the author has no access to a series of exports and imports in constant prices. Brook (1983) estimates that imports fell in real terms between 1963 and 1978, a period when New Zealand moved from being a net importer to a net exporter of clothing.

It is not possible to examine the trends in import shares and net import shares and production because of the lack of data on value of production in New Zealand (see Department of Trade and Industry 1988: Appendix VI). Employment statistics are available, however, from the Department of Labour's Quarterly Employment Survey. The clothing industries have accounted for more than one-half of employment in the textile and clothing industries in New Zealand. For the 'textile' and 'apparel' (= clothing) industries, total employment has trended downwards. Total employment in the 'apparel' industry for 1971 to 1987 fell by 23 per cent, when total employment in the manufacturing sector as a whole fell by only 6 per cent. That is, the clothing industry has declined substantially in terms of employment relative to the whole manufacturing sector.

Given the lack of output statistics it is also not possible to attempt a decomposition of the trends in employment in New Zealand in the manner reported above for Australia. The general picture, though, is of an industry group which has stagnated in terms of output rather than declined as in most advanced industrial countries.

There are two obvious hypotheses which might explain the apparent relatively favourable performance of this group of industries in New Zealand. First, it may be that the New Zealand government has been more willing to give increased protection to domestic producers as their international competitiveness declined. Unfortunately, once again, this hypothesis cannot be tested precisely as there is no annual time series of nominal or effective rates of protection for New Zealand, but the levels of protection for these commodities have been very high. The Department of Trade and Industry (1988: Appendix VII) estimates that the nominal rates of protection due to quantitative restrictions and *ad valorem* and specific duties in 1988 in the 'apparel' industry ranged from 31 per cent (ties, bow ties and cravats) to 290 per cent (corsets). As these estimates apply to a period after considerable liberalization of import licensing restrictions it is apparent that the protection given to New Zealand manufacturers of apparel has been very high indeed throughout the sample period. In its recent review of the apparel industry the Textile Overview Committee reported that 'Manufacturers' representatives generally consider that domestic apparel production is price competitive with OECD sources and almost double the costs of LDC production' (Department of Trade and Industry 1988: 44).

It is difficult to estimate the levels of protection which are implied by a regime of quantitative restrictions. Quantitative restrictions provide increasing implicit rates of protection if foreign supplies become more competitive or if domestic demand expands. Moreover, the increase of licences for some fabrics, the removal of protection for nylon and polyester yarn manufacture, and the introduction of the woven woollen bounty scheme and the 'predominant fibre rule' under the 1980 plan, lowered the cost of supplies of materials to fabric knitters and clothing producers and thereby increased their effective rates of protection.

Recently, as a result of a contract let by the New Zealand government to the Australian consulting firm Syntec, estimates of the nominal and effective rates of assistance for the groups 'Manufacturing Textiles' and 'Manufacturing Clothing except Footwear' have become available for the three years 1981–82, 1985–86 and 1987–88. These estimates are reported in Table 9.7. They reveal a general structure of protection broadly similar to that in Australia. For all three years the effective assistance given to downstream clothing industries is much greater than that given to textile producers. Both are much higher than the

Table 9.7:   *Effective rates of assistance for textile and clothing industries, New Zealand, 1981 to 1988*
(per cent)

NZSIC code	Industry	1981–82	1985–86	1987–88
32112	Woollen fibres, spinning and weaving	50	41	35
32115	Man-made fibres, spinning and weaving	29	28	32
32117	Dyeing, printing and finishing yarns and textiles	87	87	88
32121	Canvas goods and similar articles	139	219	95
32129	Other made-up textile goods	35	37	16
32130	Knitting mills	249	220	197
32140	Carpets and rugs	53	321	44
32190	Textiles, nec	33	61	36
32211	Leather gloves and clothing	205	363	145
32212	Natural and synthetic fur clothing	–19	–17	–13
32219	Clothing other than leather and fur	154	145	128
	Total manufacturing	39	37	26

Source: Syntec (1988: Table A.2.7).

average for the manufacturing sector which was estimated at 26 per cent in 1987–88, and at the 3-digit level the effective protection for the clothing industry is easily the highest in the manufacturing sector. Over the five years from 1981–82 to 1985–86 the broad structure of protection was fairly stable.

The second hypothesis to explain the favourable New Zealand experience in this commodity group is that the comparative disadvantage of New Zealand producers has declined over the period. At first sight this may seem surprising, given the emergence of new highly competitive suppliers in the Asian region. Yet real per capita incomes have grown relatively very slowly in New Zealand over the last 30 years and did not grow at all in the 1980s. Since hourly labour costs are positively and significantly correlated with per capita incomes (OECD 1983: Chart IX), this hypothesis is plausible. However, it appears that this factor would be less important than reductions in the cost of imports associated with the rapid emergence of new competitors, especially China in recent years. Consequently, this author concludes that the high level of protection is the primary explanation of the relatively favourable performance of New Zealand's industries.

While the New Zealand industries have been very highly protected during the sample period, there have been substantial reductions in the levels of industry assistance in recent years, chiefly as a result of unilateral reforms and secondarily as a result of the operation of the

Closer Economic Relations Agreement with Australia. It was noted above that the 1980 plan introduced a number of relaxations of import licensing restrictions on upstream yarns and fabrics and reductions in some tariffs and the substitution of bounties for the protection of woven woollen fabric manufactures which were designed to increase the availability of materials. In 1981 tenders were introduced for apparel import licences with the intention of replacing the import licences by tariffs when the tender premiums fell below trigger levels. Import licences were liberalized. In 1985 seventeen tender categories of textiles were put into the category of global licences on demand as a result of the import licensing tender scheme. The Syntec estimates of effective protection in Table 9.7 show that the average levels of effective protection fell sharply in the two years between 1985–86 and 1987–88.

Most recently the Apparel Tariff and Access Review conducted by the Textile Overview Committee in 1988 (Department of Trade and Industry 1988) put forward a slew of recommendations which, if implemented, will dramatically reduce the average levels of protection and induce a radical restructuring of the industries. It recommended an increase in apparel tender licence allocations each year of 3 per cent (instead of the present 2 per cent per year), the continuation of the existing tender and provision for categories to move first to global licences on demand and one year later to import licensing exemption, and the ending of all licensing controls on 1 July 1992. In addition, it recommended a major tariff reduction program and the phasing out of alternative specific and alternative composite tariff rates to commence on 1 July 1989. Finally, it recommended an ending of the industry plan status for the clothing industry by 1 July 1992.

Moreover, trade in textiles and clothing between New Zealand and Australia has been liberalized as a part of the Closer Economic Relations (CER) Agreement which came into effect in 1983. Initially the progress in freeing trade bilaterally in these commodities was slow because they were exempt from the automatic tariff and quota liberalizations as the industries were subject to plans in both countries. The CER arrangements for apparel were concluded in November 1986. These provided for the elimination of both tariffs and quantitative controls on the trans-Tasman clothing trade by 1995. In August 1988 the two governments decided to accelerate all products to free trade in 1990 and in April 1989 the timetable for the freeing of trade was again accelerated to 1 July 1989. Consequently trans-Tasman trade in apparel products is now completely free.

This recent experience shows that substantial unilateral (and bilateral) reductions in barriers to international trade in this group of industries are possible, though they have been rare. In this instance they came about not because of pressures for reform in this group of industries from either domestic consumers/users or from suppliers who have borne the burden of protection, but because of an unprecedented freeing up of the whole economy which included across-the-board trade liberalization along with major deregulation, privatization and other microeconomic reforms. This in turn is based on a wholesale change in attitudes towards government interventions. The 1988 review of the apparel industry in the Textile Industry Development Plan, for example, is a model of a critical and constructive review of the traditional methods of protection and regulation in the textile and clothing industries.

Country specialization within the global industry

In looking at the structure of the industries and the costs of protection in one country, one needs to consider further the pattern of production and intra-industry specialization among countries in the world economy.

Textile and clothing industries are commonly regarded as labour intensive. Globally this is no longer true of the textile industry though it is still true of the clothing industry in all countries. Australia conforms to this pattern. Enterprise statistics show that the value of fixed assets per employee is lower than the average for all manufacturing enterprises in the clothing industries and that the textile industry is close to the average. However, there is considerable variation *within* textile and clothing enterprises because of differences in the composition of output and the associated differences in technologies. In a survey of these industries the OECD (1983: 84) noted that 'the clothing industry's capital intensity is everywhere much lower than that of textiles and within clothing, cutting and patterning can be one hundred times as capital intensive as sewing'. Again there is a similarly wide variation in the capital intensities of individual enterprises in Australia.

One might endeavour to model the industry in terms of differences in capital intensities for different commodities. However, there is one other feature of production which is basic. Capital–labour intensities apply only to the value-added component. The distinguishing feature of these industries is the materials-intensive multi-stage nature of the production processes. Intermediate inputs account for about 60 per cent of total costs in these industries. This is roughly equal to the average for all manufacturing. However, the use of electricity, transport and other service industry inputs is much less for the group than in manufacturing in general and the use of intermediate inputs from within the group is correspondingly higher. The Australian input–output tables for 1974–75 show that 62 per cent of total intermediate inputs were of materials from other producers in the textile and clothing group.

Traditionally the production of final commodities from textile materials is divided into four stages. First, there is the production of natural and man-made fibres. The second and third stages are the spinning, and the weaving or knitting activities. The fourth and final stage is the production of the final articles: clothing and other household products such as carpets and curtains and other made-up products. This is a considerable simplification. Some of the production processes do not involve weaving (for example, the manufacture of carpets). More importantly, each of these stages really consists of a number of processing activities done in sequence. For example, the production of woven or knitted fabrics goes through the stages of broad weaving or fabric knitting followed by fabric dyeing, finishing, brushing and printing, and other preparations. (A simplified flow diagram of the industries is provided in the report of the former Textile and Apparel Industry Advisory Council 1980: 16.)

Differences in primary factor intensities can be linked to the stages of processing of materials. Dixit and Grossman (1982) have developed an elegant model of manufactures whch are produced via a vertical production structure with many stages. At each stage value is added to an intermediate material to yield a good-in-process for the next stage. The good at stage $i+di$ is produced from one unit of stage i output. All stages produce pure intermediates except the last stage which produces the final product. The stages are assumed to differ in factor intensities and it is convenient to order the stages by increasing labour intensities. At any stage a good can be produced in any country in the world economy and therefore in moving downstream through the stages a good-in-process can be shipped from one country to a second country and to a third country and so on before the final product is made. This model captures the realism of processing and international trade in materials at every stage.

Comparative advantage determines the pattern of specialization among countries if trade is free. In this model countries specialize by stages. Consider two countries, one country and the rest of the world: specialization by stages will be determined by the country's wage/capital rental ratio. There is a borderline commodity in the continuum such that the country either exports all commodities below this commodity and imports all of those above it, or vice versa. The country with the highest wage–rental ratio specializes in the production of the most capital-intensive end of the spectrum, and so on. When the actual physical sequence of stages differs from the economic ordering by factor intensities, it is possible for a country to produce and export the output of some stage and to reimport these materials after they have been processed abroad for further processing in the home country. This happens to some of the wool fibres which Australia exports.

This model is the most suitable of the trade models for analysing the effects of protection and the pattern of intra-industry specialization in the textile and clothing industries. The multi-stage production process with stages varying in capital intensities describes the main features of the industries. In reality there are many final products but each of the final goods can be considered as the end-product of a good-in-process.

The effects of protection can readily be analysed in this model. Uniform protection has the effect of increasing the range of stages that are produced in the protecting country. However, a tariff also raises the cost of intermediates downstream and this effect by itself lowers the effective protection for downstream stages. It is possible for protection to be anti-protective in that the aggregate demand for labour may be reduced if the volume effects dominate the range effect.

In the case of Australia, the wage–rental ratio is high by world standards and much higher than the major Asian trading partners from whom most textile and clothing commodities are imported. In such a country the effect of protection will be to permit it to produce goods which are more labour intensive than those in which it would specialize under free trade. If protection is non-uniform, as it is in reality, goods with higher labour intensity would require higher rates of protection if they are to be produced. The textile industry is on average much more capital intensive than the clothing industry and we do find that the levels of nominal and effective protection required to sustain clothing production in Australia are much higher than those for the textile industry.[5] It is also true that the Australian government had to modify earlier assistance to the manufacturers of some yarns and fabrics, provided by means of quotas, by substituting bounties. The latter avoided the anti-protective effects on downstream industries.

The Australian government is currently seeking to increase value added in the country's exports by further processing of raw materials. As part of this policy it has introduced a Raw Materials Processing Program for the Textile, Clothing and Footwear Industries which is administered by the TCF Development Authority. In particular, it is considering methods of promoting further processing of Australia's large exports of raw wool.

One component of this policy is to identify the factors which have impeded the growth of processing and to assess future market opportunities. The government has recognized that 'it is important that wool processing activities should achieve long-term viability without

[5] This line of analysis could be pursued further by correlating the measures of capital-labour intensity with the rates of effective protection.

government assistance'. (Department of Primary Industries and Energy 1989: 41). Any assistance will impose the usual deadweight loss on the economy through the reduction in aggregate national output and consumer welfare. The model also indicates that this strategy may not achieve an increase in aggregate value added in the industry group if the increase in domestic content of a unit of output is offset by a reduction in the number of units produced for domestic sale or export.

This model can also be used to interpret the trends in the region in relation to the trends in the global industry. As the relative costs of production of each commodity (i.e. each good-in-process at some stage) among the countries in the world economy changed there would be a corresponding relocation among countries of world production, provided the structure of protection in all countries remained constant. There have been major changes in the sourcing of imports and supplies in Australia, New Zealand and other advanced industrial countries but it is apparent that many of the changes that would have resulted from the continually shifting pattern of comparative advantage have been designed to slow down the adjustments and to maintain domestic production of particular groups of products.

Looking to the future, consider the effects of possible changes to future trading policies on the world economy. At present world trade in fibres is mostly free of border restrictions and the restrictions on world trade in the products of the group are concentrated at the upper end of the chain, especially the most labour-intensive products. These restrictions raise the average price in industrial countries of the final products of the industry relative to other commodities. This in turn reduces the volume of sales of the final products in the group and of all the materials embodied in these final products.[6] A reduction in these restrictions would increase world sales and output of the final products and all materials. Thus this protection harms fibre producers and exporters as well as the efficient textile and clothing producing countries. A global reduction in protection would also lead to changes in the location of production of semi-processed goods at lower stages since these stages are protected by some countries. These changes will increase the intra-industry efficiency of the global industry and lower the real costs of production as well as lower the final price to consumers via the removal of the tariffs and tariff equivalents of non-tariff restrictions.

A country such as Australia specializes largely in the production of fibres and other products which are at the bottom of the processing chain or continuum. While trade in these commodities is free, it is penalized by the restrictions on processed textile and clothing products. There is both a volume and a price effect as some of the tariffs or

---

[6] This follows because at every stage of production exactly one unit of the good-in-process from the previous stage is used to produce a unit of output.

tariff equivalents are passed backwards to the suppliers of goods-in-process. Consequently, upstream producers would share in a reduction in the restrictions on world trade in products at higher stages by being able to sell a greater volume of their output at a higher average price. On the other hand, higher stage producers in such countries fear a reduction in their output. This would be inevitable for some. However, given the range of final outputs produced by the commodity group, and recognizing that some of these producers are currently harmed by protection of upstream producers of some of their manufactured fibres or fabrics and other materials, some of these higher-stage producers also will benefit. Under a regime of free trade in all products of the textile and clothing industries, the effects on production in industrial countries such as Australia is such that while the outputs of commodities which were heavily protected would contract, there would be offsetting expansions in the outputs of other commodities which could now be produced with lower-price inputs and/or which could be sold at higher prices in international markets.

III
CONCLUSIONS

10

Future prospects and policy implications

Kym Anderson

In concluding the study, this chapter first draws out the lessons that emerge from East Asia's experience in becoming more involved in world markets for textile, clothing and fibres. It then examines the extent to which China needs to be considered as a special case, before turning to review what the political developments in Europe of the late 1980s/early 1990s could mean for East Asian and other exporters of textiles, clothing and fibres. A speculative section then assesses the prospects for liberalization of trade in textiles and clothing, and is followed by a few suggestions of ways to enhance those prospects for reform. Finally, some implications are mentioned for policies affecting other manufacturing industries in advanced industrial economies.

Lessons from East Asia's experience

The clearest lesson to emerge from Part I of this study is that textiles and clothing are industries which tend first to increase and then to decrease in relative importance to an economy as it gradually changes from being largely agrarian to being a modern industrial state. This rise and demise will not occur uniformly across economies as they develop and their comparative advantages change, because the latter will depend heavily on changes in a country's relative factor endowments as compared with average global endowment ratios. Specifically, industrial competitiveness will begin with more labour-intensive products, and will occur at a lower level of industrial capital per worker, the more poorly is an economy endowed with natural resources per worker. It is therefore not surprising that the economic growth of densely populated Japan, following the opening up of that economy after 1868, was accompanied by growth in production and exports of labour-intensive manufactures such as textiles and clothing. Nor is it surprising, given the large size and rapid expansion of Japan's economy, that its exports gradually eclipsed exports from the United Kingdom and Europe in international markets.

It is also not surprising that this international relocation of textile production from Europe (and North America) to Japan was accompanied by a parallel change in the direction of trade in natural fibres. The importance of the United Kingdom and continental Europe as a destination for natural fibre exports, including silk from East Asia along the so-called Silk Road, gradually dwindled in relative importance as Japan's demand for fibre imports grew.

Furthermore, we saw that in the 1950s/early 1960s the newly emerging economies of Hong Kong, South Korea and Taiwan – which are even more densely populated than Japan (see Table 10.1) – began

Table 10.1: *Population and population density, selected economies, 1986*

	Population (millions)	Population density (persons per square km)
Industrial market economies		
Japan	122	327
European Community-12	323	143
European Free Trade Association	32	26
North America and Australasia	266	10
TOTAL	743	24
Centrally-planned Europe		
USSR	281	13
Other Eastern Europe	135	109
TOTAL	416	18
East Asia		
Hong Kong	5	5400
Korea	42	423
Taiwan	19	539
ALL 3 NIEs	66	491
China	1054	110
North Korea and Vietnam	84	187
South Asia	1000	240
Other developing economies	1557	28

Source: World Bank, *World Development Report 1988*, New York, Oxford University Press, 1988.

to duplicate the Japanese development pattern. Following their economic liberalization and opening up, the production and imports of
textiles and clothing from those economies grew very rapidly, as did
their demand for imports of natural fibres. As a group these NIEs
made substantial inroads into international markets for textiles and
clothing. Just as Japan in earlier decades had put competitive pressure
on the United Kingdom and continental Europe, which brought about
the relative demise of their textile and clothing industries, so these
Northeast Asian NIEs began to reduce the competitiveness of these
industries in Japan.

However, the competitiveness of the Northeast Asian NIEs grew so
rapidly, and Japan's response to their growth was so prompt and
positive (e.g. developing new labour-saving technologies for these
industries, specializing in the more capital-intensive processes within
these industries and sub-contracting other processes offshore), that
Northeast Asia's aggregate share of textile and clothing exports and
natural fibre imports continued to increase despite some decline in
Japan's share. Moreover, this expansion occurred in spite of the
increasingly protectionist policies of the more advanced industrial
economies, beginning with the barriers to Japan's exports in the 1930s
and escalating steadily from the 1950s with the Short Term Cotton
Textile Trade Agreement (STA) which became the Long Term Cotton
Textile Trade Agreement (LTA) and then four successive Multi-fibre
Arrangements (MFA).

Since the late 1970s we have seen a third generation of export-led
NIEs emerge, most notably with China but also in Southeast Asia,
especially Thailand. They have added further to the relocation of
production and exports of textiles and clothing from, and imports of
natural fibres by, East Asia. This development is beginning to cause
these industries, not just in the high-income countries but also in Korea
and Taiwan, to move to producing and exporting more capital-
intensive manufactures and skill-intensive products. Again, though,
the growth in trade due to these third-generation NIEs is more than
offsetting the declining contributions of Japan and the advanced NIEs,
so East Asia's importance in world markets for textiles, clothing and
fibres continues to grow.

Thus the historical experience of this region does *not* suggest there
is reason to be pessimistic about the export growth prospects for
would-be newly emerging exporters of textiles and clothing, particularly when the international relocation of production and trade has
occurred despite very high and rising levels of protection against
imports of these products into advanced industrial economies. All that
those protectionist policies have done is slow the process of adjustment
to long-term changes in comparative advantage and therefore the rate
of growth of incomes in both advanced and emerging industrial
economies.

Will China's experience be different?[1]

To what extent does the fact that China is such a populous economy, and that it has been only marginally involved in international commerce for most of the postwar period, affect the likelihood of China following the development path of its more industrialized neighbours? This question is important both to politicians and others in advanced industrial economies concerned about job losses and the collapse of textile firms, as well as to producers in other third-generation NIEs. In Chapter 5 above, John Whalley cautions that China may have special difficulties for itself and cause special problems for others. Nonetheless, there is considerable evidence supporting an optimistic view of China's role in international markets for textiles and clothing. For example, the successful growth experience of Thailand in these markets in the 1980s (see Chapter 4 above) during the same period as China's emergence is a strong counter-example to the claim that China is crowding out other newcomers.

Whether China – which is not as resource-poor as its Northeast Asian neighbours but is nonetheless densely populated by world standards (Table 10.1) – continues to expand its importance in world textile, clothing and fibre markets depends both on how China reacts to its current internal macroeconomic and political problems and on how the rest of the world responds to China's growth. On the first of these, it seems more likely than not that history will judge the Tiananmen Square incident of mid-1989 and its aftermath as a temporary interruption to China's long-run economic growth path. The economic reform process seems likely to continue again from the early 1990s, if only because the Chinese people have observed a decade of what is possible, in terms of rapid incomes growth, when markets are freed. It seems unlikely that the leadership could for long deny those people a continuation of that opportunity and survive. Assuming the leadership recognizes this and adjusts its policies accordingly, thereby avoiding further internal disruptions, rapid growth may be resumed well before the turn of the century.

In the likely event that a return to 'business as usual' will still leave China struggling to overcome some major macroeconomic problems, textiles and clothing will have an even more important role to play as an export earner in the 1990s. Hard-currency export earnings are needed not only to purchase essential imports but also to service China's sizeable foreign debt. Chinese farmers are unlikely to contribute much to the earning of foreign exchange. On the contrary, the country is likely to become increasingly dependent on imports of food, feed and fibre as domestic demand growth for these products exceeds the growth in farm output and resources are attracted to industrial

[1] This section draws to some extent on Anderson (1990b).

and service sectors. Nor are mineral and energy products a likely source of expanding foreign exchange earnings, because as China's industrial development proceeds, domestic demand for these raw materials also is likely to grow faster than domestic supply. The mining sector's contribution to gross export earnings fell from more than one-quarter to only one-eighth during the 1980s, and to keep it from falling even further the domestic economy has been starved of energy to the point that many industrial plants have been grossly under-utilized for lack of power (see Anderson 1990a). Thus exports of light manufactures such as textiles and clothing are going to be critically important for China's prosperity during the next decade or so.

Moreover, China's need for greater access to industrial-country markets for textiles is *immediate*, given its current economic and political difficulties. For the open-door policy to remain credible domestically, and for foreign investment and joint ventures not to dry up, improved textile export prospects are essential. They are essential not only to allow for an increasing quantity of textile and clothing exports but also to ensure that prices of these exports do not collapse under the weight of increasing volumes in the international market-place. In short, for China's economic growth and reform process as a whole to continue, the industrial countries of the world need to signal to China – and indeed to all struggling economies in the Third World – that an economy is able to trade its way out of its economic and political difficulties.

It follows from the above assessment that reforming the trade-restricting MFA is very much in the political and strategic interests of industrial countries, for otherwise China may turn inwards again as it did during the dark age of the so-called Cultural Revolution.[2] But more than that, allowing China's exports of textiles and clothing to grow via a liberalization of the MFA is also in the narrow *economic* interests of many other countries, for it would allow a continuation of rapid growth in imports by China. It would expand the demand for natural fibres not only from the United States and Australia but also from cotton-exporting developing countries such as Egypt and Sudan. It would also expand the demand for synthetic fibre imports, for example from Japan, Korea and Western Europe, as well as the demand for foreign capital inflow from such more-established pro-ducers of textiles. But, more generally, an expansion in exports of light manufactures would strengthen the economy's industrial com-petitiveness and raise consumer incomes, thereby expanding China's net imports (reducing its net exports) of primary products as well as increasing its imports of capital equipment, high-technology products and the like from advanced industrial countries.

2 A further contribution to political stability in China from liberalizing the MFA would be the reduction in the administrative task of allocating export quotas, and hence in the corruption bred by such arrangements.

Table 10.2: *Import penetration by China into various industrial-country markets for labour-intensive manufactures,*[a] *1970 to 1986*
(per cent)

	All industrial market economies	EC	EFTA	Japan	United States	Canada	Australia
Textiles, clothing and footwear (ISIC 32)							
1970–73	0.3	0.2	0.4	1.0	—	0.5	1.2
1974–77	0.4	0.4	0.5	0.9	0.1	0.6	1.4
1978–81	0.7	0.6	0.8	1.3	0.4	0.8	1.9
1982–85	1.2	1.0	1.2	1.9	1.0	1.2	2.3
1986	1.6	1.2	1.5	1.8	1.7	1.6	2.4
Other light manufactures (ISIC 39)							
1970–73	0.2	0.3	0.3	0.3	—	0.1	0.6
1974–77	0.3	0.6	0.6	0.4	0.1	0.1	0.6
1978–81	0.5	0.9	1.0	0.4	0.3	0.1	1.0
1982–85	0.7	1.2	1.4	0.5	0.7	0.2	1.5
1986	0.9	1.2	1.8	0.5	1.1	0.5	2.1

[a] Imports from China as a percentage of apparent consumption of the industrial country(-ies), where apparent consumption is production plus imports minus exports. Intra-EC trade is excluded.
Source: See Appendix to this volume.

To what extent might industrial country markets be swamped by Chinese exports of textiles and clothing? Having seen China's share of world exports of these products grow from 3 to 10 per cent during the past decade, many politicians understandably have been concerned at the prospect of widespread unemployment of textile workers in industrial countries as Chinese goods flood in. These concerns are much greater than the evidence would suggest is appropriate, however, for two reasons. One is that China's exports to some extent would simply replace exports of other, more advanced economies. As is clear from Figures 3.1 and 3.3 in Chapter 3 above, Japan has made way for the Asian NIEs since the 1950s, just as the United Kingdom and other European countries did for Japan earlier this century. These countries can reasonably be expected to do likewise for China, as indeed is predicted by Trela and Whalley's (1988b) general equilibrium modelling results. That is, industrial country imports, and those from China's Northeast Asian neighbouring economies, would increase by less than the gross expansion in China's exports.

The second reason to discount the expressed fear of a potential flood of textile products from China has to do with the current degree of China's import penetration. It is true that China's share of textile, clothing and footwear sales in advanced industrial economies has quadrupled since the mid-1970s, and that its penetration has been uniformly spread across all major regions (Table 10.2). But this growth

Table 10.3:   *Import penetration by China and other economies into
all industrial country markets for manufactures,*[a] *1970 to 1986*
(per cent)

	China	Hong Kong, Korea, Taiwan	Other developing countries	All developing countries	All countries
Textiles, clothing and footwear (ISIC 32)					
1970–73	0.3	1.7	1.6	3.6	13.6
1974–77	0.4	3.1	2.3	5.8	18.3
1978–81	0.7	4.2	3.2	8.1	22.6
1982–85	1.2	5.4	3.8	10.4	24.1
1986	1.6	5.6	4.3	11.5	26.8
Other light manufactures (ISIC 39)					
1970–73	0.2	2.4	1.9	4.5	20.4
1974–77	0.3	2.8	2.9	6.0	25.2
1978–81	0.5	4.1	3.9	8.5	34.1
1982–85	0.7	5.4	4.6	10.7	30.7
1986	0.9	5.5	5.0	11.4	30.7
All manufactures (ISIC 3)					
1970–73	—	0.3	1.2	1.5	12.4
1974–77	0.1	0.5	1.5	2.1	15.1
1978–81	0.1	0.8	1.7	2.6	17.0
1982–85	0.2	1.0	1.9	3.1	17.7
1986	0.2	1.1	1.6	2.9	17.6

[a] Imports from the countries shown as a percentage of apparent consumption in all
industrial market economies.
Source: See Appendix to this volume.

has been from a low base, so the share of Chinese goods is still very
small both in absolute terms and relative to other suppliers. As of
1986, China supplied only 1.6 per cent of domestic sales of textiles
and clothing in all industrial market economies, which is similar to
the shares held by Northeast Asia's NIEs or all other developing
economies in the early 1970s (Table 10.3). Even if China's exports of
these products were to grow at the same frenetic pace as those from
Hong Kong, Korea and Taiwan did during the 1970s, China by the
turn of the century would be supplying barely 5 per cent of textile
and clothing sales in advanced economies.

On the other hand, if China's access to textile and clothing markets
were to continue to be limited, its desperate need to earn foreign
currency would simply force it to expand exports of other light
manufactures. As is clear from Tables 10.2 and 10.3, China's share
of those product markets in industrial countries has also been growing
rapidly, trebling since the reforms. Thus trying to prevent any disruption to one group of manufacturers in industrial countries will simply

transfer the pressure to another group. And in the case of the United States and Australia it would also harm the interests of cotton and wool growers.

For the more advanced developing countries such as the Asian NIEs, growth in China would certainly force them also to move to more capital- and skill-intensive activities, but those activities would still include some textile production processes. In addition, through joint ventures in China the expertise of producers elsewhere in Northeast Asia could continue to be used. Hong Kong and Macao would be likely to find they are also able to expand in productive areas that are highly complementary to China's, most notably in the provision of international marketing services for Chinese manufacturers.[3]

In short, a great deal hangs on whether textile trade is liberalized in the early 1990s. Should the opportunity be provided for China to expand its exports substantially during this decade, that may be just what is needed to reaffirm the Chinese government's resolve to push on with its economic reforms and to open that economy even further, which is something that would boost economic welfare in both China and the rest of the world. On the other hand, if current restrictions were to continue, China's capacity to expand might well be seriously thwarted. Moreover, other densely populated economies which may be thinking of becoming more outward looking, such as in South Asia or the centrally planned economies of Vietnam or North Korea (see Table 10.1 above), would also be discouraged from doing so if markets in rich countries are not opened up more.

What impact will developments in Europe have?

As Carl Hamilton's analysis in Chapter 7 makes clear, the political changes that began to sweep Eastern Europe in the late 1980s, together with the 1992 program and the completion of the integration of Southern Europe with the economies to its north, will have important implications for East Asia's prospects in European and indeed global markets for textiles and clothing. Should the European Community accommodate the wish of the three most recent entrants to the EC (Greece, Portugal and Spain) in retaining high barriers to external imports into that bloc, then these low-wage Southern European

[3] The general equilibrium model used by Whalley in Chapter 5 above suggests Hong Kong and Macao would be (the only) losers from a liberalization of the MFA. However, had the model explicitly included an international marketing service activity, it is likely that the sign of the effect on these two economies also would have been positive.

countries will be more able to supply the rest of Western Europe with textiles and clothing, although probably at a higher cost than East Asia. And if Turkey and other Mediterranean suppliers also were to be given greater preferential access to Western European markets through their associate membership of the EC, Asian and other suppliers would be further squeezed out of European markets.

The recent political developments in Eastern Europe will have a less immediate impact than the continuing integration of Southern and Northwestern Europe. But in the longer run they may have a much more profound impact. As Table 10.1 above shows, Eastern Europe (excluding the USSR) is as densely populated as Western Europe as a bloc. Should it begin to specialize its production in order to exploit its comparative advantage to the full, the likelihood is that it would use its low wage level to compete at the labour-intensive end of the manufacturing spectrum. And if Western Europe provides preferential access for goods from Eastern Europe, as seems very likely, this would further reduce European sales prospects for East Asian and other suppliers. On the other hand, if Europe were to open its markets and East European economies were to grow rapidly as a consequence of economic reforms, at least the volume if not the share of sales in Europe supplied by East Asia is likely to continue to rise in the 1990s.

How liberal will the textile and clothing trade be in the 1990s?

In assessing the prospects for substantial liberalization of industrial-country markets for textiles and clothing, several points need to be made. First, the perceived growth during the 1970s and 1980s in import barriers facing developing-country exporters may be more apparent than real. Certainly the trade from developing to industrial countries has continued to grow rapidly, as demonstrated by the import penetration data in Table 10.3. This supports the contention of Hughes and Waelbroeck (1981), Yoffie (1983), Bhagwati (1988) and others that protection policies provide somewhat porous rather than impenetrable barriers. The porosity results partly from the ingenuity of producers in developing countries in finding ways around barriers by altering their export product mixes, by relocating production in countries with unfilled export quotas, and so on. But it can also be the result of authorities in the importing country turning a blind eye to the over-filling of trade quotas in situations where not to do so would be against the country's broader foreign policy interests. The dramatic import penetration by China during the 1980s may be a case in point (Cline 1987). Thus while it is generally true that quantitative limitations on trade are more inefficient policy instruments than *ad valorem* trade taxes (Takacs 1978, Anderson 1988), there are situations where the administrative flexibility offered by import quotas and 'voluntary' export restraints actually lead to more rather than less trade.

This is not to downplay the harm done by the MFA and related barriers to textile and clothing trade. As the modelling results reported in Chapters 4 and 5 above show, the MFA does cause wasteful trade restrictions and diversions, and its removal would benefit virtually all developing countries – not to mention the fact that it would give a boost to incomes in the liberalizing advanced industrial economies themselves. Moreover, the covert nature of quantitative trade restrictions used under the MFA is such that consumers and other would-be opponents in high-income countries are less informed about the extent and hence cost of these trade barriers than they would be with, say, a tariff, and hence are less active lobbyists against the MFA.

Rather, the point is that newly and would-be emerging economies should not be discouraged by the MFA from adopting an export-led, open-economy industrialization strategy because, as China and Thailand in the 1980s and the more advanced NIEs in earlier decades have demonstrated, rapid and equitable economic growth based on such a strategy is clearly possible.

Ways to enhance the prospects for trade liberalization

An important way in which the prospects for reforming the MFA can be and indeed have been recently improved is through the dissemination of more information on the costs and distributional consequences of existing policies. The global, general equilibrium modelling work of Trela and Whalley's, for example, is able to add greatly to the quantitative information on the costs of these policies. More such work is needed, however, particularly on the distributional consequences within both exporting and importing countries. Such models can demonstrate clearly that volume-dominated quotas under the MFA hurt poorer consumers in importing countries disproportionately by raising most the prices of low-value standard clothing items, and cause job losses elsewhere in their country that may more than offset the jobs saved in declining textile and clothing firms, and reduce the foreign exchange earnings of those other industries. Disseminating more widely the results of such studies, as the World Bank has been doing recently (see, for example, Hamilton 1990), can add significantly to the political pressure for reform from within protected economies.

Likewise, exposing the very uneven distribution within exporting countries of rents from VERs would undermine support for the use of this policy instrument.

There are also ways of adding external pressures for reform. Unilaterally China has successfully been able to seek greater access for its textile goods by threatening otherwise to reduce its grain and other imports from those protecting countries (Cline 1987). While most other developing economies are too small individually to be able to so threaten, they would have some prospect of doing so if they were to become more active and cohesive participants in the GATT negotiations process. Moreover, exporters of fibres, both natural and synthetic, have a common interest in an expanding, less restricted trade in textiles and clothing. As tolerance of high protectionist barriers weakens in high-income economies, it may pay fibre exporters to act together to lobby in multilateral and national forums for such liberalization, in a manner similar to that adopted by the so-called Cairns group of non-subsidizing, food-exporting countries.

Efforts might also be intensified to disseminate in Southern and Eastern Europe the results of analyses which show the virtues of an export-led industrial development strategy which is based on an open economy approach rather than being dependent on discriminatory preferential access to a protected European Community–EFTA market. While the latter preferential approach may seem attractive in the short run, its effects in the longer run will not be as great as an approach based on exploiting their global as distinct from local comparative advantage. Now is a particularly opportune time to intensify the dissemination of such liberal ideas – with MFA IV due to expire in mid-1991, with the completion of the integration of the EC by 1992 and with the reconstruction of Eastern Europe's economies getting underway at long last.

One area where further research is still required is in understanding the reasons for the persistence of protection against textile and clothing imports. Like the agricultural sector, textiles and clothing are declining industries in advanced industrial countries. In fact they are typically the first significant manufacturing industries to come under pressure to decline in a growing economy. Being reasonably concentrated geographically and being major employers, firms in these industries have found it worthwhile investing in lobbying for the raising and maintaining of high trade barriers.[4] While this may continue to be the case for a while yet, the time may well come when the benefits to politicians in these countries from protecting these producers is more than offset by the political benefits forgone from other constituents harmed by the protection (Cassing and Hillman 1986; Hillman 1982,

[4] For a discussion of why agricultural protection persists in high-income countries also, see Anderson (1989) and Tyers and Anderson (forthcoming).

1989). In fact such a collapse of protection has already occurred in the case of footwear in some countries (Hamilton 1989). A better understanding of the reasons for existing policies and their changes can only help in identifying ways to facilitate reform.[5]

Implications for other industries

Finally, a rather obvious but nonetheless important inference should be drawn from the textile and clothing experience. It is that where there are long-run market forces dictating changes in comparative advantage, there is no economic point in trying to prevent those changes from making an impact on an economy by adopting protectionist policies. The effects of declining comparative advantage in a product group can be offset by protection policies only if the level of protection continues to increase over time. We have seen governments having to do that with agricultural markets (Tyers and Anderson forthcoming) and it has been done in vain for textiles and clothing. If domestic productivity cannot be increased sufficiently rapidly for an industry to remain competitive internationally in the face of a long-term decline in real output prices, it would pay to encourage that industry to decline overall and to concentrate only on those parts in which the country is able to retain a competitive edge.

[5] For a review of earlier studies of the political economy of manufacturing protection in industrial countries, see, for example Baldwin (1984) and Anderson and Baldwin (1987).

Data on world production, consumption and trade in textiles, clothing and fibres

Prue Phillips and Kym Anderson

This Appendix provides details of the data summarized in various chapters on East Asia's role in world markets for natural fibres, textiles and clothing (and other manufactured goods, for comparative purposes).

The first set of tables shows the extent of import penetration by East Asia, all developing countries and all countries into the main industrial market economies for textiles and clothing (separately and as a group with footwear and other leather products), for other light manufactures and for all manufactured goods for the period 1970 to 1986. Data are presented in Table A1 for each high-income importing country/country group. Import penetration is defined as gross imports as a percentage of consumption, the latter being determined as production plus gross imports minus gross exports.

Also of interest is net imports (gross imports minus gross exports) as a percentage of consumption, and exports as a percentage of production. These data are presented in Table A2 for the various high-income importing countries/country groups. Also in the same table is an index of import specialization, defined as net imports as a percentage of gross imports plus gross exports. The closer that index is to +100 (−100) the stronger the country is specialized in importing (exporting) the product in question as distinct from being involved in intra-industry trade.

The final two sets of tables are concerned with natural fibre markets for the period 1961 to 1986. Table A3 shows the shares of various East Asian and other countries in world production, consumption imports and exports of natural fibres, of raw cotton and of raw wool. Table A4 shows the extent to which various countries are self-sufficient in natural fibres (production as a percentage of production plus imports

Table A1.1: *Import penetration from East Asia and elsewhere into markets for textiles, clothing and other manufactures in industrial market economies, 1970 to 1986*
(imports as a percentage of domestic consumption)

| | East Asia | | | | | All | |
	NE Asian NIEs	China	ASEAN	Japan	All E. Asia	developing countries	All countries
Textiles							
1970–73	1.1	0.4	0.2	0.8	2.4	3.3	14.5
1974–77	1.5	0.4	0.2	0.7	2.8	4.2	17.5
1978–81	1.7	0.7	0.3	0.7	3.5	5.3	20.6
1982–85	2.2	1.1	0.4	0.9	4.5	6.2	20.8
1986	2.6	1.2	0.5	0.9	5.2	6.9	22.5
Clothing							
1970–73	3.4	0.1	0.1	0.7	4.4	4.4	13.5
1974–77	6.4	0.3	0.5	0.4	7.6	9.0	20.9
1978–81	8.7	0.7	1.1	0.4	10.9	13.2	27.6
1982–85	10.7	1.6	1.6	0.5	14.3	17.4	30.6
1986	10.9	2.3	1.8	0.5	15.5	19.9	35.9
Textiles, clothing, footwear, leather							
1970–73	1.7	0.3	0.1	0.7	2.9	3.6	13.8
1974–77	3.1	0.4	0.3	0.5	4.3	5.8	18.3
1978–81	4.2	0.7	0.6	0.5	5.7	8.1	22.6
1982–85	5.4	1.2	0.8	0.7	8.0	10.4	24.1
1986	5.6	1.6	0.9	0.7	8.8	11.4	26.8
Other light manufactures							
1970–73	2.4	0.2	0.2	1.9	4.6	4.5	20.4
1974–77	2.8	0.3	0.4	1.8	5.4	6.0	25.2
1978–81	4.1	0.5	0.8	1.9	7.2	8.5	34.1
1982–85	5.4	0.7	0.9	2.3	9.4	10.7	30.7
1986	5.5	0.9	1.1.	2.5	10.1	11.5	30.7
All manufactures							
1970–73	0.3	—	0.1	0.8	1.3	1.5	12.4
1974–77	0.5	0.1	0.3	1.0	1.8	2.1	15.1
1978–81	0.8	0.1	0.4	1.3	2.5	2.6	17.0
1982–85	1.0	0.2	0.4	1.7	3.4	3.1	17.7
1986	1.1	0.2	0.4	2.1	3.7	2.9	17.6

minus exports) and are direct users of raw cotton and raw wool (kilograms per capita per year clean, not counting indirect use via the importing of textile products but including the use of natural fibres in producing textile products for export).

The manufacturing data (Tables A1 and A2) are shown for seven high-income importing countries or country groups, namely: all industrial market economies, the European Community, the European Free Trade Association, Japan, the United States, Canada and Australia.

Table A1.2: *Import penetration from East Asia and elsewhere into markets for textiles, clothing and other manufactures in the European Community,[a] 1970 to 1986*
(imports as a percentage of domestic consumption)

	East Asia					All developing countries	All countries
	NE Asian NIEs	China	ASEAN	Japan	All E. Asia		
Textiles							
1970–73	0.7	0.3	—	0.3	1.4	3.4	23.2
1974–77	1.1	0.4	0.2	0.3	2.1	5.0	29.5
1978–81	1.2	0.7	0.4	0.5	2.8	6.5	35.6
1982–85	1.5	1.1	0.5	0.7	3.8	7.9	40.7
1986	1.6	1.1	0.5	0.9	4.2	7.6	41.0
Clothing							
1970–73	3.6	0.1	0.4	0.2	3.9	4.5	25.0
1974–77	6.8	0.2	1.1	0.2	7.7	10.3	37.4
1978–81	8.3	0.5	2.3	0.2	10.3	14.5	47.1
1982–85	9.4	1.1	2.3	0.2	12.2	18.8	55.6
1986	8.9	1.4	2.3	0.3	12.0	20.5	60.7
Textiles, clothing, footwear, leather							
1970–73	1.4	0.2	0.1	0.3	2.0	3.7	22.6
1974–77	2.7	0.4	0.5	0.3	3.6	6.6	30.6
1978–81	3.4	0.6	1.0	0.4	5.0	9.0	37.6
1982–85	3.9	1.0	1.1	0.5	6.2	11.1	43.0
1986	3.8	1.2	1.1	0.6	6.4	11.4	44.8
Other light manufactures							
1970–73	2.0	0.3	0.2	2.4	5.0	4.8	42.8
1974–77	2.7	0.6	0.3	2.8	6.6	7.5	54.3
1978–81	4.7	0.9	0.6	3.2	9.9	11.1	57.8
1982–85	6.8	1.2	0.8	4.3	14.3	16.4	77.0
1986	5.7	1.2	0.8	4.0	12.8	14.1	61.8
All manufactures							
1970–73	0.2	0.1	—	0.5	0.9	1.8	21.3
1974–77	0.4	0.1	0.1	0.7	1.5	2.3	26.2
1978–81	0.6	0.1	0.2	1.0	2.1	2.8	30.1
1982–85	0.7	0.1	0.2	1.4	2.7	3.5	34.4
1986	0.8	0.1	0.2	1.7	3.0	3.0	33.3

[a] Belgium–Luxembourg, France, West Germany, Italy, the Netherlands and the United Kingdom only.

The exporting countries/country groups in Table A1 are the Northeast Asian NIEs (Hong Kong, Korea and Taiwan), China, ASEAN, Japan, all of these East Asian economies as a group, all developing economies as a group and all countries as a group.

These same countries/country groups are represented in Tables A3 and A4, along with (in Table A4) Portugal and Thailand individually and European centrally-planned economies as a group.

Table A1.3: *Import penetration from East Asia and elsewhere into markets for textiles, clothing and other manufactures in EFTA,[a] 1970 to 1986*
(imports as a percentage of domestic consumption)

	East Asia					All	
	NE Asian NIEs	China	ASEAN	Japan	All E. Asia	developing countries	All countries
Textiles							
1970–73	1.1	0.4	—	1.0	2.5	2.9	43.0
1974–77	1.5	0.5	0.2	0.7	2.9	4.4	46.0
1978–81	1.7	0.7	0.4	0.5	3.3	5.2	52.6
1982–85	2.2	1.0	0.4	0.5	4.2	6.5	58.0
1986	1.9	0.9	0.3	0.5	3.6	5.9	56.5
Clothing							
1970–73	5.2	0.3	0.4	0.2	6.2	7.1	44.1
1974–77	10.0	0.6	1.1	0.2	12.0	13.5	59.0
1978–81	10.0	1.1	2.3	0.6	14.0	15.9	73.8
1982–85	11.4	1.6	2.3	0.4	15.8	18.4	79.9
1986	10.9	2.5	2.3	0.3	16.1	19.7	90.3
Textiles, clothing, footwear, leather							
1970–73	2.3	0.4	0.1	0.7	3.5	4.2	41.8
1974–77	4.3	0.5	0.5	0.5	5.7	7.3	48.7
1978–81	4.7	0.8	1.0	0.5	7.0	9.2	58.0
1982–85	5.9	1.2	1.1	0.4	8.6	11.3	64.0
1986	5.5	1.5	1.1	0.4	8.4	11.5	67.1
Other light manufactures							
1970–73	1.4	0.3	0.2	3.6	5.7	2.2	42.2
1974–77	2.2	0.6	0.3	3.9	7.0	3.7	48.0
1978–81	3.8	1.0	0.6	4.8	10.2	6.4	55.0
1982–85	5.6	1.4	0.8	6.4	14.2	8.7	58.1
1986	6.1	1.8	0.8	6.2	14.9	9.6	56.0
All manufactures							
1970–73	0.2	0.1	—	1.2	1.5	1.4	31.2
1974–77	0.4	0.1	0.1	1.6	2.2	1.7	34.3
1978–81	0.5	0.1	0.2	1.6	2.4	2.0	35.7
1982–85	0.8	0.1	0.2	2.2	3.4	2.1	38.0
1986	0.8	0.1	0.2	2.6	3.8	1.9	36.8

[a] Finland, Norway and Sweden only.

The commodity groups included in the tables are textiles (International Standard Industrial Classification (ISIC) 321 and Standard International Trade Classification (SITC) 65), clothing (ISIC 322 and SITC 84), textiles, clothing, footwear and other leather products (ISIC 32 and SITC 61, 65, 84 and 85), other light manufactures (ISIC 39 and selected items from SITC 69 and 89), all manufactures (ISIC 3 and SITC 5 to 8 plus 266), raw cotton (SITC 263), raw wool (SITC 262) and all natural fibres (SITC 26 less 266).

Table A1.4: *Import penetration from East Asia and elsewhere into markets for textiles, clothing and other manufactures in Japan, 1970 to 1986*
(imports as a percentage of domestic consumption)

	East Asia				All developing countries	All countries
	NE Asian NIEs	China	ASEAN	All E. Asia		
Textiles						
1970–73	1.8	1.2	0.2	3.2	4.6	7.1
1974–77	2.3	1.0	0.2	3.5	4.6	7.7
1978–81	2.8	1.4	0.3	4.5	5.4	8.9
1982–85	2.3	2.0	0.3	4.6	5.9	9.6
1986	1.9	1.8	0.2	4.0	4.9	7.8
Clothing						
1970–73	3.3	0.6	0.1	4.0	4.1	5.4
1974–77	6.0	0.8	0.1	6.9	7.1	9.0
1978–81	6.7	1.4	0.2	8.3	8.6	11.4
1982–85	7.0	2.4	0.2	9.6	9.9	12.3
1986	6.5	2.2	0.2	8.9	9.1	11.1
Textiles, clothing, footwear, leather						
1970–73	2.0	1.0	0.1	3.2	4.3	6.6
1974–77	3.1	0.9	0.2	4.2	5.1	7.8
1978–81	3.6	1.3	0.3	5.2	6.0	9.3
1982–85	3.5	1.9	0.3	5.6	6.6	9.9
1986	3.3	1.8	0.2	5.2	5.9	8.5
Other light manufactures						
1970–73	1.5	0.3	0.4	2.3	4.5	8.9
1974–77	1.9	0.4	0.4	2.6	4.4	8.5
1978–81	2.1	0.4	0.7	3.3	5.3	9.5
1982–85	2.2	0.5	0.6	3.3	5.0	8.8
1986	2.5	0.5	0.5	3.5	5.1	9.0
All manufactures						
1970–73	0.3	0.1	0.2	0.6	1.4	4.5
1974–77	0.5	0.1	0.4	1.0	1.9	5.1
1978–81	0.6	0.2	0.5	1.2	2.0	5.3
1982–85	0.6	0.3	0.5	1.4	2.0	5.5
1986	0.6	0.2	0.3	1.1	1.5	4.3

The data are from the Market Penetration Tapes and the Agricultural Trade Tapes of the International Economic Data Bank of the Australian National University, Canberra. The former are based on World Bank/ OECD files held at the OECD in Paris and described in Brodin and Blades (1986). The latter are compiled from files generated by the UN's Food and Agriculture Organisation in Rome and, in the case of stocks data, the US Department of Agriculture in Washington, DC.

Table A1.5: *Import penetration from East Asia and elsewhere into markets for textiles, clothing and other manufactures in the United States, 1970 to 1986*
(imports as a percentage of domestic consumption)

| | East Asia | | | | | | |
	NE Asian NIEs	China	ASEAN	Japan	All E. Asia	All developing countries	All countries
Textiles							
1970–73	0.9	—	0.1	1.2	2.2	2.3	5.5
1974–77	1.1	0.1	0.2	0.9	2.2	2.6	5.2
1978–81	1.4	0.3	0.2	0.9	2.8	3.4	6.3
1982–85	2.2	0.6	0.3	1.0	4.2	4.6	8.1
1986	3.3	1.0	0.5	1.3	6.1	6.6	11.2
Clothing							
1970–73	3.1	—	0.4	1.1	4.6	4.1	6.8
1974–77	6.0	0.1	0.6	0.6	7.2	8.7	10.0
1978–81	9.7	0.6	1.2	0.6	12.0	13.8	15.8
1982–85	12.3	1.6	2.0	0.7	16.6	18.9	21.9
1986	13.9	2.9	2.7	0.8	20.2	24.2	28.9
Textiles, clothing, footwear, leather							
1970–73	1.7	—	0.2	1.1	3.0	3.0	6.1
1974–77	3.0	0.1	0.3	0.7	4.1	4.9	7.2
1978–81	4.9	0.4	0.6	0.7	6.6	7.9	10.5
1982–85	6.8	1.0	1.0	0.9	9.7	11.1	14.4
1986	7.9	1.7	1.3	1.0	12.0	14.1	18.7
Other light manufactures							
1970–73	2.9	—	0.1	2.0	5.0	4.4	11.5
1974–77	3.4	0.1	0.3	1.6	5.4	6.0	13.6
1978–81	4.7	0.7	0.6	1.7	7.3	8.7	18.2
1982–85	6.4	0.7	0.7	2.3	10.1	11.1	22.1
1986	7.1	1.1	1.2	3.0	12.3	14.2	26.8
All manufactures							
1970–73	0.4	—	0.1	1.1	1.6	1.3	6.1
1974–77	0.6	—	0.2	1.3	2.2	2.1	7.4
1978–81	0.9	0.1	0.3	1.9	3.2	2.7	9.0
1982–85	1.4	0.1	0.4	2.5	4.4	3.5	11.0
1986	1.6	0.2	0.4	3.2	5.4	3.6	12.2

Table A1.6: *Import penetration from East Asia and elsewhere into markets for textiles, clothing and other manufactures in Canada, 1970 to 1986*
(imports as a percentage of domestic consumption)

	East Asia						
	NE Asian NIEs	China	ASEAN	Japan	All E. Asia	All developing countries	All countries
Textiles							
1970–73	1.3	0.4	0.1	2.9	4.8	3.9	26.4
1974–77	2.2	0.8	0.2	2.4	5.4	5.2	29.5
1978–81	2.3	0.9	0.4	1.6	5.2	5.4	27.6
1982–85	3.3	1.1	0.5	1.5	6.3	6.5	25.7
1986	5.1	1.4	0.6	1.7	8.9	9.4	29.7
Clothing							
1970–73	3.6	0.6	0.1	1.1	5.3	4.6	11.3
1974–77	6.8	0.8	0.2	0.4	8.2	8.7	15.6
1978–81	8.2	0.9	0.5	0.2	9.9	10.5	16.4
1982–85	10.5	1.5	1.1	0.3	13.5	14.4	20.5
1986	11.3	2.1	1.6	0.4	15.5	16.9	25.4
Textiles, clothing, footwear, leather							
1970–73	2.2	0.5	0.1	2.0	4.7	4.0	19.5
1974–77	4.2	0.6	0.2	1.3	6.3	6.6	22.8
1978–81	4.7	0.8	0.4	0.9	7.1	7.7	22.3
1982–85	6.4	1.2	0.7	0.9	9.2	9.9	22.7
1986	7.7	1.6	1.0	1.0	11.3	12.4	27.0
Other light manufactures							
1970–73	1.7	0.1	0.1	3.2	5.2	2.7	22.0
1974–77	2.2	0.1	0.3	2.7	5.3	3.6	25.3
1978–81	2.9	0.1	0.4	2.1	5.4	5.0	40.1
1982–85	3.4	0.2	0.2	2.2	6.1	5.1	31.9
1986	4.4	0.5	0.3	2.6	7.9	6.8	34.0
All manufactures							
1970–73	0.4	0.1	0.1	1.5	2.1	1.2	28.2
1974–77	0.7	0.1	0.1	1.5	2.3	1.5	30.3
1978–81	0.9	0.1	0.1	1.7	2.8	1.8	32.0
1982–85	1.1	0.1	0.2	2.0	3.4	2.3	30.6
1986	1.4	0.2	0.2	2.6	4.3	3.0	34.4

Table A1.7: *Import penetration from East Asia and elsewhere into markets for textiles, clothing and other manufactures in Australia, 1970 to 1986*
(imports as a percentage of domestic consumption)

	East Asia						
	NE Asian NIEs	China	ASEAN	Japan	All E. Asia	All developing countries	All countries
Textiles							
1970–73	3.4	1.7	0.4	7.0	12.7	7.7	25.6
1974–77	5.3	1.8	0.8	6.3	14.2	10.1	29.6
1978–81	6.6	2.4	1.3	5.2	15.6	13.0	32.7
1982–85	8.3	2.6	1.5	6.1	18.5	14.8	34.1
1986	9.0	2.6	2.0	5.1	18.6	15.9	33.9
Clothing							
1970–73	3.1	0.7	0.1	0.3	4.2	4.3	7.3
1974–77	7.8	1.1	0.8	0.4	10.2	10.8	14.8
1978–81	7.8	1.8	1.3	0.3	11.2	11.9	15.4
1982–85	8.6	2.4	1.0	0.3	12.4	13.3	16.9
1986	6.9	2.8	0.9	0.4	10.9	12.2	16.8
Textiles, clothing, footwear, leather							
1970–73	3.0	1.2	0.3	4.5	9.1	6.1	18.1
1974–77	6.0	1.4	0.8	3.8	11.9	9.9	22.7
1978–81	6.7	1.9	1.2	3.0	12.8	11.9	24.1
1982–85	8.1	2.3	1.3	3.5	15.1	13.6	25.8
1986	7.8	2.4	1.5	3.0	14.7	13.9	26.1
Other light manufactures							
1970–73	3.3	0.6	0.9	6.2	10.7	5.6	27.7
1974–77	5.0	0.6	1.1	7.0	13.7	8.8	36.0
1978–81	7.2	1.0	2.0	6.6	16.8	12.3	39.7
1982–85	10.2	1.5	2.2	8.2	22.1	16.1	41.4
1986	12.1	2.1	2.5	8.2	24.9	19.3	43.8
All manufactures							
1970–73	0.5	0.2	0.3	2.6	3.5	1.5	15.2
1974–77	1.0	0.2	0.6	3.9	5.7	3.0	18.5
1978–81	1.3	0.2	0.9	4.1	6.6	3.7	20.2
1982–85	1.7	0.3	0.9	5.4	8.3	4.2	22.0
1986	2.0	0.3	1.0	5.8	9.1	4.3	24.5

Table A2: *Trade specialization in textiles and clothing, industrial market economies, 1970 to 1986*
(per cent)

	Gross imports/ consumption	Net imports/ consumption	Gross exports/ production	Net imports/ imports plus exports
(a) *All industrial market economies*[a]				
Textiles				
1970–73	14.5	–0.3	14.7	–1.1
1974–77	17.5	–0.2	17.7	–0.5
1978–81	20.6	0.8	20.0	1.9
1982–85	20.8	2.0	19.2	5.1
1986	22.5	3.3	19.8	8.9
Clothing				
1970–73	13.5	4.0	9.9	17.6
1974–77	20.9	8.7	13.3	26.5
1978–81	27.6	12.8	17.0	30.1
1982–85	30.6	16.8	16.6	37.8
1986	35.9	19.9	20.0	38.3
(b) *European community*[b]				
Textiles				
1970–73	23.2	–4.1	26.3	–8.2
1974–77	29.5	–2.2	31.0	3.5
1978–81	35.6	0.3	35.4	0.4
1982–85	40.7	–0.5	41.0	–
1986	41.0	–1.0	41.6	–1.2
Clothing				
1970–73	25.0	2.1	23.4	4.3
1974–77	37.4	8.6	31.5	12.9
1978–81	47.1	12.4	39.6	15.2
1982–85	55.6	12.5	49.2	12.7
1986	60.7	12.4	55.2	11.3
(c) *France*				
Textiles				
1970–73	15.8	–5.9	20.6	–15.8
1974–77	21.7	–0.4	22.1	–1.0
1978–81	29.9	2.9	25.8	5.5
1982–85	32.9	4.9	29.5	8.0
1986	33.8	6.5	29.1	10.7
Clothing				
1970–73	12.2	–9.1	19.5	–27.1
1974–77	17.6	–6.6	22.7	–15.7
1978–81	25.0	0.5	24.6	1.1
1982–85	32.3	6.8	27.4	11.7
1986	37.9	11.5	29.8	179.9

Table A2 (cont'd)

	Gross imports/ consumption	Net imports/ consumption	Gross exports/ production	Net imports/ imports plus exports
(d) West Germany				
Textiles				
1970–73	25.5	4.0	22.4	8.4
1974–77	30.8	4.2	27.7	7.4
1978–81	38.4	8.0	33.0	11.6
1982–85	44.3	4.5	41.7	5.3
1986	43.4	1.8	42.4	2.1
Clothing				
1970–73	30.9	17.7	16.0	40.3
1974–77	45.2	27.6	24.3	44.0
1978–81	57.1	34.6	34.4	43.4
1982–85	70.3	39.6	50.8	39.2
1986	73.7	39.2	56.8	36.2
(e) Italy				
Textiles				
1970–73	14.5	−13.5	24.7	−31.7
1974–77	20.4	−14.3	30.4	−25.9
1978–81	23.5	−17.3	34.8	−26.9
1982–85	25.3	−20.9	38.3	−29.3
1986	25.4	−21.8	38.7	−30.0
Clothing				
1970–73	8.7	−51.1	39.6	−74.5
1974–77	16.3	−85.6	54.9	−72.4
1978–81	29.1	−147.6	71.4	−71.7
1982–85	43.1	−210.8	82.1	−71.8
1986	57.6	−276.7	88.7	−70.6
(f) United Kingdom				
Textiles				
1970–73	16.0	−2.3	17.9	−6.6
1974–77	22.0	0.1	22.0	0.2
1978–81	29.8	5.8	25.5	10.8
1982–85	39.3	15.6	28.0	24.9
1986	41.1	18.2	28.3	28.2
Clothing				
1970–73	16.3	6.4	10.6	24.4
1974–77	25.6	10.7	16.7	26.5
1978–81	33.7	13.1	23.7	24.1
1982–85	40.8	19.7	26.4	31.7
1986	43.5	21.4	28.1	32.6

(cont'd)

Table A2: *(cont'd)*

	Gross imports/ consumption	Net imports/ consumption	Gross exports/ production	Net imports/ imports plus exports
(g) EFTA[c]				
Textiles				
1970–73	43.0	29.3	19.4	51.6
1974–77	46.0	30.2	22.6	48.9
1978–81	52.6	33.1	29.2	45.9
1982–85	58.0	35.4	34.9	44.0
1986	56.5	34.8	33.3	44.5
Clothing				
1970–73	44.1	20.6	29.6	30.5
1974–77	59.0	29.2	42.1	32.9
1978–81	73.8	35.9	59.1	32.2
1982–85	79.9	44.0	64.0	38.0
1986	90.3	58.4	76.8	47.7
(h) *Sweden*				
Textiles				
1970–73	40.5	26.4	19.2	48.4
1974–77	44.5	27.8	23.2	45.3
1978–81	53.3	30.5	32.8	40.1
1982–85	62.2	32.3	44.1	35.1
1986	58.8	29.2	41.9	33.0
Clothing				
1970–73	46.3	31.5	21.6	51.6
1974–77	63.3	46.4	31.5	57.9
1978–81	78.0	61.3	43.1	64.7
1982–85	87.5	69.9	58.3	66.5
1986	94.5	76.8	76.5	68.4
(i) *Japan*				
Textiles				
1970–73	7.1	–8.6	14.5	–37.7
1974–77	7.7	–8.9	15.3	–36.5
1978–81	8.9	–6.4	14.3	–26.4
1982–85	9.6	–7.6	15.9	–28.3
1986	7.8	–4.6	11.9	–22.7
Clothing				
1970–73	5.4	–5.4	10.3	–33.4
1974–77	9.0	4.3	4.9	31.5
1978–81	11.4	7.8	3.9	52.2
1982–85	12.3	7.4	5.3	43.3
1986	11.1	7.9	3.5	55.4
(j) *United States*				
Textiles				
1970–73	5.5	2.3	3.3	26.7

Table A2: *(cont'd)*

	Gross imports/ consumption	Net imports/ consumption	Gross exports/ production	Net imports/ imports plus exports
1974–77	5.2	0.0	5.2	0.3
1978–81	6.3	–0.3	6.5	–2.2
1982–85	8.1	3.9	4.4	31.7
1986	11.2	7.5	4.0	50.5
Clothing				
1970–73	6.8	5.6	1.3	70.0
1974–77	10.0	8.0	2.1	67.1
1978–81	15.8	13.2	3.0	71.9
1982–85	21.9	20.2	2.2	85.4
1986	28.9	27.2	2.4	88.7
(k) *Australia*				
Textiles				
1970–73	25.6	18.7	8.5	57.4
1974–77	29.6	21.7	10.2	57.7
1978–81	32.7	20.5	15.3	45.6
1982–85	34.1	21.1	16.4	44.9
1986	33.9	17.8	19.6	35.6
Clothing				
1970–73	7.3	6.0	1.4	70.2
1974–77	14.8	13.9	1.1	88.4
1978–81	15.4	14.5	1.0	89.6
1982–85	16.9	16.4	0.7	93.5
1986	16.8	16.0	0.9	91.0
(l) *Canada*				
Textiles				
1970–73	26.4	21.9	5.7	71.1
1974–77	29.5	25.4	5.5	75.7
1978–81	27.6	22.7	6.3	70.2
1982–85	25.7	21.3	5.7	70.4
1986	29.7	23.8	7.8	66.5
Clothing				
1970–73	11.3	6.6	5.1	41.1
1974–77	15.6	11.8	4.3	60.8
1978–81	16.4	11.7	5.3	55.7
1982–85	20.5	15.8	5.6	62.3
1986	25.4	19.5	7.3	62.2

[a] Australia, Belgium, Canada, Finland, France, West Germany, Italy, Japan, the Netherlands, Norway, Sweden, the United Kingdom and the United States only.
[b] Belgium–Luxembourg, France, West Germany, Italy, the Netherlands and the United Kingdom only.
[c] Finland, Norway and Sweden only.

Table A3.1: *Shares of world's natural fibre production, consumption, imports and exports, selected countries, 1961 to 1986*
(per cent)

| | EC-12 | EFTA | United States | Canada | Australia | New Zealand | East Asia | | | | | All industrial market economies | All developing countries | European CPEs |
							Japan	NE Asian NIEs	China	ASEAN	All East Asia			
Share (%) of world:														
Production														
1961–64	3.4	0.1	16.7	0.1	7.7	2.8	1.8	0.2	7.2	0.6	9.8	32	52	16
1965–69	2.9	0.1	11.0	0.1	7.5	3.0	1.6	0.3	12.2	0.8	14.9	26	57	17
1970–74	2.6	0.1	11.2	0.1	7.3	2.7	1.4	0.4	12.3	0.7	14.4	25	57	18
1975–79	2.5	0.1	11.0	0.1	6.4	2.7	1.1	0.5	12.9	0.7	15.2	24	57	19
1980–84	2.4	0.1	9.9	0.1	5.9	2.9	0.7	0.2	20.2	0.6	21.7	22	60	18
1985–86	2.6	0.1	8.8	0.1	6.7	2.6	0.5	0.1	19.7	0.5	20.8	21	63	16
Consumption														
1961–64	10.4	0.6	15.2	0.2	4.9	1.7	4.4	0.7	7.3	0.3	12.7	38	45	17
1965–69	8.7	0.5	10.6	0.2	5.0	2.2	4.3	0.9	12.0	0.5	17.7	32	50	18
1970–74	8.5	0.5	9.3	0.2	4.3	1.7	5.4	1.4	12.3	0.7	19.8	30	50	20
1975–79	10.5	0.7	6.8	0.2	2.5	1.1	6.3	3.3	13.2	1.3	24.1	28	51	21
1980–84	10.5	0.8	4.3	0.2	1.0	0.8	6.1	3.8	20.5	1.6	32.0	24	56	20
1985–86	9.9	0.8	5.9	0.2	1.7	0.9	4.5	3.0	18.3	1.5	27.3	24	58	18

Gross imports

1961–64	46.2	3.3	6.4	0.6	0.6	0.1	15.1	2.7	1.5	0.6	19.9	73	11	15
1965–69	42.2	2.9	5.6	0.6	0.6	0.1	16.5	3.7	1.5	0.8	22.5	69	14	17
1970–74	35.7	2.6	2.2	0.7	0.5	0.1	19.6	5.9	3.4	1.5	30.4	62	19	20
1975–79	34.2	2.6	1.5	0.4	0.4	0.1	17.2	10.1	4.5	2.8	34.6	57	25	18
1980–84	31.3	2.6	1.6	0.3	0.3	0.1	15.7	12.0	6.9	3.3	37.9	52	30	18
1985–86	34.2	2.8	1.6	0.3	0.3	0.1	14.1	12.4	3.3	3.6	33.4	54	29	18

Gross exports

1961–64	9.8	0.3	12.9	0.2	15.8	5.7	1.0	0.2	0.7	2.3	4.2	45	48	7
1965–69	8.5	0.3	8.6	0.1	16.2	4.8	0.3	0.5	1.3	2.8	4.9	39	52	9
1970–74	7.5	0.3	11.5	0.1	15.6	5.2	0.2	1.1	2.5	1.6	5.4	40	50	9
1975–79	8.7	0.4	15.6	0.1	13.7	5.6	0.2	1.1	2.7	0.7	4.7	44	43	12
1980–84	8.1	0.4	18.6	—	15.4	6.3	0.1	1.4	4.1	0.5	6.1	49	40	11
1985–86	9.8	0.4	11.5	—	18.9	6.2	0.2	2.7	7.7	0.3	10.9	47	42	11

Table A3.2: *Shares of world's raw cotton production, consumption, imports and exports, selected countries, 1961 to 1986* (per cent)

	EC-12	EFTA	United States	Canada	Australia	New Zealand	Japan	NE Asian NIEs	China	ASEAN	All East Asia	All industrial market economies	All developing countries	All European CPEs
Share (%) of world:														
Production														
1961–64	1.5	—	24.3	—	—	—	—	0.1	8.6	0.2	8.9	26	60	14
1965–69	1.2	—	15.7	—	0.2	—	—	0.1	15.9	0.2	16.2	17	68	15
1970–74	1.1	—	16.1	—	0.2	—	—	—	14.9	0.2	15.1	17	66	17
1975–79	1.1	—	16.0	—	0.2	—	—	—	14.8	0.3	15.1	17	68	19
1980–84	1.0	—	14.1	—	0.6	—	—	—	23.4	0.4	23.8	16	70	17
1985–86	1.4	—	12.3	—	1.2	—	—	—	22.0	0.3	22.5	15	64	15
Consumption														
1961–64	14.3	1.1	14.8	0.7	0.2	—	6.2	2.0	9.1	0.6	17.9	38	44	18
1965–69	12.1	0.9	10.5	0.6	0.2	—	5.7	2.2	16.3	0.8	25.0	30	52	18
1970–74	9.7	0.8	10.0	0.5	0.2	—	5.4	2.8	16.1	1.0	25.3	27	54	19
1975–79	8.4	0.8	8.2	0.4	0.2	—	5.2	4.5	16.4	1.7	27.8	23	58	19
1980–84	7.5	0.7	5.2	0.3	0.1	—	4.8	4.5	20.7	1.9	31.9	19	65	17
1985–86	7.5	0.7	7.1	0.2	0.3	—	3.8	4.0	24.3	2.0	34.1	19	65	16

Gross imports

Year														
1961–64	37.0	3.1	1.4	1.2	0.6	—	16.6	5.0	2.0	1.2	24.8	61	18	22
1965–69	34.1	2.7	1.0	0.9	0.4	—	16.4	6.3	2.5	1.7	26.9	57	21	23
1970–74	28.7	2.4	0.4	0.4	0.2	—	16.7	8.8	5.2	2.5	33.2	50	27	23
1975–79	25.2	2.4	0.3	0.2	0.1	—	16.0	14.5	6.9	4.6	42.0	45	35	20
1980–84	23.4	2.5	0.1	0.1	0.1	—	16.1	15.7	9.5	5.2	46.5	43	39	18
1985–86	25.4	2.9	0.2	0.1	0.1	—	14.1	16.0	0.1	6.3	36.5	43	35	21

Gross exports

Year														
1961–64	3.3	0.1	26.1	—	—	—	0.1	0.1	0.1	—	0.3	30	60	11
1965–69	3.2	0.1	16.7	—	—	—	0.1	0.2	0.2	—	0.5	20	65	14
1970–74	3.0	0.1	19.2	—	0.2	—	0.2	0.3	0.4	—	0.9	23	62	15
1975–79	2.5	0.1	25.1	—	0.3	—	0.1	0.8	0.9	0.1	1.9	28	52	20
1980–84	2.3	0.2	31.1	—	1.7	—	0.2	1.2	1.7	0.2	3.3	36	46	18
1985–86	2.9	0.3	19.8	—	4.0	—	0.2	0.6	7.5	0.1	8.4	27	54	19

Table A3.3: *Shares of world's raw wool production, consumption, imports and exports, selected countries, 1961 to 1986 (per cent)*

| | EC-12 | EFTA | United States | Canada | Australia | New Zealand | East Asia | | | | | All industrial market economies | All developing countries | All European CPEs |
							Japan	NE Asian NIEs	China	ASEAN	All East Asia			
Share (%) of world:														
Production														
1961–64	6.7	0.2	4.9	0.1	29.0	10.5	0.1	—	3.6	—	3.7	52	31	17
1965–69	6.2	0.2	3.6	0.1	29.1	11.6	0.1	—	3.8	—	3.9	51	32	18
1970–74	5.6	0.2	2.8	0.1	29.8	11.4	0.1	—	4.5	—	4.6	50	31	19
1975–79	5.4	0.2	1.8	—	27.1	11.5	0.1	—	5.2	—	5.3	46	32	21
1980–84	5.3	0.2	1.7	—	25.0	13.0	—	—	6.6	—	6.6	45	34	21
1985–86	5.5	0.2	1.3	—	27.6	12.4	—	—	6.1	—	6.1	47	33	20
Consumption														
1961–64	31.3	1.2	10.8	0.4	3.5	1.3	10.1	0.2	3.7	—	13.9	59	20	22
1965–69	27.7	1.0	9.0	0.4	2.3	3.6	11.4	0.6	3.5	—	15.5	55	22	23
1970–74	24.5	0.8	4.8	0.2	4.0	2.5	12.1	1.2	4.3	—	17.6	49	24	27
1975–79	22.6	0.8	3.4	0.3	4.0	2.0	9.5	1.9	5.1	0.1	16.6	43	28	30
1980–84	18.3	0.6	3.5	0.2	2.7	3.1	7.3	2.5	8.4	0.2	18.4	36	34	30
1985–86	20.1	0.5	3.1	0.2	2.7	2.9	7.0	2.6	10.7	0.2	20.5	36	37	27

Gross imports														
1961–64	53.8	2.0	10.1	0.6	0.2	—	16.4	0.3	1.3	—	18.0	83	5	12
1965–69	48.2	1.6	9.7	0.6	0.3	0.1	19.6	1.0	0.6	—	21.2	80	6	13
1970–74	44.9	1.4	4.3	0.4	0.6	0.1	22.0	2.3	0.5	—	24.8	74	9	18
1975–79	45.4	1.5	3.3	0.4	0.8	0.1	18.4	3.9	0.8	0.2	23.2	69	12	19
1980–84	38.7	1.2	4.1	0.4	0.8	0.1	15.0	6.2	4.2	0.4	25.8	60	19	21
1985–86	39.9	0.9	3.8	0.4	0.8	0.1	13.6	7.0	9.8	0.3	30.7	59	24	17
Gross exports														
1961–64	13.7	0.3	0.1	0.2	43.4	15.6	0.1	—	0.9	—	1.0	73	24	3
1965–69	11.4	0.3	0.2	0.1	47.9	14.1	0.1	—	1.0	—	1.1	74	23	3
1970–74	11.4	0.4	0.3	0.1	49.6	16.8	0.2	0.1	0.4	—	0.7	79	20	2
1975–79	13.7	0.4	0.2	—	46.7	19.0	0.2	0.4	0.5	—	1.1	80	19	1
1980–84	11.6	0.3	0.2	—	47.6	20.7	0.1	1.1	0.2	—	1.4	81	18	1
1985–86	12.7	0.3	0.2	—	51.6	19.2	0.1	2.2	0.1	—	2.4	84	15	1

Table A4: *Fibre self-sufficiency and per capita consumption, East Asian and other countries, 1961 to 1986*

	All industrial countries	EC-10	EFTA	Portugal	United States	Australia	New Zealand	United Kingdom	Japan
Self-sufficiency in natural fibres (%)									
1961–64	85	27	10	32	108	155	157	23	39
1965–69	82	28	12	30	102	150	134	27	37
1970–74	83	27	9	17	119	167	156	26	26
1975–79	81	22	7	12	157	247	243	24	17
1980–84	90	21	6	9	226	591	342	33	12
1985–86	86	24	6	9	142	384	272	35	10
Per capita consumption of raw cotton (kg/yr)									
1961–64	8.1	6.9	5.4	10.5	10.8	3.0	0.3	6.7	8.9
1965–69	6.8	6.0	4.6	12.6	7.9	3.6	0.5	5.4	8.5
1970–74	6.2	4.9	4.1	14.9	7.8	2.6	0.4	3.8	8.3
1975–79	5.3	4.2	4.0	14.1	6.2	2.2	0.3	2.8	7.5
1980–84	4.7	4.0	4.1	12.5	4.2	1.5	0.2	1.4	7.6
1985–86	5.4	4.4	4.8	19.8	6.3	3.5	0.3	1.4	6.6
Per capita consumption of raw wool (kg/yr)									
1961–64	2.57	3.28	1.18	1.82	1.60	9.05	14.33	5.21	2.90
1965–69	2.44	2.89	0.99	2.26	1.32	5.77	38.86	4.40	3.30
1970–74	2.09	2.48	0.78	2.13	0.68	8.95	25.47	3.17	3.34
1975–79	1.68	2.21	0.72	1.59	0.43	8.07	18.59	2.57	2.37
1980–84	1.41	1.81	0.60	1.72	0.44	5.28	28.38	1.83	1.79
1985–86	1.54	2.14	0.55	1.88	0.42	5.42	28.22	2.00	1.85

	Taiwan	Korea	Hong Kong	All three NE Asian NIEs	China	Thailand	All ASEAN	All developing countries	European CPEs
Self-sufficiency in natural fibres (%)									
1961–64	42	52	—	32	98	178	190	114	90
1965–69	36	63	—	37	100	181	162	112	92
1970–74	9	63	—	30	99	120	102	112	89
1975–79	3	27	—	14	95	62	49	108	90
1980–84	2	8	—	5	96	52	39	105	87
1985–86	1	7	—	4	104	42	34	104	87
Per capita consumption of raw cotton (kg/yr)									
1961–64	6.3	2.6	37.1	6.5	1.8	1.1	0.5	2.8	3.6
1965–69	7.0	3.0	41.0	7.2	3.2	1.6	0.6	3.2	3.8
1970–74	9.7	4.2	38.2	8.5	2.9	2.2	0.8	3.2	4.2
1975–79	12.7	8.3	46.4	12.6	3.1	3.0	1.2	3.1	4.0
1980–84	10.5	30.4	13.2	3.9	3.2	1.3	3.5	3.9	3.9
1985–86	9.7	24.0	12.8	4.9	3.7	1.4	3.7	4.0	4.0
Per capita consumption of raw wool (kg/yr)									
1961–64	0.10	0.11	0.10	0.11	0.15	—	—	0.25	0.88
1965–69	0.54	0.27	0.49	0.37	0.13	—	—	0.26	0.93
1970–74	1.06	0.48	0.76	0.67	0.15	—	—	0.26	1.06
1975–79	1.09	0.90	0.63	0.93	0.15	—	—	0.26	1.08
1980–84	1.21	1.25	0.34	1.17	0.24	—	—	0.29	1.06
1985–86	1.27	1.42	0.43	1.30	0.33	—	—	0.32	1.02

Bibliography

Ajanant, J. and Speafico, L., 1984. *Industrial Restructuring in Textile Industries*, an interim report to UNOP/UNIDO-NESDB Industrial Restructuring Project, Industrial Management Co. Ltd, Bangkok.

Akimatsu, K., 1961. 'A theory of unbalanced growth in the world economy', *Weltwirtschaftliches Archiv* 86(2): 196–217.

Allen, G.C., 1981. *A Short Economic History of Modern Japan*, New York, St Martins Press.

Anderson, J.E., 1988. *The Relative Inefficiency of Quotas*, Cambridge, MIT Press.

Anderson, K., 1983. 'Economic growth, comparative advantage and agricultural trade of Pacific Rim countries', *Review of Marketing and Agricultural Economics*, 51(3): 231–48.

—— 1987. 'On why agriculture declines with economic growth', *Agricultural Economics*, 1(3): 195–207.

—— 1989. 'Rent-seeking and price-distorting policies in rich and poor countries', Seminar Paper No. 428, Institute for International Economic Studies, University of Stockholm, January.

—— 1990a. *Changing Comparative Advantages in China: Effects on Food, Feed and Fibre Markets*, Paris, OECD.

—— 1990b. 'China and the Multifibre Arrangement', in C. Hamilton (ed.), *Textile Trade and Developing Countries: Eliminating the MFA in the 1990s*, Washington, DC, World Bank.

—— 1991. 'China's Industrialization and Fibre Self Sufficiency', in C. Findlay (ed.), *Challenges of Economic Reform and Industrial Growth: China's Wool War*, London and Sydney, Allen and Unwin.

—— and Baldwin, R., 1987. 'The political market for protection in industrial countries', in A.M. El-Agraa (ed.), *Protection, Cooperation, Development and Integration: Essays in Honour of Kiroshi Kitamura*, London, Macmillan.

—— and Garnaut, R., 1987. *Australian Protectionism: Extent, Causes and Effects*, London and Sydney, Allen and Unwin.

—— and Park, Y.I., 1989. 'China and the international relocation of world textile and clothing activity', *Weltwirtschaftliches Archiv*, 125(1): 129–48.

—— and Smith, B., 1981. 'Changing economic relations between Asian ADCs and resource-exporting developed countries', in W. Hong and L. Krause (eds), *Trade and Growth of the Advanced Developing Countries in the Pacific Basin*, Seoul, Korea Development Institute Press.

— and Tyers, R., 1987. 'Economic growth and market liberalisation in China: implications for agricultural trade', *The Developing Economies*, 25(2): 124–51.

Armington, P.S., 1969. 'A theory of demand for products distinguished by place of production', *IMF Staff Papers*, 16(1) 159–78.

— 1970. 'Adjustment of trade balances: some experiments with a model of trade among many countries', *IMF Staff Papers*, 17(2): 488–526.

Asian Development Bank (various issues). *Key Indicators of Developing Member Countries of ADB*, Manila.

Australian Wool Corporation, 1988. Wool information paper (mimeo), Melbourne.

Author unknown, 1988. 'China and GATT', *Intertrade* 5: 2–26.

Balassa, B., 1965. 'Trade liberalization and "revealed" comparative advantage', *Manchester School of Economic and Social Studies*, 33(2): 99–124.

— 1979. 'The changing pattern of comparative advantage in manufactured goods', *Review of Economics and Statistics*, 61(2): 259–66.

— and Bauwens, L., 1988. *Changing Trade Patterns in Manufactured Goods: An Econometric Investigation*, Amsterdam, North-Holland.

— and Michalopoulos, C., 1985. 'Liberalizing world trade', World Bank Discussion Paper, Washington, DC.

Baldwin, R.E., 1984. 'Trade policies in developed countries', in P.B. Kenen and R.W. Jones (eds), *Handbook of International Economics*, vol. 1, Amesterdam, North-Holland.

— and Green, R.K., 1988. 'The effects of protection on domestic output', in R.E. Baldwin (ed.), *Trade Policy Issues and Empirical Analysis*, Chicago, University of Chicago Press.

Bank of Thailand (various issues). *Bank of Thailand Monthly Bulletin*, Bangkok.

Barnard, A., 1958. *The Australian Wool Market: 1840–1900*, Melbourne, Melbourne University Press.

Bhagwati, J.N., 1988. *Protectionism*, Cambridge, MIT Press.

Bowen, H.P., 1983. 'Changes in the international distribution of resources and their impact on U.S. Comparative Advantage', *Review of Economics and Statistics* 65(3): 402–14.

Brodin, A. and Blades, D., 1986. 'The OECD Compatible Trade and Production Data Base, 1970–1983', Working Paper No. 31, Department of Economics and Statistics, OECD Secretariat, Paris.

Brook, P., 1983. *A Preliminary Assessment of Restructuring in the Textile Industry*, Wellington (NZ), The Treasury.

Bureau of Agricultural Economics, 1973. *Statistical Handbook of the Sheep and Wool Industry* (4th ed.), Canberra, Australian Government Publishing Service.

Cable, V., 1981. 'An evaluation of the Multi-fibre Arrangement', Commonwealth Economic Paper No. 15, London, Overseas Development Institute.

— 1987. 'Textiles and clothing in a new round of trade negotiations', *World Bank Economic Review* 1(4): 619–46.

— 1990. 'Adjusting to textiles quotas – a summary of some Commonwealth countries' experience as a pointer to the future', in C.B. Hamilton (ed.),

Textile Trade and Developing Countries: Eliminating the MFA in the 1990s, Washington, DC, World Bank.

Cassing, J.H. and Hillman, A.L., 1986. 'Shifting comparative advantage and senescent industry collapse', *American Economic Review*, 76(3): 516–23.

Caves, R.E. and Barton, D.R., 1989. 'Efficiency, productivity growth, and international trade', in D.B. Audretsch, L. Sleuwaegen and H. Yamawaki (eds), *The Convergence of International and Domestic Markets*, Amsterdam, North-Holland.

—— and Uekesa, M., 1976. *Industrial Organization in Japan*, Washington, DC, Brookings Institution.

Chambers, R. and Just, R.E., 1979. 'Critique of exchange rate treatment in agricultural trade models', *American Journal of Agricultural Economics*, 61(2): 249–57.

Chan, G., 1988. 'Market socialism and economic development in China', Econometric Research Memorandum No. 340, Econometric Research Program, Princeton University, Princeton, NJ.

Chaudhry, S.A. and Hamid, J., 1988. 'Foreign trade barriers to exports: Pakistan', *Foreign Trade Barriers and Export Growth*, Manila, Asian Development Bank.

Chen, K., Wang, H.C., Zheng, Y., Jefferson, G.H. and Rawski, T.G., 1988. 'Productivity change in Chinese industry: 1953–1985', *Journal of Comparative Economics*, 12(4): 570–91.

Chen, X., 1988. 'The effects of Chinese economic reforms on agricultural and industrial productivity' (mimeo), Institute of Systems Science, Chinese Academy of Sciences, Beijing.

Chenery, H., Robinson, S. and Syrquin, M., 1986. *Industrialization and Growth: A Comparative Study*, New York, Oxford University Press for the World Bank.

—— and Syrquin, M., 1975. *Patterns of Development, 1950–1970*, New York, Oxford University Press.

Cline, W.R., 1987. *The Future of World Trade in Textiles and Apparel*, Washington, DC, Institute for International Economics.

Commission of the European Communities, 1988. 'The Economics of 1992', *European Economy*, 35 (March).

Congressional Budget Office, 1985. 'Protecting the textile and apparel industries', Staff Working Paper, Washington, DC, Congressional Budget Office.

Corden, W.M., 1987. 'Protection and liberalisation: a review of analytical issues', Occasional Paper No. 54, Washington, DC, International Monetary Fund.

Cross, J.W. and Spinks, M.L., 1986. 'The Australian-Chinese wool trade: recent developments and policy implications', *Economic Papers*, 5(4): 53–72.

Davies, S. and Caves, R.E., 1987. *Britain's Productivity Gap*, Cambridge, Cambridge University Press.

Deardorff, A.V., 1984. 'An exposition and exploration of Krueger's trade model', *Canadian Journal of Economics*, 17(4): 731–46.

—— and Stern, R.M., 1984. 'The effects of the Tokyo Round on the structure of protection', in R.E. Baldwin and A.O. Krueger (eds), *The Structure and Evolution of Recent U.S. Trade Policy*, Chicago, University of Chicago Press.

de Melo, J. and Robinson, S., 1989. 'Product differentiation and the treatment of the foreign trade sector in computable general equilibrium models of small economies', *Journal of International Economics*, 27(1): 47–67.

Department of Primary Industries and Energy, 1989. *Prospects for Further Processing of Wool in Australia*, Discussion Paper prepared for the Primary and Allied Industries Council, Canberra, Australian Government Publishing Service.

Department of Trade and Industry (New Zealand), 1988. *Apparel Tariff and Access Review*. Wellington, Department of Trade and Industry.

Desai, P. and Bhagwati, J., 1981. 'Three alternative concepts of foreign exchange difficulties in centrally planned economies', in J.N. Bhagwati (ed.), *International Trade: Selected Readings*, Cambridge, MIT Press.

Diao, X.S., 1987. 'The role of the two-tier price system', in Chinese Economic System Reform Institute (CESRI), *Reform in China*, Armonk, NY, East Gate Press.

Dixit, A.K. and Grossman, G.M., 1982. 'Trade and protection with multi-stage production', *Review of Economic Studies*, 49(158): 583–94.

Dixon, P., Parmenter, B., Sutton, J. and Vincent, D., 1982. *ORANI: A Multisectoral Model of the Australian Economy*, Amsterdam, North-Holland.

Do Rosario, L., 1989. 'One star for debt control', *Far Eastern Economic Review*, 19 January: 48–50.

Du, Y.T., 1987. 'The wool market in China' (mimeo), Centre for Asian Studies, University of Adelaide.

Eaton, J., 1987. 'A dynamic specific-factors model of international trade', *Review of Economic Studies*, 54(2): 325–38.

Eckstein, A. (ed.), 1971. *China Trade Prospects and U.S. Policy*, New York, Praeger.

Erzan, R., Goto, J. and Holmes, P., 1990. 'Effects of the Multi-fibre Arrangement on the developing countries' trade: an empirical investigation', in C. Hamilton (ed.), *Textile Trade and the Developing Countries: Eliminating the MFA in the 1990s*, Washington, DC, World Bank.

Feder, G., 1983. 'On exports and economic growth', *Journal of Development Economics*, 12(1/2): 59–73.

Finger, M. and Messerlin, P., 1989. 'The industry–country incidence of unfair imports cases in the United States and European Community', paper presented at The Hague Group Meeting at Thoresta, Stockholm, October.

Garnaut, R., 1988. 'Asia's giant', *Australian Economic Papers*, 27(51): 173–86.

— and Anderson, K., 1980. 'ASEAN export specialization and the evolution of comparative advantage in the Western Pacific region', in R. Garnaut (ed.), *ASEAN in a Changing Pacific and World Economy*, Canberra, ANU Press.

GATT, 1975. 'Arrangement regarding international trade in textiles', in GATT, *Basic Instruments and Selected Documents*, 21st Supplement, Geneva.

— 1982. *International Trade 1981–82*, Geneva, GATT.

— 1984. *Textiles and Clothing in the World Economy*, Geneva, GATT.

— 1986. *International Trade 1985–86*, Geneva, GATT.

— 1987. *International Trade 1986–87*, Geneva, GATT.

— 1988. *International Trade 1987–88*, Geneva, GATT.

Goto, J., 1988. 'Impacts of the Multi-fibre Arrangement (MFA) on developing countries: a survey', draft paper prepared for the World Bank, Washington, DC.

Granger, C.W.J., 1969. 'Investigating causal relations by econometric models and cross-sectional methods', *Econometrica*, 37(3): 424–38.

Grilli, E.R. and Yang, M.C., 1988. 'Primary commodity prices, manufactured goods prices, and the terms of trade of developing countries: what the long run shows', *World Bank Economic Review*, 2(1): 1–48.

Grossman, G.M. and Helpman, E., 1989. 'Endogenous product cycles', NBER Working Paper No. 2913, Cambridge, Mass.

— and —, 1990. 'Comparative advantage and long-run growth', *American Economic Review*, 80(4): 796–815.

Grubel, H.G. and Lloyd, P.J., 1975. *Intra-industry Trade*, London, Macmillan.

Guo, C.D., 1987. 'China', in J. Whalley (ed.), *Dealing with the North*, Research Monograph, Centre for the Study of International Economic Relations, University of Western Ontario, London, Canada.

— 1988. 'The developing world and the Multi-fiber Arrangement', in J. Whalley (ed.), *Developing Countries and the Global Trading System*, vol. 2, London, Macmillan.

Hamilton, C.B., 1984. 'Voluntary export restraints on Asia: tariff equivalents, rents and trade barrier formation', Seminar Paper No. 276, Stockholm, Institute for International Economic Studies.

— 1985. 'Follies of policies for textile imports in Western Europe', *The World Economy*, 8: 219–34.

— 1986. 'An assessment of voluntary restraints on Hong Kong exports to Europe and the U.S.A.', *Economica* 53(1): 339–350, August.

— 1988. 'Restrictiveness and international transmission of the "new" protectionism', in R.E. Baldwin, C.B. Hamilton and A. Sapir (eds), *Issues in US–EC Trade Relations*, Chicago, University of Chicago Press for the NBER.

— 1989. 'The political economy of transient "new" protection', *Weltwirtschaftliches Archiv*, 125(3): 522–46.

— (ed.), 1990. *Textile Trade and Developing Countries: Eliminating the MFA in the 1990s*, Washington, DC, World Bank.

— and Kim, C., 1990. 'Korea: rapid growth in spite of protectionism abroad', in C. Hamilton (ed.), *Textile Trade and Developing Countries: Eliminating the MFA in the 1990s*, Washington, DC, World Bank.

Harris, D.N., 1988. Substitution Between Raw Fibres: Apparel Manufacturing in the United States, a thesis submitted for the Master of Economics and Politics, Monash University, September.

Hausman, J.A., 1978. 'Specification tests in econometrics', *Econometrica*, 46(5): 1251–71.

Herin, J., 1986. 'Rules of origin and differences between tariff levels in EFTA and in the EC', EFTA Occasional Paper No. 13, Geneva, European Free Trade Association.

Hickman, B.G. and Lau, L.J., 1973. 'Elasticities of substitution and export demands in a world trade model', *European Economic Review*, 4(2): 347–80.

Higgs, P.J., Parmenter, B.R., and Powell, A.A.L., 1984. 'The scope for tariff reform created by a resources boom: simulations with the ORANI model', *Australian Economic Papers*, 23(June): 1–26.

Hillman, A.L., 1982. 'Declining industries and political-support protectionist motives', *American Economic Review*, 72(5): 1180–7.

—— 1989. *The Political Economy of Protection*, New York, Harwood Academic Publishers.

Hindley, B., 1989. 'Drifting (or steering) towards bilateralism', paper presented at The Hague Group Meeting at Thoresta, Stockholm, October.

Hine, R.C., 1985. *The Political Economy of European Trade*, Brighton (Eng.), Wheatsheaf Books Ltd.

Hiranyakit, K., 1986. Sales Taxes and Industrial Development, unpublished M.A. thesis, Thammasat University, Bangkok (in Thai).

Hsiao, L.L., 1974. *China's Foreign Trade Statistics 1864–1949*, Cambridge, Harvard University Press.

Hufbauer, C.G., Berliner, D.T. and Elliott, A.K., 1986. *Trade Protection in the United States: 31 Case Studies*, Washington, DC, Institute of International Economics.

Hughes, H., 1985. 'Asian and Pacific developing economies: performance and issues', *Asian Development Review* 3(1): 1–23.

—— and Waelbroeck, J., 1981. 'Can developing-country exports keep growing in the 1980s?', *The World Economy*, 4(2): 127–48.

IFCT, 1986. *Thai Textile Industry*, Bangkok (in Thai).

Indonesia, Biro Pusat Statistik, 1984. *Input-Output Table Indonesia 1980*, vols 1–4, Central, Jakarta.

Industries Assistance Commission, 1980. *Textiles, Clothing and Footwear*, Canberra, Australian Government Publishing Service.

—— 1986a. *The Changing Industrial Composition of the Economy*, Canberra, Australian Government Publishing Service.

—— 1986b. *The Textile, Clothing and Footwear Industries*, Canberra, Australian Government Publishing Service.

—— 1988. *Annual Report 1987–88*, Canberra, Australian Government Publishing Service.

—— 1989. *Annual Report 1988–89*, Canberra, Australian Government Publishing Service.

International Wool Secretariat, 1987. *Wool Facts*, IWS, Ilkley (Eng.).

Itoh, M. and Kiyono, K., 1988. 'Foreign trade and direct investment', in R. Komiya, M. Okuno and K. Suzumura (eds), *Industrial Policy of Japan*, San Diego, Academic Press.

James, W.E., Naya, S., and Meier, G.M., 1987. *Asian Development: Economic Success and Policy Lessons*, Madison, University of Wisconsin Press for the International Center for Economic Growth.

Japan Tariff Association, 1989. *Kanzeikaisei no subete* [The Manual of the Revision of Tariff Structure], Tokyo, Japan Tariff Association.

Johnson, D.G., 1973. *World Agriculture in Disarray*, London, Fontana.

Johnson, H.G., 1968. *Comparative Cost and Commercial Policy Theory for a Developing World Economy*, Stockholm, Almqvist and Wiksell.

Jones, R.W., 1971. 'A three-factor model in theory, trade and history', in J. Bhagwati *et al.* (eds), *Trade, Balance of Payments and Growth*, Amsterdam, North-Holland.

Jungenfelt, K. and Hague, D. (eds), 1985. *Structural Adjustment in Developed Open Economies*, London, Macmillan.

Katano, H., 1981. *Japan Enterprise in ASEAN Countries*, Kobe, Research Institute for Economics and Business Administration, Kobe University.

Keesing, D.B. and Sherk, D.R., 1971. 'Population density in patterns of trade and development', *American Economic Review* 61(5): 956–61.

— and Wolf, M., 1980. *Textile Quotas Against Developing Countries*, Thames Essay No. 23, London, Trade Policy Research Centre.

Kis, P., Robinson, S. and Tyson, L., 1986. 'Computable general equilibrium models for socialist economies', Working Paper No. 394, Division of Agriculture and Natural Resources, University of California, Berkeley.

Komiya, R. and Itoh, M., 1988. 'Japan's international trade and trade policy', 1955–1984, in T. Inoguchi and D.I. Okimoto (eds), *The Political Economy of Japan Vol. 2: The Changing International Context*, Stanford, Stanford University Press.

Kravis, I.B., Heston, A. and Summers, R., 1982. *World Product and Income: International Comparisons of Real Gross Product*, Balitmore, Johns Hopkins University Press.

—, — and — 1983. 'The share of services in economic growth', in F.G. Adams and B.G. Hickman (eds) *Global Econometrics*, Cambridge, MIT Press.

Krueger, A., 1977. *Growth, Distortions and Patterns of Trade Among Many Countries*, Princeton, NJ, International Finance Section.

Kumar, K. and McLeod, M., 1981. *Multinationals from Developing Countries*, Lexington, Lexington Books.

Kumar, R. and Khanna, S.R., 1990. 'India, the Multi-Fibre Arrangement and the Uruguay Round', in C.B. Hamilton (ed.), *Textile Trade and Developing Countries: Eliminating the MFA in the 1990s*, Washington, DC, World Bank.

Kuznets, S.S., 1966. *Modern Economic Growth: Rate, Structure and Spread*, New Haven, Yale University Press.

— 1971. *Economic Growth of Nations: Total Output and Production Structure*, Cambridge, Harvard University Press.

Lam, W., 1989. 'Is the Chinese economy compliant with the GATT?', Term Paper, University of Western Ontario, London, Canada.

Lardy, N., 1983a. *Agriculture in China's Modern Economic Development*, Cambridge, Cambridge University Press.

— 1983b. 'Agricultural prices in China', World Bank Staff Working Paper No. 606, World Bank, Washington, DC.

— 1987. 'Technical change and economic reform in China: a tale of two sectors' (mimeo), University of Washington, Seattle, June.

Lary, H.B., 1968. *Imports of Manufactures from Less Developed Countries* New York, Columbia University Press.

Leamer, E.E., 1984. *Sources of International Comparative Advantage: Theory and Evidence*, Cambridge, MIT Press.

Lin, J.Y., 1988. 'The household responsibility system in China's rural reforms', paper presented to the XXth International Congress of the International Association of Agricultural Economists, Buenos Aires, August.

Lloyd, P.J., 1985. 'The Australian textile and clothing industry group: untoward effects of government intervention, in K. Jungenfelt and D. Hague (eds), *Structural Adjustment in Developed Open Economies*, London, Macmillan.

—— 1989. 'Textiles, clothing and fibres in Australia and New Zealand', CIES Seminar Paper 89–11, University of Adelaide, December.

Lluch, C., Powell, A.A. and Williams, R.A., 1977. *Patterns in Household Demand and Savings*, New York, Oxford University Press.

McMillan, J., Whalley, J. and Zhu, L., 1989. 'The impact of China's economic reforms on agricultural productivity growth', *Journal of Political Economy*, 97(4): 781–807.

Maddison, A., 1982. *Phases of Economic Development*, London, Oxford University Press.

Maizels, A., 1963. *Industrial Growth and World Trade*, Cambridge, National Institute of Economic and Social Research.

Marin, D., 1989. 'Trade and scale economies: a causality test for the US, Japan, Germany and the UK', in D.B. Audretsch, L. Sleuwaegen and H. Yamawaki (eds), *The Convergence of International and Domestic Markets*, Amsterdam, North-Holland.

Mark, J., 1985. 'The Multi-fibre Arrangement: unravelling the costs', Briefing Paper, The North-South Institute, Ottawa.

Medalla, E.M. and Tecson, G.R., 1988. 'Foreign trade barriers to exports: Philippines' in *Foreign Trade Barriers and Export Growth*, Manila, Asian Development Bank.

Messerlin, P., 1989. 'The EC anti-dumping regulations: a first economic appraisal, 1980–85', *Weltwirtschaftliches Archiv*, 125(3): 563–87.

Ministry of Commerce, 1987. 'Report on textiles and clothing trade of 1986–87' (mimeo), Bangkok, Department of Economics and Business (in Thai).

Ministry of International Trade and Industry (MITI) (ed.), 1986. *Dai 2 kai kaigaijigyokatsudo kihonchosa: kaigaitoshi tokei soran* [The 2nd Report on Foreign Activity: The Statistical Report of Foreign Investment], Tokyo, Keibunshuppan.

—— 1988. *Toshin: kongo no sen' isangyo oyobi sonoshisaku no arikata* [Report on the Future of the Textile Industry and its Policy Measures], Tokyo, MITI's Textile Industry Council.

—— 1989. *Sen'isangyo no genjyo* [Current Report on the Textile Industry], Tokyo, MITI.

Mitchell, B.R., 1962. *Abstracts of British Historical Statistics*, Cambridge, Cambridge University Press.

—— 1978. *European Historical Statistics 1750–1970, abridged edition*, London, Macmillan.

Mitsubishi Economic Research Bureau, 1936. *Japanese Trade and Industry*, London, Macmillan.

Morkre, M.E., 1984. *Import Quotas on Textiles: The Welfare Effects of United States Restraints on Hong Kong*, Washington, DC, Bureau of Economics Staff Report to the Federal Trade Commission.

Mukaiyama, M., 1989. 'NIES karano sen'inijiseihin yunyujittai to ryutsukiko no henkaku' [Apparel imports from industrializing countries and the evolution of the distribution system], *Shoko kinyu*, June: 18–35.

National Statistical Office (various issues). *National Income Accounts*, Bangkok.

Niu, R. and Calkins, P., 1986. 'Towards an agricultural economy for China in a new age: progress, problems, response and prospects', *American Journal of Agricultural Economics*, 68(2): 445–50.

Nogues, J., Olechowski, A. and Winters, L.A. 1986. 'The extent of nontariff barriers to industrial countries' imports', *World Bank Economic Review*, 1(1): 181–99.

Oda, H., 1984. 'The administration of foreign trade in the People's Republic of China', *The Developing Economies*, 22(2): 155–68.

OECD, 1981. *Structural Problems and Policies Relating to the OECD Textile and Clothing Industries*, Paris, OECD, Directorate for Science, Technology and Industry.

—— 1983. *Textile and Clothing Industries: Structural Problems and Policies in OECD Countries*, Paris, OECD.

—— 1985. *The Costs and Benefits of Protection*, Paris, OECD.

Ohkawa, K., Shinohara, M. and Umenura, M. (eds), 1979. *Estimates of Long Term Economic Statistics of Japan Since 1868*, vol. 14, *Foreign Trade and Balance of Payments*, Tokyo, Toyo Keizai Shimposha.

Padoa-Schioppa, T., King, M., Paelinck, J., Papademos, L., Pastor, A., Scharp, F. and Emerson, M., 1987. *Efficiency, Stability and Equity. A Strategy for the Evolution of the Economic System of the European Community*, London, Oxford University Press.

Park, Y.I., 1988. 'The changing pattern of textile trade in Northeast Asia', *Pacific Economic Papers*, No. 157, Canberra, Australian National University.

—— and Anderson, K., 1991. 'The rise and demise of textiles and clothing in economic development: the case of Japan', *Economic Development and Cultural Change*, 39(3) (CIES Seminar paper 89-04, University of Adelaide, August 1989).

Pelkmans, J. and Winters, L.A., 1988. *Europe's Domestic Market*, London, Routledge.

Pelzman, J., 1987. 'The Multifiber Arrangement: the third reincarnation', in I.W. Zartman (ed.), *Positive Sum: Improving North–South Negotiations*, New Brunswick, NJ, Transaction Books.

—— 1988a. 'The Multifiber Arrangement: is there a future post Uruguay Round?', in R.E. Baldwin and D. Richardson (eds), *Issues in the Uruguay Round*, Cambridge, Mass., NBER Conference Report.

—— 1988b. 'The tariff equivalents of the existing quotas under the Multifiber Arrangement', Washington, DC, US Department of Labor, Bureau of International Labour Affairs (Contract No. B9K63381).

—— 1989a. 'Textiles and apparel', ch. 4 and appendixes F and G in United States International Trade Commission, *The Economic Effects of Significant U.S. Import Restraints . . . Phase I: Manufacturing*, USITC Publication 2222, Washington, DC, Government Printing Office.

—— 1989b. 'The MFA: U.S. refinements or on with the cartels', in S. Rajaptirana and A. MacBean, *Trade Issues in the 1980s*, Washington, DC, World Bank.

—— 1989c. 'The re-direction of United States imports of textiles and clothing: the role of the United States Bilateral Restraint Program', CIES Seminar Paper 89-09, University of Adelaide, November.

Perkins, D.H., 1986. *China: Asia's Next Economic Giant?* Seattle, University of Washington Press.

Roemer, M., 1986. 'Simple analytics of segmented markets: what case for liberalisation?', *World Development*, 24(3): 429–39.

Rostow, W.W., 1960a. *The Process of Economic Growth*, Oxford, Clarendon Press.

—— 1960b. *The Stages of Economic Growth*, Cambridge, Cambridge University Press.

Sampson, G.P., 1987. 'Pseudo-economics of the MFA – a proposal for reform', *The World Economy*, 10(4): 455–68.

Sapsford, D., 1985. 'The statistical debate on the net barter terms of trade between primary commodities and manufactures: a comment and some additional evidence', *Economic Journal*, 95(379): 718–88.

Saxonhouse, G.R. and Stern, R.M., 1988. 'An analytical survey of formal and informal barriers to international trade and investment in the United States, Canada, and Japan', Discussion Paper No. 215, Research Seminar in International Economics, University of Michigan, Ann Arbor, January.

Schultz, T.W., 1945. *Agriculture in an Unstable Economy*, New York, McGraw Hill.

Sekiguchi, S. and Horiuchi, T., 1988. 'Trade and adjustment assistance', in R. Komiya, M. Okuno and K. Suzumura (eds), *Industrial Policy of Japan*, San Diego, Academic Press.

Sepala, A. and Lee, D., 1989. 'Export-led industrialization and employment creation in Sri Lanka', paper contributed to the Annual Conference of Economists, University of Adelaide, 10–13 July.

Shirk, S.L., 1985. 'The politics of industrial reform', in E. Perry and C. Wong (eds), *The Political Economy of Reform in Post-Mao China*, Harvard Contemporary China Series 2, Cambridge, Harvard University Press.

Shoven, J.B. and Whalley, J., 1984. 'Applied general equilibrium models of taxation and international trade', *Journal of Economic Literature*, 22(3): 1007–51.

Siamwalla, Ammar and Setboonsarng, Suthad, 1987. *Agricultural Pricing Policies in Thailand 1960–1984*, Bangkok, Thailand Development Research Institute (a report submitted to the World Bank).

Sicular, T., 1988. 'Plan and market in China's agricultural commerce', *Journal of Political Economy*, 96(2): 383–7.

—— 1989. 'China: food pricing policy under socialism', in T. Sicular (ed.), *Food Price Policy in Asia*, Ithaca, Cornell University Press.

Silbertson, Z.A., 1989. *The Future of The Multi-Fibre Arrangement*, Department of Trade and Industry, London, HMSO.

Simmons, P., Trendle, B. and Brewer, K., 1988. 'The future of Chinese wool production', ABARE paper presented to 32nd Annual Conference of the Australian Agricultural Economics Society, La Trobe University, Melbourne, 8–12 February.

Sims, C.A., 1972. 'Money, income and causality', *American Economic Review*, 62(4): 540–52.

—— 1980. 'Macroeconomics and reality', *Econometrica*, 48(1): 1–48.

Siriwardana, M., 1986. 'An initial model of the Chinese economy: a framework for discussion' (mimeo), Bureau of Agricultural Economics, Canberra, June.

Sit, V.F.S., 1985. 'The special economic zones of China: a new type of economic processing zone?', *The Developing Economies*, 23(1): 69–87.

Spraos, J., 1980. 'The statistical debate on the net barter terms of trade between primary commodities and manufactures', *Economic Journal*, 90(357): 107–28.

Srinivasan, T., 1987. 'Economic liberalization in China and India: issues and an analytical framework', *Journal of Comparative Economics*, 11(3): 427–43.

State Planning Commission and State Statistical Bureau, 1987. *Input-Output Tables for China*, China Statistical Information Centre, Beijing and the East West Center, Hawaii.

Stern, R.M. and Deardorff, A.V., 1985. 'The structure of tariff protection: effects of foreign tariffs and existing NTBs', *Review of Economics and Statistics*, 67(4): 539–48.

Stoeckel, A., 1979. 'Some general equilibrium effects of mining growth on the economy', *Australian Journal of Agricultural Economics*, 23(1): 1–22.

Sung, Y.W., 1987. 'The role of microeconomic reforms in the decentralization of China's foreign trade', China Working Paper 87/1, National Centre for Development Studies, Canberra.

—— and Chan, T.M., 1987. 'China's economic reforms: the debates in China', *Asian-Pacific Economic Literature* 1(1): 1–24.

Suphachalasai, Suphat, 1988. 'Impact of MFA on world clothing markets with emphasis on Thailand', paper presented to 1988 Australian Economic Congress, Australian National University, Canberra, 28 August–2 September.

—— 1989a. The Effects of Government Intervention and the Multi-fibre Arrangement on the Thai Clothing and Textiles Industry, unpublished Ph.D dissertation, Australian National University, Canberra.

—— 1989b. 'Thailand's growth in textile exports', CIES Seminar Paper 89-08, University of Adelaide, November.

Summers, R. and Heston, A., 1988. 'A new set of international comparisons of real product and prices: estimates for 130 countries, 1950–1985', *Review of Income and Wealth*, 34(1), March.

Syntec, 1988. *Industry Assistance Reform in New Zealand*, Syntec Economic Services.

Takacs, W.E., 1978. 'The non-equivalence of tariffs, import quotas and voluntary export restraints', *Journal of International Economics*, 8(4): 565–73.

Tambunlertchai, Somsak, 1987. 'Development of the manufacturing sector in Thailand', paper presented at the International Conference on Thai Studies, Australian National University, Canberra, 3–6 July.

—— and Yamazawa, I., 1981. 'Manufactured exports and foreign direct investment: a case study of textile industry in Thailand', Research Report Series No. 29, Faculty of Economics, Thamasat University, Bangkok.

Textile and Apparel Industry Advisory Council, 1980. *The Australian Textile and Apparel Industries*, Canberra, Australian Government Publishing Service.

Tharakan, M., 1989. 'The political economy of anti-dumping undertakings in the European Communities', paper presented at The Hague Group Meeting at Thoresta, Stockholm, October.

Theil, H. and Clements, K.W., 1987. *Applied Demand Analysis: Results from System-wide Approaches*, Cambridge, Mass., Ballinger.

Theravaninthorn, Supee, 1982. The Roles of Domestic Demand and Production Conditions in Export Performance: The Case of the Thai Textile Industry, unpublished Ph.D. dissertation, Hitosubashi University, Tokyo.

Tidrick, G. and Chen, J., 1987. *China's Industrial Reforms*, New York, Oxford University Press.

Trela, I. and Whalley, J., 1988a. 'Global effects of developed country trade restrictions on textiles and apparel' (mimeo), Centre for the Study of International Economic Relations, University of Western Ontario, London, Canada.

— and — 1988b. 'Do developing countries lose from the MFA?', National Bureau of Economic Research, Working Paper No. 2618, Cambridge, Mass.

— and — 1990. 'Unravelling the threads of the MFA', in C. Hamilton (ed.), *Textile Trade and Developing Countries: Eliminating the MFA in the 1990s*, Washington, DC, World Bank.

Tsurumi, Y., 1976. *The Japanese are Coming: A Multinational Interaction of Firms and Politics*, Cambridge, Mass., Ballinger.

Tyers, R. and Anderson, K., forthcoming. *Disarray in World Food Markets*, Cambridge, Cambridge University Press.

—, Phillips, P. and Findlay, C., 1987. 'ASEAN and China exports of labour-intensive manufactures: performance and prospects', *ASEAN Economic Bulletin*, 3(3): 339–67.

United Nations (various issues). *Yearbook of International Trade Statistics*, New York.

— 1983. *Monthly Bulletin of Statistics*, New York, United Nations Statistical Office, June.

— 1988. *Monthly Bulletin of Statistics*, New York, United Nations Statistical Office, August.

United States Department of Commerce, 1976. *Historical Statistics of the United States* (bicentennial edition), Washington, DC, US Department of Commerce.

United States General Accounting Office, 1983. *Implementation of Trade Restrictions for Textile and Apparel*, Report to the Chairman, Subcommittee on Ways and Means, House of Representatives, November, Washington, DC, Government Printing Office.

United States International Trade Commission, 1978. *The History and Current Status of the Multifiber Arrangement*, Washington, DC, Government Printing Office.

Vernon, R., 1966. 'International investment and international trade in the product cycle', *Quarterly Journal of Economics* 80(2): 190–207.

Vincent, D.P., 1985. 'Exchange rate devaluation, monetary policy and wages: a general equilibrium analysis for Chile', *Economic Modelling*, 2(1): 17–32.

Wallace, H., 1989. 'Dealing in multiple currencies: negotiations in the European Community' (mimeo), Royal Institute of International Affairs, London.

Wallace, W., Naylor, T.H. and Sasser, W.E., 1971. 'An econometric model of the textile industry in the United States', *Review of Economics and Statistics*, 65(1): 13–22.

Werner Associates Inc., 1988a. *Australian Cotton Market Survey: Final Report*,

Brussels, Werner Associates Inc.

—— 1988b. *Australian Wool Market Survey: Final Report*, Brussels, Werner Associates Inc.

Williamson, P.J. and Yamawaki, H., 1989. 'Distribution: Japan's hidden advantage', Discussion Paper No. FSIV 89-11, Wissenschaftszentrum Berlin.

Wolf, M., 1989. 'The battle between liberalism and mercantilism: the external impact of the single market programme', paper presented at The Hague Group Meeting at Thoresta, Stockholm, October.

——, Glismann, H.H., Pelzman, J. and Spinager, D., 1984. *Costs of Protecting Jobs in Textiles and Clothing*, Thames Essay No. 37, London, Trade Policy Research Centre.

World Bank, 1984. *World Tables*, 3rd ed., Baltimore, Johns Hopkins University Press.

—— 1985a. *World Development Report 1985*, New York, Oxford University Press.

—— 1985b. *China: Economic Model and Projections*, Annex 4 to *China's Long-Term Development Issues and Options*, World Bank, Washington, DC.

—— 1985c. *China: Economic Structure in International Perspective*, Annex 5 to *China: Long-Term Development Issues and Options*, World Bank, Washington, DC.

—— 1986. *World Development Report 1986*, New York, Oxford University Press.

—— 1987. *World Development Report 1987*, New York, Oxford Univerity Press.

—— 1988. *World Development Report 1988*, New York, Oxford University Press.

Wu, J.L. and Zhao, R., 1987. 'The dual pricing system in China's industry', *Journal of Comparative Economics*, 11(3): 309–18.

Yamawaki, H., 1989. 'International competition and domestic adjustment: the case of the Japanese textile industry', *Pacific Economic Papers* No. 177, Australia–Japan Research Centre, Canberra.

Yamazawa, I., 1983. 'Renewal of the textile industry in developed countries and world textile trade', *Hitotsubashi Journal of Economics*, 24(1): 25–41.

—— 1988. 'The textile industry', in R. Komiya, M. Okuno and K. Suzumura (eds), *Industrial Policy of Japan*, San Diego, Academic Press.

—— and Yamamoto, Y., 1979. *Estimates of Long Term Economic Statistics of Japan since 1868*, vol. 14: *Foreign Trade and Balance of Payments*, Tokyo, Toyo Keizai Shimposha.

Yang, Y. and Tyers, R., 1989. 'The economic costs of food self-sufficiency in China', *World Development*, 17(2): 237–53.

Yang, Z., 1989. 'The performance and issues of Chinese foreign trade', paper presented to the Annual Conference of Economists, University of Adelaide, 10–13 July.

Yoffie, D.B., 1983. *Power and Protectionism: Strategies of the Newly Industrializing Countries*, New York, Columbia University Press.

Young, N. and Hood, S., 1985. 'Foreign direct investment and the Hong Kong textile and clothing industry', in *Textile Outlook International*, London, Economist.

Index